D1103891

When Sunday Comes

MUSIC IN AMERICAN LIFE

*A list of books in the series appears
at the end of this book.*

When Sunday Comes

Gospel Music in the Soul and Hip-Hop Eras

CLAUDRENA N. HAROLD

UNIVERSITY OF
ILLINOIS PRESS
Urbana, Chicago, and Springfield

Library of Congress Cataloging-in-Publication Data
Names: Harold, Claudrena N., author.
Title: When Sunday comes: gospel music in the
    soul and hip-hop eras / Claudrena N Harold.
Description: Urbana: University of Illinois Press,
    2020. | Series: Music in American life | Includes
    bibliographical references and index. |
Identifiers: LCCN 2020020770 (print) | LCCN
    2020020771 (ebook) | ISBN 9780252043574
    (cloth) | ISBN 9780252085475 (paperback) |
    ISBN 9780252052453 (ebook)
Subjects: LCSH: Gospel music—20th century—
    History and criticism. | African Americans—
    Music—History and criticism.
Classification: LCC ML3187 .H34 2020 (print) |
    LCC ML3187 (ebook) | DDC 782.25/409—dc23
LC record available at https://lccn.loc.gov/
    2020020770
LC ebook record available at https://lccn.loc.gov/
    2020020771

Contents

Acknowledgments

When Sunday Comes: Gospel Music in the Soul and Hip-Hop Eras is a labor of love. Much of the book was written in the city of Charlottesville, Virginia. In the late spring and summer of 2017, Charlottesville was the site of a series of white supremacist marches that received international attention. In the aftermath of the "Unite the Right" rallies of August 11 and 12, I agreed to coedit, with my colleague Louis Nelson, *Charlottesville 2017*, a collection of essays written by University of Virginia (UVA) faculty. That volume examined the legacy of slavery and racial segregation in Charlottesville, situated the controversy over the Robert E. Lee and Stonewall Jackson statues within a larger historical context, explored various First and Second Amendment issues, and sought to provide some answers to the pressing question "Where do we go from here?" Working on this volume was not an easy task, but it was a manageable one. My earlier work on the Garvey movement had familiarized me with the history of white supremacy in Virginia. And I was quite familiar with UVA's history of racism and the ongoing battle to make the institution a more just and democratic place. Knowing that history proved useful as students returned to campus two weeks after the "Unite the Right" rallies. Equally helpful was my ongoing work on the history of gospel music, which on many days provided sonic relief. During this hectic time, it was a pleasure to spend hours listening to Aretha Franklin, Sam Cooke and the Soul Stirrers, the Winans, the Hawkins Family, Commissioned, and other gospel favorites. My indebtedness to these and other artists stemmed from much more than the sheer brilliance of their artistry; their theological reflections provided spiritual sustenance as our university grappled with difficult existential and ethical questions. I recall a conversation with an undergraduate entering her first semester at the university. I met her after a forum hosted by the Corcoran Department of History, which sought to historicize recent events. At one of the breakout sessions, this student introduced herself and then relayed her fears about the possibility of the white supremacists following through with their promise/threat to return to Charlottesville in defense of their name, in defense of their cause, and in defense of what they saw as their First and Second Amendment rights. After sharing her concerns, she asked me a question that still lingers with me: How have black people maintained hope given the persistence of white supremacy?

Writing this book has provided me with some answers to her difficult question; so too have the many people and institutions who have supported my work and affirmed its importance. I have benefited immensely from the backing of colleagues in the history department at UVA. I especially appreciate the assistance of the department's staff: Kathleen Miller, Scott Roberts, Kelly Robeson, and Courtney Lazore. Beyond the history department, my colleagues Lawrie Balfour, Bonnie Gordon, Kevin Jerome Everson, Marlon Ross, and Ian Grandison have been extremely supportive of this work. Bonnie and Lawrie have been especially encouraging, and it is hard to imagine completing this book without their friendship, advice, and brilliance.

The same can be said of my comrade Corey D. B. Walker. I have leaned heavily on his critical insights on art, aesthetics, theology, and politics. In addition to offering stimulating conversations, Corey has provided me with challenging yet nurturing spaces to think about these issues. In 2016, for example, he hosted a conference at Winston-Salem State University titled "Black Genius," which featured several scholars, including Farah Jasmine Griffin, Greg Carr, Aldon Nielsen, and Steven Thrasher. At that conference, I presented on James Cleveland, shared my concerns about the challenges of biography, and received the affirmation necessary to press forward.

I am very thankful for family, friends, and colleagues who read or engaged parts of the manuscript at various stages: Dave Crawford, Bonnie Gordon, Greg Tate, Yolanda Willis, Andrew Kahrl, John Mason, Dana Cypress, Grace Hale, Lawrie Balfour, Rhon S. Manigault-Bryant, James Manigault-Bryant, Mark Burford, Julian Hayter, Darren Dochuk, Joseph Thompson, Davarian Baldwin, John McGreevy, Daryl Scott, Penny Von Eschen, Kevin Gaines, Reg Jones, and Corey D. B. Walker. I am also thankful to my dear friends Brandi Hughes, Nicole Ivy, Sarah Haley, and Cheryl Hicks, who asked tough questions about the work, my engagement with the artists, and my targeted audience. Another source of support and intellectual rigor has been Jonathan Fenderson, whose work on Hoyt Fuller greatly informed my treatment of gospel music in the 1960s and 1970s. As I wrestled with difficult questions regarding the personal politics of my subjects, I drew heavily on his treatment of Fuller and other figures in the Black Arts movement. The intellectual work and institution-building efforts of my comrade J. T. Roane has also been important in shaping my approach to the politics, theology, and aesthetics of gospel music.

This book has additionally been enhanced by the critical feedback of David Stowe and Robert Marovich. Both of these scholars have had a profound impact on my work. Their suggestions enhanced my analysis of the politics, culture, and business of gospel music, and their attention to tone, narrative structure, and sources enhanced the final product considerably. I am deeply appreciative to the University of Illinois Press for finding such thoughtful and insightful readers. I am especially thankful for the assistance and support of editor Laurie Matheson, as well as for the encouragement of Dawn Durante. And in the final stages of production, Julie Bush's meticulous copyediting made this a much stronger book. Madeleine Molyneaux has been an invaluable source of information as I have navigated the business aspects of the book. Moreover, her support of my collaborative work with Kevin Everson is deeply appreciated. Speaking of Kevin, it is hard to put into words how much he has shaped this book. Over the past five years, he has listened attentively to my perspectives on various gospel artists, most notably James Cleveland and Aretha Franklin; provided valuable suggestions with regard to photography; and helped me make sense of the pregnant silences in the music. More importantly, he has taught me about the power and beauty of collaboration and community. Through Kevin, I have also found a trusted comrade in Kahlil Pedizisai. For several years, Kahlil has provided a sounding board on critical questions and issues in the book and affirmed the importance of the work and my voice. And because of my work in film, I have had the good fortune to discuss music and art with such brilliant minds as Arthur Jafa, Greg de Cuir Jr., Nzingha Kendall, Michael Gillespie, and Cauleen Smith. One of my most important interlocutors has been my cousin Dave Crawford, who always puts me in revisionist mode. I am deeply thankful for his love, care, and intellect.

The value of thinking within the context of community has also been reinforced through my teaching at UVA. Students in several of my courses, most notably Introduction to African American and African Studies, Sounds of Blackness, From Motown to Hip-Hop: The Evolution of African American Music, and Black Fire, have been incredibly supportive during the writing process. I was also helped immensely by my graduate students and teaching assistants Benji Cohen, Gillet Rosenblith, Adair Hodge, Kamille Seward, Niya Bates, Joseph Thompson, Joseph Foley, Christopher Mathis, Diane-Jo Bart-Plange, Alexander Hyres, Tyrabia Womble, Tracie Canada, Kayla Kauffman, Clayton Butler, and Kevin Caprice.

Many institutions have been supportive of my research and writing. I am especially indebted to the Gospel Music Workshop of America; God's World record store in Detroit; Barky's record store in Richmond; What Cha Like Gospel store in North Charleston; New Sound Gospel Records and Tapes in Chicago; DJ's record store in Jacksonville; Reid's Records in South Berkeley; the Southern Historical Collection, Wilson Library, University of North Carolina, Chapel Hill; the William R. Perkins Special Collections Library, Duke University; the Stuart A. Rose Manuscript, Archives, and Rare Book Library, Emory University; the Archives of African American Music and Culture, Indiana University; the University of Notre Dame; the National Gallery of Art; the Library of Congress; the Urban Historical Association; the Association for the Study of the World-wide African Diaspora; Winston-Salem State University; the *Journal of Africana Religions*; the McIntire Department of Music at the University of Virginia; and the Association for the Study of African American Life and History. In working on this book, I received critical funding from my home institution, UVA, particularly from the Department of History, the Vice Provost of the Arts, the Office of the Vice President for Research, and the College and Graduate School of Arts and Sciences. I am also indebted to the Religion, Race, and Democracy Lab at UVA, which in the spring of 2019 hosted a wonderful symposium on the fiftieth anniversary of James Cone's groundbreaking book, *Black Theology and Black Power*. The symposium participants—Corey D. B. Walker, Tshepo Chéry, Paul Jones, Bonnie Gordon, Mark Burford, Kai Parker, Kevin Gaines, Josef Sorett, Suzanne Smith, Rob Sevier, Kevin Everson, Todne Thomas, Sabrina Pendergrass, Ashon Crawley, and Maurice Wallace—delivered papers that really pushed me in new and exciting directions.

This book reflects my deep love of and profound respect for gospel music. That love and respect developed at an early age and within the context of a family passionate about African American music. Long talks with my mother about Motown, James Brown, Aretha Franklin, James Cleveland, and Gladys Knight, among other artists, had a significant impact on me. So too did my weekend visits with my aunt JoAnn, who listened incessantly to the local gospel radio station in Jacksonville. Interspersed in their conversations about music were stories about the two professional musicians in my family: my uncle David Crawford (a songwriter and producer responsible for such songs as "What a Man," "Young Hearts Run Free," and "I Like to Live the Love") and my cousin Jackie Moore, known for the disco hit "This Time Baby" and the soul hit "Precious, Precious." Their stories were foundational to my intellectual and political development. It is my hope that the book's contents and spirit provide a modest return on my family's investment.

Introduction

My song is a serious matter.
—DAVID BERNARD CRAWFORD, "I Like to Live the Love"

I fell in love with the music before I fell in love with the Lord.
—AL HOBBS INTERVIEW, Mellonee V. Burnim Collection,
1861–1996, Archives of African American Music
and Culture, Indiana University

On February 2, 1972, 6,000 mourners jammed into Arie Crown Theater in Chicago, Illinois, for the public funeral of gospel icon Mahalia Jackson. Though Jackson had previously requested "no big fanfare when I'm gone," her homegoing service was a star-studded event.[1] During the ninety-minute funeral, attendees heard tributes from Mayor Richard Daley, Sammy Davis Jr., Studs Terkel, Ella Fitzgerald, Aretha Franklin, and Coretta Scott King, among other luminaries. In her reflections, King eulogized Jackson as "proud, black, and beautiful."[2] Even amid their grief, most speakers offered tributes reflective of Jackson's ebullient spirit and dogged determination. "We didn't come here to cry," Reverend C. L. Franklin informed the crowd in his moving invocation; "we didn't come here with hung-down heads; we come here to rejoice. For we know, now, that she has laid her heavy burden down."[3] Covered extensively in both black and white newspapers, Jackson's Chicago funeral was but one event in a weeklong period of mourning that ended with her burial at Providence Memorial Park in Metairie, Louisiana, a New Orleans suburb on the south shore of Lake Pontchartrain.

Six months after the gospel world mourned the death of its most beloved star, one of Jackson's biggest admirers, Reverend James Cleveland, convened the fifth annual convention of the Gospel Music Workshop of America (GMWA) in Los Angeles, California. The three-day event, which included workshops, lectures, and performances from some of the biggest names in the gospel industry, drew thousands of participants from cities across the nation. A jubilant Cleveland congratulated the attendees on a fine convention and promised a crowd of at least 10,000 at the next gathering in his hometown of Chicago. "We just might get Mayor Daley to join us in a good old gospel song," he jokingly noted to supporters gathered at the Los Angeles Hilton.[4]

Cleveland departed the convention ecstatic over the direction of not just the GMWA but also the black gospel industry. Much like soul and funk, gospel claimed a dedicated group of innovative artists who were proven hitmakers in their field. Established and rising stars like Cleveland, Shirley Caesar, Edwin Hawkins, Andraé Crouch, and the Mighty Clouds of Joy provided gospel radio stations with a steady supply of hits. Across the country, black gospel fans had at their disposal music as wide ranging as the gutbucket soul of Caesar and Cleveland, the praise and worship songs of Crouch, and the funk-laced rhythms of Rance Allen.

The good times did not end in the 1970s. As new artists built on the sonic innovations of their predecessors and the rise of cable television transformed the media landscape, the gospel industry experienced monumental growth and change during the last two decades of the twentieth century. The total sales for Christian/gospel music, including CDs, cassettes, and videos, increased from

FIGURE I. Gospel icon James Cleveland (*left*) and civil rights activist Jesse Jackson onstage at PUSH's Save the Children concert in 1972. Photo by Michael Ochs Archives/Getty Images.

$190 million in 1980 to $390 million in 1994. With this growing market for religious music, gospel stars like the Clark Sisters, Take 6, the Winans, Yolanda Adams, and Kirk Franklin became household names in black communities across the nation and throughout the African diaspora.

One place in which gospel music definitely had a strong presence was my Jacksonville, Florida, home. The music of James Cleveland, the Dixie Hummingbirds, Andraé Crouch, Walter Hawkins, the Winans, Vanessa Bell Armstrong, and Milton Brunson and the Thompson Community Singers were as much a part of my childhood sonic landscape as the pop ballads and infectious grooves of Michael Jackson, Whitney Houston, Luther Vandross, and Prince. Thanks in large part to my mother's refusal to compartmentalize the secular and the sacred, no genre of African American music was excluded from our working-class home. The joy with which she discussed her first time seeing James Cleveland when she was a student at Florida A&M University in Tallahassee equaled her passionate recollections of James Brown's brilliant performances at the Veterans Memorial Coliseum in Jacksonville. The youngest child of Beulah Mae Crawford, my mother made the concert rounds at an early age, tagging along with her mom whenever the famed Caravans performed at Mount Ararat Baptist Church during the late 1950s and early 1960s. All of the Caravans' members were stellar, but my mother was especially fond of Shirley Caesar, a dynamic performer whose youthful energy wowed concertgoers of all ages. The electrifying Caesar would dance and "shout" down the aisles of Mount Ararat as men and women, young and old, cheered her on. My mother's stories of Caesar's masterful performances, along with her endless tales of her beloved Motown artists, nurtured my love not only for African American music but also for a certain kind of storytelling deeply rooted in black working-class oral traditions.

Frequently in her stories about music, my mother included recollections of her brother David Crawford, who worked as a songwriter and producer for Atlantic, ABC, and Warner Brothers during the late 1960s and 1970s.[5] Primarily known for songs like Linda Lyndell's "What a Man," Candi Staton's "Young Hearts Run Free," B. B. King's "I Like to Live the Love," Jackie Moore's "Precious, Precious," and the Mighty Clouds of Joy's crossover hit "Mighty High," my uncle David first entered the music world as a radio announcer for WOBS in Jacksonville. Locally known as "The Demon," he captivated listeners with his youthful energy, encyclopedic knowledge of music, and sly humor. Always on the move, he had short stints as a radio announcer in Tampa, Florida, and Washington, D.C. Then in 1967 he moved to Atlanta's WAOK. Shortly thereafter, Uncle David joined Atlantic Records as a staff writer, producer, and musician, working with the likes of Wilson Pickett, Aretha Franklin, the Dixie Flyers, the J. Geils Band, and Dee Dee Warwick. To keep up with my uncle and the music world, my mother dutifully read *Billboard* magazine and *Cashbox* with an intensity her teenage friends reserved for *Jet* and *Ebony*. That practice deepened her interest in the business side of the music industry, which she passed down to me.

By the mid-1980s, when my passion for African American gospel music intensified, my engagement with the art form bore the imprint of my family's influence. Listening to gospel on the radio and in church was not enough. I religiously purchased the records of my favorite musicians and devoured publications like *Billboard*, *Totally Gospel*, *Score/Gospel Today*, and *CCM Magazine*. An important source for any student of gospel music, *Billboard* featured several stellar writers,

FIGURE 2. The famous gospel group the Caravans pose for a portrait in New York City in 1960. Photo by Michael Ochs Archives/Getty Images.

including Lisa Collins and Robert Darden, who in 2004 published the seminal book *People Get Ready! A New History of Black Gospel Music*. Darden's column in *Billboard* often featured artist interviews that brought readers closer to gospel's major stars as well as stories on the controversies surrounding the sonic shifts in the genre. An even more in-depth look into the black gospel industry came with the arrival of the Detroit-based monthly *Totally Gospel*, which, under the direction of its founder and publisher, T. J. Hemphill, ran from 1986 to 1989. The monthly's three-year run coincided with one of the most exciting times in urban contemporary gospel, when artists like the Winans and Take 6 achieved widespread success in the secular market and sparked new debates about the direction of black sacred music.

Not everyone was comfortable with gospel music's commercial success, and some wondered if the art form had betrayed its sacred roots and lost its connection to the prophetic tradition of the black church. Across the media landscape, from radio to television, gospel artists, fans, and industry insiders raised new and old questions about the art form's evolution: Were the contemporary gospel artists who experimented with the rhythms of funk, disco, and hip-hop more concerned with selling records than with saving souls, and if so, was gospel music on the same path of decline as its secular sibling R&B, which many music critics insisted had lost its soul? Were the new artists guilty of not only diluting gospel's religious message but also engaging in a form of cultural suicide by pulling the music away from its roots? Or were they simply doing what their predecessors had done—employing new technologies and marketing strategies to fulfill their broader evangelical mission? These questions frequently grabbed the headlines of black publications like *Ebony* and *Jet*, which set aside space in their pages to rehash and contemporize old debates about the evolution and commercialization of African American gospel music.[6]

As the black gospel industry became more successful in the commercial market, the genre also attracted increased attention from some of the nation's finest music journalists and cultural critics. Geoffrey Himes and Richard Harrington of the *Washington Post* and Carol Cooper of the *Village Voice* regularly covered gospel's biggest stars. Throughout her tenure at the *Voice*, Cooper wrote thought-provoking pieces on Thomas Dorsey, the Clark Sisters, and Kirk Franklin, among other gospel artists. Though much of Cooper's writing covered pop music, her works on gospel music and film are essential reading for scholars interested in the genre and its community of artists and fans. Like Cooper, Geoffrey Himes treated gospel as a vibrant art form worthy of historically and culturally informed analysis. On the pages of the *Post*, he offered incisive commentary on gospel's major players, as well as on the genre's evolution in sound. Not one to pull punches, Himes often vented his frustration with certain trends in contemporary gospel: "It was inevitable that gospel music would evolve to keep up with changes within the African American community," Himes reasoned. "But why did it have to go from the raw, impassioned singing of Julius Cheeks to the super-slick, tightly controlled productions of Andraé Crouch? Why did gospel, once the religious analogue of B. B. King and James Brown, become the churchly equivalent of Lionel Richie? There must be a hundred different Winanses out there, but none of them ever found a rough edge they couldn't sand down to a polished sheen."[7] Himes and other writers provided me with a critical language and historical context to process music debates taking place on AM radio stations, at churches, and in the homes of family and friends.

My expanding knowledge of gospel music benefited not just from the critical insights offered in the pages of major newspapers and periodicals but also from Christian television, particularly the hugely popular *Bobby Jones Gospel Show*, which began airing on Robert and Sheila Johnson's Black Entertainment Television (BET) in 1980. Especially among those living in black households where secular entertainment was outlawed on the "Lord's Day," *Bobby Jones* was among the best options in a rather limited selection of cable television programming. The hour-long program, which had a 9 a.m. start time, featured some of the biggest acts in the industry and also introduced young fans like me to gospel trailblazers who had made vast contributions to the art form.

In many ways, this book represents the continuation of a long communal conversation involving a host of individuals and institutions. On the pages that follow, I examine gospel music's creative shifts, sonic innovations, theological tensions, and political assertions within the larger framework of the socioeconomic and cultural transformations taking place in post–civil rights black America. Through an in-depth look at some of the genre's best-selling artists, my work explores gospel music's importance as an outlet for African Americans to express their spiritual, cultural, and regional identities. *When Sunday Comes* also details how larger political developments in the United States, such as the rise and fall of the Black Power movement as well as the emergence and growing power of the Christian Right/Moral Majority, shaped the music and politics of black gospel performers.

Very much like the artists who occupy the center of my narrative, this book takes the music seriously by paying close attention to its formal qualities, detailing some of the heated debates among musicians, fans, and journalists over the aesthetic merits of certain sonic shifts, and documenting the public's reception to groundbreaking recordings. In telling the story of gospel's evolution during the last three decades of the twentieth century, I have relied on a wide range of source material, including but not limited to released and unreleased music, newspapers, readers' letters to popular magazines, comic books, concert memorabilia (including my own), biographies, and some of the administrative papers of the Gospel Music Workshop of America.

No source proved more valuable than the gospel industry's hardcore fans, particularly those who endured my questions during the GMWA's fiftieth annual convention, held in Atlanta during the summer of 2017. Conversations with elders at the historic gathering not only provided me with rare insight into iconic figures like James Cleveland and Andraé Crouch but also underscored the importance of understanding the network of churches, record shops, radio stations, and black businesses that nurtured these talented individuals. On their trips down memory lane, GMWA supporters and historians like Norma Jean Pender and Sandra Rose of Detroit reflected on critical institutions and people in their local community, such as King Solomon Baptist Church, Prayer Tabernacle, and Ed Smith's flower shop. Their recollections pushed me toward an even deeper engagement with gospel music's living archives—the people, churches, record stores, and studios still standing despite economic hardships, gentrification, and loss of members. To be certain, sifting through archival materials in research libraries and digging through album crates at obscure record shops consumed a large amount of my time. But my research travels also included visits to historic spots like Nashville's Woodland and Quadrafonic Studios, where Shirley Caesar cut several of her classic albums for Word in the 1980s; Bishop E. E. Cleveland's Ephesian Church of God in Christ in Berkeley, California, where Walter Hawkins recorded his legendary 1975 *Love Alive* album with a small loan from his then mother-in-law, Lois "The Pie Queen" Davis; Milton Brunson's Christ Tabernacle Baptist Church in Chicago, where hundreds of gospel lovers encountered the fictive character Shouting John for the first time; and New York's famed Carnegie Hall, where black and white Christians flocked to see Andraé Crouch during the height of his popularity.

Though few in number, black-owned record stores also became critical research sites. During my time at Reid's Records in South Berkeley, DJ's in Jacksonville, New Sound Gospel in Chicago, Barky's in Richmond, and God's World in Detroit, owners and longtime customers reflected on these stores' historical importance as popular hangout spots for aspiring musicians, as key partners in local concert promotion, as sites of affirmation for everyday folk navigating the trials and tribulations of life, and as invaluable repositories of gospel music history. So much more than businesses, these stores were cultural centers. "It was like a train station," noted owner Larry Robinson in his description of God's World during the 1980s.[8]

First located on Livernois Avenue and then West Seventh Mile Road, God's World was and remains an institutional center of Detroit's gospel scene. As Robinson pointed out, "We've tried to bless people and to be there for a lot of churches, artists, 'wanna-be' artists." Indeed, during their formative years, many Detroit-based gospel musicians relied on God's World and Robinson for assistance. "I guess we have given a platform for people to start," Robinson reflected.

"I remember when Commissioned would use God's World for a practice area. When the store would close at night, they would move things around so they could rehearse. God has helped us to be there in the early stages of artists' careers."[9] The same can be said of Reid's Records in South Berkeley. Started by Mel Reid and Betty Reid Soskin in 1945, Reid's sold gospel music, promoted gospel concerts, outfitted local church choirs, and functioned as an important network center for rising stars in the gospel industry, including members of the Hawkins family. Taking over the operation of Reid's in the 1990s, David Reid still has vivid memories of the store's importance to local gospel lovers. "Reid's was like the happening place for all the newest music coming out, when people were actually depending on physical product. . . . We had about six employees and we would have two cash registers going and people would be coming in Friday after work and all through the weekend. . . . We had tickets for all kinds of concerts. From sunup to sundown, we would just be swamped in here, people coming from all over the Bay Area."[10] This bustling scene described by Reid is a

FIGURE 3. Reid's Records, South Berkeley. Founded in 1945, Reid's was an epicenter of black gospel music in the Bay Area. Photo by author.

thing of the past. "Gentrification has taken over," Reid bluntly told me in 2018. "All the main black businesses have gone and been replaced by housing or not replaced. Back in the day we had doctors and lawyers and restaurants, pool halls. There were things going on up and down the street twenty-four hours a day, but now it has become very quiet and culturally very sparse."[11]

Spending time in the Bay Area, Detroit, Chicago, and other cities forced me to grapple with the fragmentary artifacts of history: empty lots where vibrant neighborhoods and churches once stood, promising business plans that never materialized, record stores struggling to survive under the pressures of gentrification, and emotionally scarred musicians who would rather do anything than look back. And then there is the understandable element of distrust among gospel insiders fatigued by those scholars and journalists more interested in sensational stories than in the art form. All of these things pushed me to find meaning in the pregnant silences and reconcile myself with the fact that some questions will remain shrouded in mystery and uncertainty.

The story of black gospel music's evolution in post–Jim Crow America is a beautifully complex one that can be told from a variety of angles and perspectives. Structured along the lines of a collective biography, *When Sunday Comes* centers on some of gospel's biggest stars, most notably James Cleveland, Andraé Crouch, Shirley Caesar, Walter Hawkins, Al Green, the Clark Sisters, the Winans family, Milton Brunson and the Thompson Community Singers, Vanessa Bell Armstrong, John P. Kee, Take 6, the Sounds of Blackness, Kirk Franklin, and Yolanda Adams. Looking at the evolution of gospel music through these performers deepens our understanding of how the genre's changing landscape reflected broader trends in African American life. These artists also offer important insight into critical debates and issues rarely covered in other forms of black popular music. The lyrical content of contemporary gospel music, for example, highlights the growing political tensions created by the coexistence of liberal and neo-Pentecostal viewpoints within the African American Christian community, the religious forces that sought to add legitimacy to some of the most salient features of the underclass debate, and African Americans' ongoing quest to forge new conceptions of freedom and human possibility in the United States and the larger world.

In analyzing the politics and art of some of gospel's biggest stars, *When Sunday Comes* seriously considers the power of region in shaping their perspectives, their aesthetic practices, and even their self-fashioning. My individual chapters on Shirley Caesar, Al Green, and John P. Kee explore the complex ways these musicians asserted their identity as southerners to distinguish themselves from their peers, to transgress industry-constructed racial divides, to present themselves and their southern communities as sources of deep cultural wisdom, and to address intraracial debates regarding class, social standing, and culture. The importance of region in shaping the soundscapes of African American gospel music also surfaces in my analysis of the California-born artists Andraé Crouch and Walter Hawkins. Their music, politics, and theological perspectives reflected their West Coast rearing and experiences. The power of the local is equally apparent in the Detroit-based artists covered in this book: the Clark Sisters, the Winans family, Commissioned, and Vanessa Bell Armstrong. Simply put, Detroit was to urban contemporary gospel music what New York was to hip-hop. The city's rich musical legacies, segregated landscapes, and entrenched economic inequality penetrated every aspect of Detroit gospel.

FIGURE 4. Andraé Crouch performing in the 1970s. Photo courtesy of Photofest.

Just as region shaped the evolving sound of gospel music, so did the political economy of the music industry in general and Christian entertainment in particular. No different from their secular counterparts, African American gospel artists had to respond to changes within the music industry, from label mergers and marketing cutbacks to swings in record executives' views on the profitability of black gospel music. To bolster their album sales and increase their profit margins, artists experimented with a variety of label arrangements. Rance Allen recorded for Stax Records between 1971 and 1975, then signed with Capitol Records, where he worked briefly with the Mizell Brothers. A decade into his recording career, Andraé Crouch signed with Warner Brothers but remained on Light's roster. Crouch's unique deal involved him recording different albums for both companies, an arrangement that presented its share of distribution nightmares. During their commercial heyday, BeBe and CeCe Winans released their music through Sparrow and Capitol, while Take 6 released their music through Warner Brothers and Reunion. Another industry trend involved established gospel artists leaving their Christian labels and signing exclusively with secular ones. The Winans quartet, for example, left Light in 1985 and signed with Quincy Jones's label, Qwest, which was distributed by Warner Brothers. The move brought the group a wider audience and garnered them a gold-certification record with *Return*, a gospel/New Jack Swing hybrid featuring the production of Teddy Riley. Likewise, Yolanda Adams achieved crossover success when she signed with Elektra, partnered with super-producers James "Jimmy Jam" Harris and Terry Lewis, and scored a platinum hit with *Mountain High . . . Valley Low*.[12]

Another important though often neglected aspect of this crossover story involves white Christian labels' recruitment and signing of African American gospel artists. Within the Christian music world, the color line was a reality. In fact, the Christian music industry's biggest label, Word, did not aggressively recruit African American artists until 1980. That year, the company hired James Bullard as the head of its black division. It also signed Shirley Caesar and Al Green. Caesar and Green increased the company's share of the black gospel market considerably, as did the label's later signing of the Clark Sisters, Milton Brunson and the Thompson Community Singers, the Richard Smallwood Singers, Tramaine Hawkins, and the Mighty Clouds of Joy. Slowly but surely, companies like Benson and Sparrow added more African Americans to their lineups. Yet even as several Christian labels integrated their rosters, accusations of racism continued to surface among African American artists. Their complaints ranged from insufficient budgets for recording and marketing to the discriminatory practices of the Gospel Music Association, particularly its annual Dove Awards ceremony. African Americans' complaints were amplified in March 1992, when *Ebony* magazine ran a story detailing the entrenched racism within the Christian music industry. In the article, Marvin Winans recalled how his group had been given a seat in the balcony at the Dove Awards, while Alvin Chea of Take 6 reflected on how a white attendee at a gospel festival told him his group didn't sound black. "It's a sad commentary that the most blatant racism has occurred at gospel festivals," an exasperated Chea complained.[13]

In light of these realities, African American gospel artists recognized the importance of exercising greater autonomy over the marketing and production of their art. Toward this end, they created artist workshops and organizations and lent their support to black-owned companies. Taking the lead in increasing black gospel artists' autonomy and advancing the interests of the art form, James Cleveland established the Gospel Music Workshop of America in 1967. A link between the gospel world and the larger African American community, the GMWA provided a space for young artists to develop their talent and a yearly platform for black gospel musicians and fans to discuss issues of importance to them. "It became a training ground for me," remembered Teresa Hairston, journalist and founding editor of *Score/Gospel Today*, who attended her first GMWA convention in 1975. Over time, the annual gathering also became a "place of reunion" for Hairston. Like many industry insiders, she marveled at the dedication of gospel music's rank and file—the women and men who performed in the mass choirs, dutifully paid their membership dues and conference fees, and yearned to be a part of something bigger than themselves. "It is amazing to me that people will pay $1,500 to $2,000 to come here and go through rehearsals that last 4 hours for 4 or 5 days a week; will go from a scheduled class that began at 7 a.m. in the morning and [doesn't] end until the afternoon ... and then go to midnight services. That kind of devotion to art form or anything is so unusual. People will come here not knowing how they are going to make it through the week financially. They just come here because they got to come to the workshop. It's amazing."[14]

Why the GMWA came to occupy such a cherished place in the hearts of black gospel music fans and practitioners is vividly described in the book's first chapter, which examines the GMWA's formation and its highly attended conventions, as well as its unsuccessful attempt to establish a black gospel college in the geographical center of Floyd McKissick's Black Power experiment, Soul City, North Carolina. In tracing African American artists' struggle for autonomy, this book also shines light on independent black gospel labels like Tyscot and GospoCentric. Indeed, one of the most exciting stories in the gospel world during the 1990s was the arrival and commercial success of Kirk Franklin. His first four records on GospoCentric spawned a commercial revolution in the gospel music industry. Owned by Vicki Mack Lataillade and Claude Lataillade, GospoCentric claimed an impressive roster of artists that included Franklin, God's Property, J. Moss, Trin-i-tee 5:7, and Kurt Carr. By the end of the 1990s, it was not uncommon to see the label's artists on the cover of mainstream magazines like *Vibe* or in heavy rotation on BET or MTV.

This commercially vibrant world of gospel music was very much a part of black popular culture. In fact, while I was an undergraduate at Temple University in the mid-1990s, gospel's ubiquity in both secular and sacred spaces was a source of great fascination for me. On a Saturday night stroll down the halls of my dormitory, Temple Towers, one might hear Kirk Franklin's "Silver and Gold," Mary J. Blige's "My Life," and Biggie's "One More Chance" in succession. Though hip-hop had the loyalty of most undergraduates, my inner circle, particularly my fellow women's basketball teammates, had a deep appreciation for gospel music. On our road trips, at the dining halls, and in our dormitories, gospel music occupied the same space as R&B and old-school soul. Fortunately, my academic work as an African American studies major and history minor reinforced many of the lessons provided during my extracurricular activities. Classes and conversations with Professors Sonia Sanchez, Bettye Collier-Thomas, Greg Carr, Valethia Watkins, and Mario Beatty, among others, strengthened my already firm sense of the importance of the spiritual lives of black folk. Seeds sown in my childhood home of Jacksonville blossomed under the guidance of these teachers and the music journalists and cultural critics whom I read over the next two decades: Horace Boyer, Mark Burford, Mellonee Burnim, Portia Maultsby, Eileen Southern, Jon Michael Spencer, Brooksie Eugene Harrington, Michael W. Harris, Robert Darden, Anthony Heilbut, Glenn Hinson, Wyatt Tee Walker, Pearl Williams-Jones, Robert Marovich, and Jerma Jackson.[15] Their respective histories of gospel music enriched my understanding of the genre's centrality to black culture, its early relationship to the recording industry, and its role as a source of individual and collective uplift for people of African descent. They also reaffirmed my belief in gospel music as a subject worthy of in-depth cultural criticism and historical analysis.

And yet, despite my admiration for their work, or perhaps because of it, these authors always left me wanting more, particularly greater engagement with the gospel music of the post–civil rights era. Why couldn't their razor-sharp analyses of gospel music's "golden era" (1945–65) extend into the 1970s and 1980s, I often wondered? Why did the black sacred music adored by so many of my generation seem inconsequential to the historians whose scholarship mattered so much to me? To be sure, Heilbut's *The Gospel Sound* and Darden's *People Get Ready!* extended their analyses beyond gospel's golden era. But their discussion of the genre's later years lacked the detailed attention given to the earlier period.

By focusing primarily on the last three decades of the twentieth century, *When Sunday Comes* shines light on gospel's golden era of commercialism. Instead of dismissing this period as one of musical decline and questionable crossover pursuits, this book treats these years as a time of great artistic innovation and advancement.[16] It details how Kirk Franklin, the Winans, Take 6, and the Clark Sisters, among others, not only advanced the black sacred music tradition but also ensured that gospel remained embedded in African American culture. That embeddedness has surfaced in a variety of cultural contexts and arenas and continues to do so: BET's annual award shows; the music of secular stars like Beyoncé, D'Angelo, Missy Elliott, Snoop Dogg, Chance the Rapper, and Kanye; the cinematic offerings of such avant-garde filmmakers as Arthur Jafa, Kevin Jerome Everson, and Cauleen Smith; and even the televised funerals of some of the entertainment industry's biggest icons. Take as a case in point the very public mourning that followed the deaths of Michael Jackson and Whitney Houston. On July 7, 2009, twelve days after Jackson's death, millions of fans watched the homegoing service of the "King of Pop." The memorial opened with Andraé Crouch and his choir humming the melody of the gospel classic "Soon and Very Soon" as Jackson's brothers rolled his casket to the center stage of Staples Center in Los Angeles.

Three years later, Crouch's music had a strong presence at the homegoing of another pop legend, Whitney Houston. This time, the musical vessel was not Crouch himself but his student Marvin Winans. Standing before a grief-stricken audience of family, friends, music legends, and curious onlookers, Winans belted out Crouch's latest hit, "Let the Church Say Amen," as he closed his eulogy of a woman who had been raised in New Hope Baptist Church under the tutelage of her mother, Cissy Houston; who had supported the careers of his younger siblings BeBe and CeCe Winans; and who fifteen years before her passing released the multi-platinum gospel album *The Preacher's Wife.* The presence of Crouch's music at both Houston's and Jackson's funerals not only symbolized his importance to the gospel sound but also showed how often African Americans have turned to this vibrant and life-affirming art form to make sense of the tragicomic reality of human existence.

As I reflected on what gospel music has meant to African Americans, my thoughts often turned to the song that inspired the book's title: Donald Lawrence and the Tri-City Singers' 1995 hit "When Sunday Comes." Seven minutes long, the song features gospel legend Daryl Coley on lead vocals. Throughout the performance, Coley titillates the crowd with a flurry of vocal riffs, drawing from the improvisational styles of both gospel and jazz. The audience's shouts of approval convey their agreement with his message of the joy that awaits Jesus's Second Coming and also their recognition of his mastery of form. "When Sunday Comes," as both a song and a metaphor, captures the wide range of emotions, relationships, and processes operating in African American gospel music: the climactic moment in a performance when a musician reaches the height of his or her artistic and spiritual powers, the gospel audience's contribution to and immediate recognition of such moments, and the deep cultural meanings the sacred songs hold for people of African descent in America.

For many of the artists in this book, singing gospel was not simply a form of self-expression or a way to magnify God but also a way to uplift people, to lighten their burden. Perhaps no one understood this more than Shirley Caesar, who envisioned her concerts as a way to elevate her audience to a higher spiritual plane. "It's not so much that I want people to shout," she explained to Geoffrey Himes in 1987. "I want them to forget that burden they left behind when they came to the concert. I want to give them a spiritual catharsis."[17]

CHAPTER 1

Lord Let Me Be an Instrument

The Artistry and Cultural Politics
of Reverend James Cleveland

The bluesman, who comes out of the black Christian culture,
is telling the story differently. He has good news, but his news
puts a different kind of hurtin' on the gospel. His news says this:
If I sing my blues, I'll lose my blues—at least for those precious
moments when I'm singing. His news says that the story of our
lives—our losses, our depression, our angst—can be simplified
and funkafied in a form that gives visceral pleasure and subversive
joy, both to the bluesman and his audience.

—CORNEL WEST, *Brother West: Living and Loving*
Out Loud, a Memoir

On Thursday night, January 13, 1972, an eclectic crowd of music lovers assembled
at New Temple Missionary Baptist Church in Los Angeles to witness Aretha
Louise Franklin deliver one of the most amazing performances of her career.
The atmosphere in New Temple was electric as Franklin's soaring shouts and
deep moans sent chills down the spines of women and men, blacks and whites,
regular churchgoers and self-proclaimed atheists. On such gospel classics as
"What a Friend We Have in Jesus," "How I Got Over," and "Precious Lord,
Take My Hand," she fused the optimistic spirit of the civil rights movement,
the cultural ethos of the Black Power era, and the prophetic vision of the black
church to create a transcendent work of art.

The following night, Franklin returned to New Temple to deliver another
round of gospel classics. Once again, she mesmerized the audience with her vocal prowess and radiant spirit. Her set included a sublime version of "Amazing
Grace," a magnificent reworking of the Caravans' "Mary Don't You Weep," and
a scorching duet with gospel legend James Cleveland.

Four months later, Atlantic records released Franklin's magical performances
as a double album titled *Amazing Grace*. Across the country, journalists heralded
Franklin's latest offering as a sonic masterpiece. "She sings like never before

on record," raved journalist Jon Landau in *Rolling Stone*. "The liberation and abandon she has always implied in her greatest moments are now fully and consistently achieved."[1]

Rarely acknowledged in public conversations about Franklin's triumphant return to gospel was her competitive spirit, specifically her desire to demonstrate a mastery of the art form—gospel music—that had been so central to her identity as an artist. Since signing with Atlantic Records in 1966, Franklin had released some of the most celebrated albums in pop music, most notably *I Never Loved a Man the Way I Love You*, *Lady Soul*, *Spirit in the Dark*, and *Young, Gifted, and Black*.[2] Despite her phenomenal success in the secular world, Franklin wanted to return, if only momentarily, to the sacred music of her youth. "I told Atlantic that it was time for me to return to my roots and make a gospel album," she stated in her autobiography.[3] Such an album, she insisted, must be recorded live with a real congregation. It also had to include her mentor and close friend Reverend James Cleveland. "No one could put together a choir like James Cleveland," Franklin recalled in her memoir.[4] Indeed, Cleveland's collaborative endeavors with Detroit's Voices of Tabernacle, the Angelic Choir of Nutley, New Jersey, and his own Southern California Community Choir had resulted in some of the most commercially successful recordings in gospel music history.

Unwavering in his commitment to expanding gospel's influence and popularity, Cleveland appreciated the opportunity to participate in what he knew would be a historic event. With approval from his record label, Savoy, he agreed to contribute to Franklin's gospel outing by directing the choir, playing the piano, emceeing the live recording, and lending his voice on the duet "Precious Memories."

Franklin's insistence on Cleveland's involvement in *Amazing Grace* was a testament not just to her faith in his artistry but also to his unrivaled stature in the gospel music industry. With his signature voice, distinctive phrasing, and innovative choir arrangements, Cleveland had scored a series of hits during the 1960s. In addition to releasing groundbreaking records like *Peace Be Still* and *I Stood on the Banks of the Jordan*, he performed sold-out concerts throughout the United States and Europe. An ambitious musician whose artistic goals extended beyond his own individual success, Cleveland wanted to secure greater respect and recognition for gospel music's integral role in the spiritual nourishment and cultural advancement of black America. Toward this end, he established the Gospel Music Workshop of America in 1967. Under his dedicated leadership, the GMWA provided an institutional space in which black artists could hone their craft, gain exposure to the latest developments and trends in gospel music, exercise greater control over the marketing of their art, and fellowship with like-minded musicians who shared their religious convictions. The GMWA's annual conventions brought together artists, concert promoters, ministers, disc jockeys, radio programmers, A&R directors, and fans. Its success led Cleveland and his associates to pursue an even bigger project in the mid-1970s: the formation of a gospel music college in Soul City, North Carolina. The proposed college would further institutionalize Cleveland's artistic vision and evangelical mission and enhance the GMWA's outreach work among black youth.

An imaginative leader with an indefatigable work ethic, Cleveland was part of a growing community of black artists, writers, and religious figures who were reevaluating and redefining the meaning of black sacred music and its place in the black freedom struggle. In many ways, his advocacy work on behalf of the GMWA complemented the intellectual pursuits of scholars like Horace Boyer, James Cone, and Pearl Williams-Jones who promoted gospel music as an integral component of African Americans' ongoing quest for self-definition.[5] Williams-Jones, in particular, led the way in challenging writers to consider seriously the religious music of African Americans in their discussions on the black aesthetic: "If a basic theoretical concept of a black aesthetic can be drawn from the history of the black experience in America, the crystallization of this concept is embodied in Afro-American gospel music."[6] No longer, she maintained, could black arts writers concern themselves solely with secular forms of black cultural expression. "In order to establish a black aesthetic definition as applied to black art forms, the implications of the black gospel church and the music associated with it should be brought into focus."[7] Echoes of Williams-Jones's arguments appear in the works of several black cultural artists, from Cannonball Adderley ("Country Preacher" and "Walk Tall") to Donald Byrd ("Pentecostal Feeling" and "Cristo Redentor") to poet Nikki Giovanni, who celebrated the black church as a "great archive of black music." Giovanni's engagement with that archive was most explicit on her 1971 recording *Truth Is on Its Way*. On this critically acclaimed record, Giovanni covered James Cleveland's classic "Peace Be Still." Her selection reflected her view of the sacred songs as an abundant cultural resource for African Americans, as well as her vision of Cleveland as the embodiment of the genre's best traditions and possibilities: "I dig gospel," Giovanni proudly proclaimed, "especially James Cleveland, he's saying a whole lot."[8]

To Giovanni and many other African Americans, the music of James Cleveland had special resonance. Songs like "Peace Be Still," "I Stood on the Banks of the Jordan," "Lord Help Me to Hold Out," "God Is," "Please Be Patient with Me," and "Lord Do It for Me" captured not just his artistic brilliance but also the complexity and beauty of the African American odyssey in the United States. To be sure, the gospel superstar enjoyed a level of material comfort that escaped most of his followers, but in the opinion of many of his working-class supporters, he spoke their language, articulated their pains, and gave voice to the hope that sustained them in the darkest times.

One night in 1968, a staff writer for *Ebony* magazine had the opportunity to bear witness to Cleveland's deep connection with his fans. Sitting in Harlem's famed Apollo Theater, watching Cleveland sing as audience members danced down the aisles, the writer struggled to process, let alone convey, the emotional power of Cleveland's artistry. That night, Cleveland wowed his audience with several hits, but one song in particular drew a visceral reaction from the crowd: "'Lord Do It' is what the song is called and the words have special meaning there in Harlem where most folks reckon that just about the only one who can ease the black-poor pain is the one that they learned about back home down South—the Lord. James Cleveland sings as if he agrees, and he squeezes the mike and tightens up his face, and his whole body shakes as he shouts the words that get to the people."[9]

Cleveland's impact on African Americans not just in Harlem but throughout the United States was profound. The same can be said for his influence on the evolution of black sacred music in the post–civil rights era. For more than twenty years, he was the dominant figure in black gospel music as both an artist and an institution builder. His accomplishments commanded the respect of fellow artists within and beyond the religious world. "I want to do for black publishing what James Cleveland does for gospels," writer Toni Morrison declared in 1974.[10]

Young James Cleveland and Chicago's New Sacred Order

A child of the Great Depression, James Edward Cleveland was born in Chicago on December 5, 1931. Much of what we know about his childhood comes from his interviews, in which he focused overwhelming on his early exposure to gospel music. His family belonged to Pilgrim Baptist Church, where the politically conscious minister Junius C. Austin served as pastor and the famed musician Thomas Dorsey directed the gospel choir.[11] Located at 3301 South Indiana Avenue, the church functioned as an important institutional anchor of Chicago's Bronzeville community.[12] The young Cleveland routinely accompanied his grandmother to choir rehearsals and eventually assumed the role of "church mascot." One Sunday, Dorsey gave the eight-year-old his first solo opportunity before the congregation. With what he would later describe as a "beautiful boy soprano voice," Cleveland sang "He's All I Need." The seriousness with which he later approached his craft as a gospel performer developed as a result of his experiences at Pilgrim. Always willing to learn, Cleveland also drew inspiration and guidance from what scholar Wallace Best refers to as "black Chicago's new sacred order." This new sacred order, according to Best, "didn't so much topple an old religious establishment as it rendered that establishment's long-held institutional priorities ineffective in a rapidly changing religious climate. In contrast to the old religious establishment that was run by a coterie of well-educated, middle-class male ministers, the new sacred order was largely a female order, as black women constituted more than 70 percent of the membership in many churches."[13] One of the most important members of this new sacred order was Mahalia Jackson, a brilliant singer from New Orleans who left an indelible impression on Cleveland: "I was Mahalia's paper boy. I'd go over to her apartment on Indiana Avenue and leave her paper and then try to put my ear to the door to hear her singing. If she wasn't at home, I'd go over to her beauty shop . . . and just sit around . . . listening to her hum songs while she was straightening hair. I grew up completely fascinated by Mahalia Jackson."[14] Another important figure in Chicago's sacred order was Roberta Martin.[15] A native of Arkansas born in 1907, Martin graduated from Wendell Phillips High School in Chicago. Her musical gifts earned her the position of lead pianist for Arnett Chapel AME and tremendous respect within the larger church world. One of the many young musicians she inspired was Cleveland, who borrowed from her style and technique.

Not just location but also timing factored significantly in Cleveland's artistic development. "He came in at the tail end of gospel's second generation," music historian Anthony Heilbut points out. "He's old enough to have seen the greatest pioneers sing their hearts out, and he learned from all of them."[16] Contact with Jackson, Martin, and Dorsey instilled within Cleveland a deep love for gospel music. It also taught him the importance of intergenerational exchange and rooting oneself in the institutional life of the African American community. Cleveland's talent and confidence developed within the matrix of extended family members, church elders, and community leaders who loved and nurtured him. He was the product of the sacred order of South Side Chicago and represented some of its best possibilities.

Paying Dues

On his journey to artistic greatness, Cleveland received enormous support and encouragement from the gospel community, particularly African American women. Taking note of Cleveland's writing talents, Roberta Martin debuted one of his compositions ("Grace Is Sufficient") at the 1948 National Baptist Convention in Houston, Texas. A year later, Cleveland moved to Detroit to serve as the minister of music at Reverend C. L. Franklin's Bethel Baptist Church, where he first met a young Aretha Franklin. Still working hard to increase membership in his church, Reverend Franklin envisioned Cleveland as an essential coworker in his efforts to transform his "nomadic choir into a powerful instrument for giving praise."[17] Franklin's confidence in Cleveland was based on the singer's connection to Pilgrim Baptist and Thomas Dorsey, as well as on his willingness to buck conventional trends. The partnership between Franklin and Cleveland came at an ideal time for both men. Franklin was on his way to becoming Detroit's most famous preacher, while Cleveland was forging his own unique sound as a musician. By the time of his arrival in the Motor City, Cleveland's once "boy soprano" had transformed into what he jokingly referred to as a "foghorn," giving him one of the genre's most recognizable voices.[18]

Never confining himself to one group during the 1950s, the independent Cleveland lent his services to several gospel acts, most notably the Gospelaires, the Chimes, and the famed Caravans. Under Albertina Walker's guidance, the Caravans had developed into one of the most revered acts in gospel music history. Hired as the Caravans' pianist and arranger, Cleveland joined the popular group in 1954. Wasting no time in establishing himself as a key contributor to the Caravans' sound, he wrote several songs for the group, two of the most notable being "What Kind of Man Is This" and "This Man Jesus."

Upon his departure from the Caravans in 1957, Cleveland forged a strong artistic bond with Detroit's Voices of Tabernacle. Under the leadership of Reverend Charles A. Craig, who pastored the spiritualist church Prayer Tabernacle, the Voices of Tabernacle revolutionized the gospel sound during the 1950s and 1960s. Listening to the Voices for the first time, according to gospel musician and scholar Charles Clency, was a mind-altering experience: "I heard sounds I never heard before in gospel. I could not believe what I was hearing; none of us could. . . . They had an organ, piano, directors, they had about one hundred singers, and they sang everything, with music and without music." The choir's sound, according to Clency, was nothing short of revolutionary. "Charles Craig and James Cleveland came out with a completely brand new idea of all kinds of contemporary chords, extended chords, chord alterations . . . a lot of jazz rhythms, where you had sevenths and ninths and thirteenths—Charles Craig could hear all that and incorporated it into his music, along with Beethoven, Mozart, all of the masters."[19] The tremendous buzz surrounding the choir eventually caught the attention of House of Beauty owner Carmen Murphy, who recorded the Voices of Tabernacle on her record label. The choir released two albums in 1959: *Today* and *The Love of God*. On these records, Cleveland's distinctive baritone adds a new spin to such gospel classics as "Down by the Riverside," "I Know It Was the Blood," and "The Love of God." During this time, Cleveland also recorded "That's Why I Love Him So," a gospel version of Ray Charles's "Hallelujah I Love Her So." Everything about the song—from the background vocals to Cleveland's piano licks—underscores the mutually beneficial and multidirectional exchange between soul artists and gospel musicians.

With the success of "That's Why I Love Him So," as well as his work with the Voices of Tabernacle, Cleveland was a hot commodity in gospel circles. On May 23, 1960, *Billboard* reported that Cleveland had signed an exclusive contract with Savoy.[20] The contract paid Cleveland an annual salary (rumored to be in the six figures) in exchange for multiple albums a year. It marked the beginning of one of the more intriguing relationships in music: the partnering of a fiercely independent, business-minded black artist with a record label whose owner, according to some musicians, exploited many of his clients.[21]

James Cleveland and Savoy

Founded in 1942 by Herman Lubinsky, Savoy specialized in bebop during its early years. Its talented roster of jazz giants included Charlie Parker, Dizzy Gillespie, Dexter Gordon, Bud Powell, Lester Young, Stan Getz, Fats Navarro, and Sonny Stitt, among others.[22] In the 1950s, Savoy ventured deeper into the world of gospel, eventually signing such talented artists as the Clara Ward Singers, the Gay Singers, the Caravans, and James Cleveland.

Within months of signing with Savoy, Cleveland released the singles "He's Alright with Me" and "Just Like He Said He Would." These standout cuts appeared on his 1961 album, *Out on a Hill.* Incorporating the rhythms of soul, pop, and gospel, Cleveland pleased both his fans and record company executives with the new release. Savoy's A&R director, Fred Mendelsohn, marveled at the album's success: "We, here at Savoy Records, have received thousands of requests for more records by James Cleveland and we are happy to comply."[23] Much to Mendelsohn's delight, the prolific Cleveland had no problem with delivering quality product at a rapid pace. In 1962, he completed two albums, *James Cleveland with the Gospel Chimes* and *This Sunday in Person.* The latter album featured the Angelic Choir, as well as a fifteen-year-old organist named Billy Preston. On the soulful "So Good," Cleveland, the choir, and Preston deliver masterful performances, drawing heavily from the energy of the crowd. Instead of recording the album in a studio, Cleveland and Savoy opted for a church setting with a live congregation. "You get something extra in a live recording," Mendelsohn later explained. "The result may not be as perfect as a record made in the studio, but it has what is perhaps more important—sincerity and soul."[24] This approach continued on Cleveland's next album, *Peace Be Still,* which was released in 1963.

Higher Ground: Peace Be Still

Nothing could have prepared Cleveland or the label for the public's overwhelming response to the single "Peace Be Still," recorded at Trinity Temple Seventh Day Adventist Church in Newark, New Jersey. The most important song in Cleveland's catalog, "Peace Be Still" hit the airwaves during a time of great political upheaval in the United States and the African diaspora. The year of its release witnessed the assassination of Medgar Evers in Jackson, Mississippi; the brutal murders of Carole Robertson, Denise McNair, Cynthia Wesley, and Addie Mae Collins at the 16th Street Baptist Church in Birmingham, Alabama; the March on Washington; the slaying of President John F. Kennedy in Dallas,

Texas; Elijah Muhammad's suspension of Malcolm X from the Nation of Islam; the independence of Kenya; and the formation of the Organization of African Unity.[25] Looking back on the tumultuous events of 1963, Dr. Martin Luther King Jr. marked the year as the beginning of "America's third revolution—the Negro revolution." The nation was in the throes of revolutionary change, and nothing—not even the assassination of President Kennedy—could be understood in isolation. Noting that the assassin's bullets "killed not only a man but a complex of illusions," King situated the president's death within the larger context of the nation's violent culture. "Negroes tragically know political assassination well. In the life of Negro civil-rights leaders, the whine of the bullet from ambush, the roar of the bomb have all too often broken the night's silence. . . . Nineteen sixty-three was a year of assassinations. Medgar Evers in Jackson, Mississippi, William Moore in Alabama, six Negro children in Birmingham—and who could doubt that these too were political assassinations?"[26]

A song that simultaneously spoke to *and* transcended the political moment, "Peace Be Still" became one of the most important recordings in gospel music history. Its unique time signatures represented a sonic departure from much of the music played on gospel radio during the early 1960s. However, its biblically inspired message was quite familiar to most gospel audiences.

Five minutes of gospel perfection, the song recounts the biblical story of Jesus and the disciples' crossing of the Sea of Galilee, a central site for many of the parables, sermons, and miracles found in the Synoptic Gospels. On one particular voyage across the sea, stormy weather threatened to overturn the boat carrying Jesus and the disciples. Frightened by the raging waters, the disciples awaken Jesus, who had been calmly sleeping through the adventurous journey. "Teacher, don't you care if we drown?" they query in a state of panic. Testing the disciples' patience and their faith, Jesus moves rather slowly before commanding the waves to "be still." After the wind and waves settle into a calm state, Jesus turns to his disciples and asks, "Why are you afraid; do you still have no faith?" Inspired by this story of Jesus calming the Sea of Galilee, Mary Ann Baker wrote "Master, the Tempest Is Raging" in 1871. Baker's hymn enjoyed great popularity among churchgoers well into the twentieth century. Then in 1949, the noted gospel composer William Herbert Brewster Sr. rearranged the hymn as "Peace Be Still." Thirteen years later, James Cleveland put his own spin on the gospel classic.

Showcasing his formidable skills as an arranger, Cleveland alters the rhythmic patterns of the hymn to maximize the talents of his surrounding musicians. The song opens with a short yet moving exchange between the pianist and the drummer. Cleveland then approaches the microphone in Trinity Temple and lays down one of the most memorable solos in gospel music history. "Master," he powerfully sings in his signature gravelly voice, "the tempest is raaaa-ging. Oh, the billows are tossing high." As the audience delivers its shouts of approval, Cleveland paints a vivid picture of the weather conditions confronting Jesus and the disciples as they cross the Sea of Galilee. "The sky," he croons, "is all shadowed with blackness."[27] The words are familiar but the delivery is not. Something about Cleveland's voice and how he bends the notes on "shadowed" and "blackness" deepens the song's emotional complexity and adds to its spiritual urgency.

Staying with the hymn's narrative theme, Cleveland then assumes the voice of the disciples during their questioning of Jesus:

> Carest Thou not that we perish?
> Oh how can Thou lie asleep?
> It seems like each moment so madly is threatening
> *Oh a grave, a grave, a grave in the angry deep*[28]

By now, the Holy Spirit has gripped the church. Through his deft storytelling and skillful manipulation of space, Cleveland has transported his audience to another time and place. The image of Jesus and the disciples crossing the sea becomes even more vivid at the song's two-minute mark, when the Angelic Choir launches into the chorus.

> The winds and the waves shall obey my will
> Peace be still, peace be still, peace be still
> Whether the wrath of the storm-tossed sea
> Or demons or men or whatever it be
> No water can swallow the ship where lies
> The Master of ocean and earth and skies
> They all shall sweetly obey my will
> *Peace, peace be still*[29]

With vocal support from Cleveland, the choir repeats the refrain as the soprano section takes the lead. As Anthony Heilbut perceptively notes, "Each line moves progressively higher, till 'The master of ocean and earth and sky' booms a solid octave over the winds and the waves."[30] The song's last minute is glorious. The drummer maintains a steady groove, the choir chants the word "peace" in unison, and Cleveland repeatedly belts out "yeah" to the delight of the crowd gathered at Trinity Temple.[31]

"Peace Be Still" did much more than confirm Cleveland's remarkable skills as a performer and arranger. It also secured him a position at the top of the gospel charts for years to come. Due to his hit single, as well as other strong tunes like "I'll Wear a Crown," "Praise God," and "The Lord Brought Us Out," *Peace Be Still* reached the top of *Billboard*'s gospel charts and remained there for more than five years. Selling more than 800,000 copies, the album achieved a level of commercial success largely unknown in the gospel music industry. On the strength of the record alone, Cleveland toured the nation, performing sellout shows in major cities like New York, Philadelphia, and his hometown of Chicago.

Gospel's New King

Working at a feverish pace, Cleveland delivered seven albums for Savoy from 1963 to 1965. With this high level of productivity, he dominated the gospel charts, typically holding several positions in the top ten. Moved by Cleveland's success, the black press frequently ran stories on his stardom in the gospel field. Throughout the 1960s, *Jet*, the *New York Amsterdam News*, the *Pittsburgh Courier*, the *Chicago Defender*, and the *Norfolk Journal and Guide*, among other black periodicals, covered his performances domestically and internationally.[32] The most extensive feature of the singer came from black America's premier monthly, *Ebony*. Its November 1968 issue included a five-page feature documenting Cleveland's ascent from his humble beginnings in South Side Chicago to the top of the gospel world. The magazine highlighted his impressive record sales, his sold-out shows in the United States and abroad, and the ways in which his music struck a responsive chord among members of the black working class. "Everything he records will sell," Fred Mendelsohn boasted to *Ebony*. "Even his new releases sell more than what we can expect from the complete sale of any of our other artists. Why, do you know the album that's our biggest seller right now? It's *Peace Be Still*, and Cleveland recorded that five years ago."[33]

Consistent with its narrative style and bourgeois sensibilities, *Ebony* detailed Cleveland's commercial success and comfortable lifestyle. There were pictures of him performing in concert, walking and shopping in New York City, and relaxing (with friends and his personal cook) in his spatial home. "I don't like anything dull," the gospel star noted as he explained his choice of red and white interior for his ten-room home, located in the Leimert Park section of Los Angeles. Fashioning himself as a man of style, Cleveland proudly boasted his possession of more than a hundred pairs of shoes and fifty suits. Noting that he had been paying his dues on the gospel highway for more than twenty years, Cleveland described his ascension as "a little more proof that if you hold out, deliverance will come."[34]

The coverage of Cleveland received positive reviews from *Ebony* readers, particularly those who identified closely with the black church and felt as if the religious dimensions of African American life did not get the proper attention. "I couldn't believe my eyes when I opened my November issue of *Ebony* and saw that beautiful spread on my favorite gospel singer," enthused Ella Lampkin of Atlanta, Georgia. "I have every album that he has ever made, and I rank him above all of the gospel stars." Noting *Ebony*'s tendency to focus largely on secular artists, Lampkin begged the magazine to feature "more stories that highlight the contributions that young people like James Cleveland are making to the church world."[35] Reverend B. W. Hamilton of Detroit echoed her sentiments. "You will never know how much joy you brought to me with your story on James Cleveland, the gospel singer. He has been a favorite of mine for a number of years, and I've often wondered why the national publications had never done a feature on him." That *Ebony* had decided to run a detailed portrait of Cleveland's life within and beyond the music industry reinforced Hamilton's perception of the monthly as "really a magazine of the people—and I mean all kinds of people, not just those who listen only to Beethoven."[36]

Where Everybody Is Somebody: The Formation of the Gospel Music Workshop of America

Though appreciative of the positive press, Cleveland was far from satisfied. His personal success only deepened his commitment to garnering greater respect for gospel music, ensuring that black youth interested in the genre had the necessary support to pursue their craft, and facilitating greater unity within the gospel industry. Toward these ends, he created the Gospel Music Workshop of America, an international organization that now claims a membership of 75,000. In building the organization, Cleveland aspired to provide an alternative to Thomas Dorsey's National Convention of Gospel Choirs and Choruses, which had been established in 1933. Cleveland belonged to Dorsey's organization but had grown frustrated with its handling of younger musicians within it. "Cleveland was part of the Youth Department of that convention," Ed Smith, Cleveland's trusted associate, later recalled. "And he had become dissatisfied with the treatment of the youth in that convention, stating that they had no platform to display their talent. Some of the older artists were just trying to hold them back so he decided to form his own convention."[37]

The genesis of Cleveland's Gospel Music Workshop of America can be traced to March 1967, when the singer convened a small group of musicians and business associates to discuss ways to advance gospel music artistically, spiritually, and commercially. In its constitution, the GMWA vowed to "perpetuate, promote and advance the Christian ideal through the medium of music by joining together gospel choirs, choruses, and analogous entities and persons affiliated . . . throughout the United States of America, in a voluntary association for education, cooperation, promotion and the communication of ideas and ideals."[38]

The GMWA's formation was not an isolated phenomenon. Across the nation, black musicians, writers, and visual artists sought greater control over their cultural productions, more interaction with each other, and more engagement with the politics of their communities. This was a moment in which black artists promoted the spirit of creativity and the power of the imagination to transform the world. "Creativity is the soul of the nation," wrote Larry Neal, one of the leading spokespersons for the Black Arts movement. "It influences and shapes the mind and direction of the struggle for national self-determination. It is concerned with the collective ethos of the people. Without it, the whole of whatever we want to be cannot be realized. For when we speak of creativity, we are, in fact, speaking about the spiritual manifestations of the people, of their will to survive beyond the merely physical."[39] To bring forth a new cultural reality, artists encouraged collaboration across a broad range of forms and disciplines. "There should be concrete moves made to bring about a working unity among the Black creative artists," Askia Touré wrote in *Black Poetry* in 1968. "Moves should be made to 'collectivize' Black culture."[40] Out of this impulse to collectivize black culture emerged several multidisciplinary art collectives, most notably COBRA (Commune of Bad Relevant Artists) and OBAC (Organization of Black American Culture) in Chicago, the Black Artists' Group in St. Louis, Harlem's New La-fayette Theatre, and Spirit House in Newark, New Jersey.[41] In many respects, the Gospel Music Workshop of America represented the sacred variant of this cultural nationalist push.

With extremely skilled leaders at both the local and national levels, the GMWA flourished during its formative years. The association's annual conventions drew musicians, industry leaders, and fans from around the country. The 1968 convention attracted more than 3,000 people and was held at King Solomon Baptist Church, a popular meeting place for black activists, musicians, and politicians in Detroit. The following year, 5,000 people attended the GMWA convention in Philadelphia. Likewise, the 1970 convention in St. Louis topped the 5,000 mark. Mindful of gospel's broad geographical base, Cleveland ventured farther west with the next few conventions, holding the fifth annual gathering in Los Angeles. A star-studded event, the LA convention in 1972 attracted youngsters from New York, Greensboro, St. Louis, New Orleans, Houston, and Detroit, among other locales. To finance their trip, the 300 attendees from New Orleans sold peanuts, washed cars, and held bake sales. Detroit youngsters held concerts and performed odd jobs around their neighborhoods. The sacrifice and dedication of the young attendees caught the attention of *Ebony*, which recounted the efforts of young musicians to attend the convention and their disciplined pursuit of artistic excellence. "When they weren't singing, the youths were in classes and seminars—some beginning as early as 8 a.m.—working hard at perfecting their piano and organ playing, at learning conducting techniques, and at mastering problems of harmony, sight-reading, and even choir administration."[42]

As *Ebony* focused its attention on the GMWA, many secular magazines were exploring the artistry of Cleveland for the first time as his recording with Aretha Franklin, *Amazing Grace*, climbed the pop charts.[43] The brilliant record piqued the curiosity of many journalists wanting to know more about Cleveland. "It's really quite a sad commentary on life," noted John Abbey of *Blues and Soul*, "that it took a pupil to bring the master to the attention of the world. But that's almost the way it has been with the Rev. James Cleveland, who was almost unknown to the world until the highly acclaimed *Amazing Grace*."[44] To provide his British readers with a deeper understanding of Cleveland, Abbey detailed the musician's relationship with Franklin and her father, his classic records on Savoy, and his efforts to augment his following among young people. Similar articles appeared in other publications as music critics applauded the artistry of *Amazing Grace* and the remarkable chemistry between Franklin and Cleveland.

Though appreciative of the positive press from his involvement in *Amazing Grace*, Cleveland remained focused on the GMWA. He was particularly interested in institutionalizing his gospel vision through the formation of a gospel college. For this task, he turned to Woodrow Ted Lewis and his most trusted ally, Edward Smith. A native of Sumter, South Carolina, Lewis served as the GMWA's director of human resources and planning. Like most GMWA leaders, his leadership skills had been honed within independent black institutions. Upon his graduation from Allen University in 1962, Lewis began graduate studies at Interdenominational Theological Center in Atlanta. The political fervor engulfing the city eventually caught the attention of Lewis.[45] Two days after the passage of the Civil Rights Act of 1964, he and two other students from the center, Albert Dunn and George Willis, attempted to integrate Pickrick Restaurant, a popular dining spot owned by former Georgia governor Lester Maddox.[46] This was not an episodic act of resistance for Lewis. After graduating from Interdenominational Theological Center and returning to his hometown of Sumter, Lewis chaired the Equal Employment Opportunity Commission, as well as reactivated the local chapter of the Congress of Racial Equality. In 1972, he served as chairman of the South Carolina Black Political Assembly, an affiliate of the National Black Political Assembly.

Edward Smith also had an impressive résumé. A native of Detroit, Smith graduated from Northwestern High School and was well respected among black Detroiters. Smith's first major foray into the world of gospel music came in 1962, when he became the business manager for the Harold Smith Majestic Choir, a group with whom Cleveland recorded his classic "Lord Help Me to Hold Out." Impressed by Smith's business savvy and his passion for gospel music, Cleveland tapped him to serve as the executive secretary of the GMWA. Smith had also been one of the twelve people the gospel star summoned in 1967 to assist him in the formation of the association. "We sat around in a hotel room in Detroit," Smith later recalled, "and he explained his idea to us."[47] Over the next few years, Smith listened to many of Cleveland's ideas and labored earnestly to transform those ideas into reality. "Ed was James' neck," gospel star Albertina Walker later noted. "And the head couldn't turn without the neck. . . . He was the man who made things happen."[48]

With guidance from Smith and Lewis, the GMWA sought to elevate gospel music's place in the art world and in the public's imagination. Lewis in particular emphasized gospel's importance as a cultural pillar of the nation, especially as elected officials, civic leaders, and the general public prepared for the country's bicentennial celebration. Much of Lewis's work as director of the GMWA's Cultural Development Project involved convincing governmental funding agencies, particularly the National Endowment for the Arts, that gospel was a "national treasure" that deserved to be respected, preserved, and financially supported in the same manner as the blues and jazz. On numerous occasions, he celebrated gospel music as the "spark of life to the depressed, hopeless blacks and poor whites." "Its artistic and soulful aspects," he continued, "comforts them when they are burdened, strengthens them when they are weak, and gives them, in part, the ingredients to 'keep on keeping.'" Now more than ever, Lewis believed, "the true meaning and awareness of this unique and particular art, culture and heritage should be preserved and brought to the light."[49] With this in mind, Lewis and other members of the GMWA sought to establish a gospel college modeled along the lines of Berklee College of Music in Boston.

The GMWA and the Soul City Experiment

The GMWA set its sights on one of the Black Power era's most interesting experiments, Soul City, North Carolina. The brainchild of civil rights leader Floyd McKissick, Soul City was the centerpiece of McKissick's efforts to assist working-class African Americans facing the challenges of unemployment and underemployment, poverty, and poor housing in the nation's urban centers.[50] Early in 1969, the civil rights leader announced plans to create a predominantly black town in Warren County, North Carolina. Not too far from the Virginia–North Carolina border, McKissick's proposed site was located in the northeastern piedmont region of the Tar Heel State. Within two decades, he predicted, Soul City would consist of a residential population of 40,000 people, quality housing, shopping centers, industrial plants, and a resort. This planned community, he argued, was not anti-white. "We don't intend to adopt the white man's racism," McKissick insisted. Rather, African Americans simply wanted to realize their own version of the American dream. "The black man has been searching for his identity and destiny in the cities. He should be able to find it on the plains of Warren County."[51]

The project struggled in its early years, but things appeared to turn around in 1974, when HUD secretary James T. Lynn announced that Soul City would receive $14 million in federal guarantee assistance.[52] There was one important restriction, however: until Soul City employed 300 workers, only $5 million could be used for the project. With this requirement in mind, McKissick focused his attention on three central tasks: hiring architects and contractors to build homes for workers, arranging water and utility services, and recruiting businesses and investors to Soul City. One interested party was Woodrow Lewis, who in August 1975 phoned McKissick to familiarize him with the GMWA's interest in establishing a gospel college in Soul City. The college, Lewis insisted, not only would push forward Black Power's cultural agenda but also would assist Soul City in its larger developmental work. In addition to focusing McKissick's attention on the financial benefits of a partnership with the GMWA, Lewis also stressed to him the political advantages of associating with the gospel organization. If institutionally linked to Soul City, the GMWA could additionally provide a base of support for McKissick in his national endeavors. "You are a national figure," Lewis noted in a follow-up letter to the Congress of Racial Equality president, and the GMWA "is a national organization of which Rev. James Cleveland is President and Founder. It is heavy with a hell of a number of members, and you know where people exist political power and strength exist also."[53]

Two months after Lewis's correspondence, Edward Smith requested a meeting with McKissick to discuss in greater detail the possibility of the GMWA purchasing land in Soul City. The first formal meeting between GMWA leaders and Soul City officials occurred on December 6, 1975, at the Sheraton-Cadillac hotel in Detroit.[54] At the meeting, GMWA officials presented Soul City officials with a 100-plus-page proposal for the college. The proposal included a blueprint of how the school would be organized in terms of physical structure and its curriculum. The twenty-six-acre site would consist of two dormitories, each containing 250 rooms. These dorms would accommodate 1,000 students drawn from cities and towns nationwide. The physical plans also included a dining facility, a state-of-the-art gymnasium, the James Cleveland Auditorium for the Performing Arts, and a main administration building. Located in the heart of the campus, the main building would consist of eighty classrooms and laboratories, sound studios, administration offices, and a library.

The executive council's plan for the college's curriculum would provide students with a strong grounding in the artistry, theological foundations, and business of gospel music. Students would be able to take courses on a variety of subjects, including but not limited to the Old and New Testaments, the history of gospel music, the sociology of the church, and the philosophy of religion. Sensing that the university would appeal to a broad range of students, the proposed curriculum consisted of four major tracks: vocal performance, instrumental performance, music administration, and commercial music.

The GMWA had lofty ambitions for the college, ambitions GMWA officials hoped Soul City would help them bring to fruition. On April 6, 1976, Smith contacted Soul City's marketing director, Jack Stewart, noting that the GMWA "would like to set aside enough land that you feel adequate to accommodate the facilities we discussed."[55] Several weeks later, Smith submitted a more specific request of twenty-five acres for the proposed college.[56]

Soul City officials appreciated the GMWA's interest, especially given the hostile political environment in which they operated. Notwithstanding McKissick's ties with the Republican Party, Soul City endured tremendous opposition from North Carolina conservatives. Senator Jesse Helms railed against governmental

FIGURE 5. Plans for the Gospel Music Workshop of America's proposed college in Soul City, North Carolina. Source: Floyd McKissick Papers, Southern Historical Collection, Wilson Library, University of North Carolina, Chapel Hill.

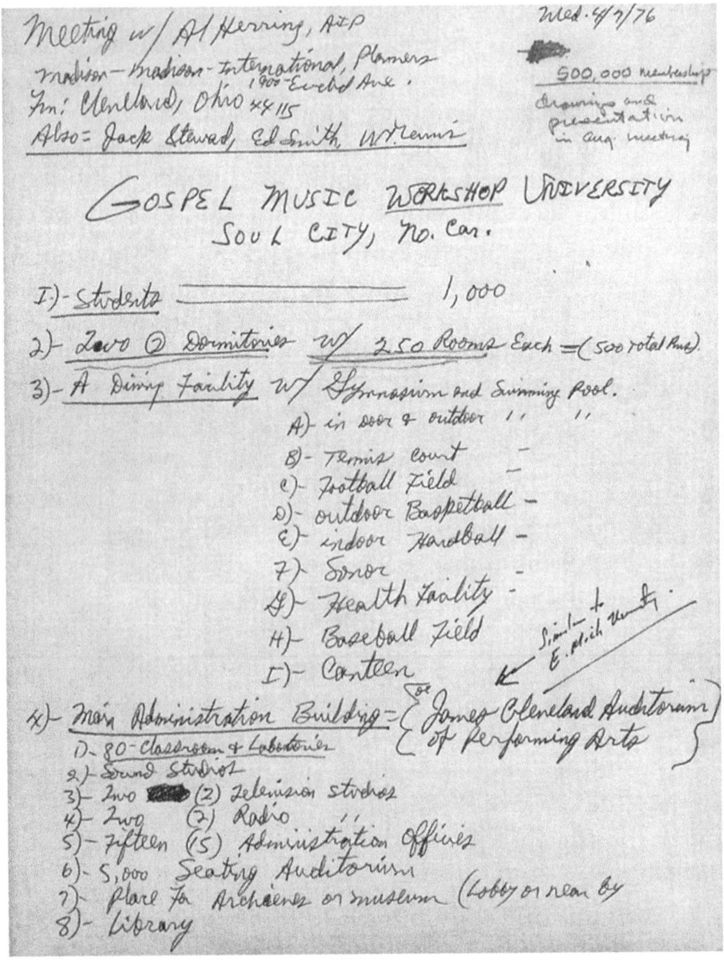
Meeting w/ Al Herring, A&P
Madison–Madison–International, Planners
1900 Euclid Ave.
Cleveland, Ohio 44115
Also = Jack Steward, Ed Smith, W. Lewis

Wed. 4/7/76
500,000 membership
drawings and presentation in Aug. meeting

GOSPEL MUSIC WORKSHOP UNIVERSITY
SOUL CITY, No. Car.

1)- Students ——— 1,000
2)- Two (2) Dormitories w/ 250 Rooms Each = (500 total Rms).
3)- A Dining Facility w/ Gymnasium and Swimming Pool.
A)- in door & outdoor " "
B)- Tennis court –
C)- Football Field –
D)- outdoor Basketball –
E)- indoor Handball –
F)- Soccer –
G)- Health Facility –
H)- Baseball Field
I)- Canteen

Similar to E. Mich University

4)- Main Administration Building = {James Cleveland Auditorium of Performing Arts}
1)- 80 - Classroom & Laboratories
2)- Sound Studios
3)- Two (2) Television studios
4)- Two (2) Radio "
5)- Fifteen (15) Administration Offices
6)- 5,000 Seating Auditorium
7)- Place For Archives or museum (Lobby or near by
8)- Library

support of black community projects, even those under the umbrella of black capitalism. Insisting that Soul City was the "greatest single waste of public money that anyone in North Carolina can remember," Helms ordered an investigation into the finances of McKissick and Soul City.[57] Although the state-appointed investigators cleared Soul City of any wrongdoing, the project and its leaders remained subjected to public attacks from GOP officials. Soul City also faced serious economic difficulties. As historian Devin Fergus explains, "The investment economy was tight and it was a buyer's market; few financiers with the means of investing large-scale venture capital or corporate earnings would waste their time or money sorting between the rumors of wrongdoing and its substance."[58]

The establishment of a gospel college at Soul City would have provided a much-needed boost to the fledging town, but Cleveland's gospel college dream went unrealized. Negotiations between the GMWA and Soul City slowed down considerably in 1977. Four years later, the entire Soul City experiment came to an end. Inadequately funded and constantly under political attack from Republican officials, Soul City never secured the necessary residents and business clients to become an oasis for African Americans seeking refuge from the nation's economic crises.

New Challenges, New Opportunities

If James Cleveland's gospel college in Soul City had panned out, one wonders how he would have balanced his multiple duties as administrator, artist, and pastor. No one in gospel music had more responsibilities than Cleveland, who reveled in his status as the leading figure in the genre. Working incessantly, he moved as if gospel's vitality depended on his productivity. "When Mahalia Jackson died, her mantle sort of fell down to me," Cleveland explained in 1975, "and unless there is a great explosion and upsurge, I'm sitting up on the mountain very secure."[59] Indeed, Cleveland's reign as gospel's "king" was quite secure. Along with his own solo tours, which commanded a fee of $8,000 in the 1970s, he also participated in Ed Smith's "World's Greatest Gospel Show." Launched by Smith in 1974, the series featured Cleveland, the Mighty Clouds of Joy, Shirley Caesar, Inez Andrews, Rance Allen, Delois Barrett Campbell, and the Swan Silvertones, along with various local acts. The tour included stops in Detroit, New York, Los Angeles, and Cleveland. On August 3, 1975, 20,000 gospel fans crammed into Art Modell's Lakefront Stadium in Cleveland to witness the "King of Gospel" alongside some of the most exciting performers in the genre.[60]

A major powerbroker, Cleveland also used his influence to promote dozens of other artists and connect them to a larger audience. During the 1970s, Savoy released recordings in the "James Cleveland Presents" series by Charles Fold, Marva Hines and Company, the White Brothers, the Donald Vails Choraleers,

Marvin Jenkins and the Musettes, and Sara Jordan Powell, among others. Savoy also released the musical proceedings of the annual GMWA conventions. Cleveland possessed a tremendous amount of power, not just in terms of providing a space for artists to hone and share their talents but also in shaping debates regarding the direction of black gospel music.

As might be expected given his stature in the field, Cleveland frequently received requests to comment on sonic transformations in gospel music. For example, in the April 29, 1976, edition of *Jet* magazine, Cleveland and the Mighty Clouds of Joy engaged in a spirited debate about the aesthetic and religious merits of gospel rock, a term commonly used to describe more disco- or funk-influenced religious music. The debate developed in response to the quartet's recent success in the pop field. With members Joe Ligon, Richard Wallace, Elmo Franklin, and Johnny Martin, the Mighty Clouds were now in the national spotlight for their smash hit "Mighty High."

Firmly established in the gospel field, the Mighty Clouds had recently come under the control of the ABC label after the company acquired Duke-Peacock Records. Feeling as if the quartet had crossover potential, ABC paired them with Dave Crawford, a talented producer whose previous tenure with Atlantic Records included work with Wilson Pickett, Sam Moore, Dee Dee Warwick, the J. Geils Band, and Jackie Moore.[61] The pairing yielded positive results as the Mighty Clouds scored a major hit with "Mighty High" from their 1975 album, *Kickin'*. The song held the top position on *Billboard*'s dance charts for five weeks, reached as high as #22 on the soul charts, and peaked at #66 on the pop charts. With the success of their hit single, they became the first gospel group to appear on Don Cornelius's popular dance show, *Soul Train*.

"Mighty High" brought the Mighty Clouds new fans while disappointing some of the group's older followers, including James Cleveland, who later produced one of their gospel hits, "I've Been in the Storm Too Long." Cleveland's friendship with the Mighty Clouds did not prevent him from expressing displeasure at their ABC material, which was being marketed as "rock gospel." "Gospel music expresses love for Christ and it cannot be sung as rock music or rock gospel. The message is paramount, not the music. In rock gospel, the music is more important than the message," Cleveland declared.[62] Taking exception with Cleveland's position, Mighty Clouds member Johnny Martin criticized the gospel star for his failure to take into account the unique marketing challenges facing gospel quartets: "It's easy for him to say that rock gospel isn't gospel. He's making plenty of money and his records, since they are choir-oriented, are always being played on the radio." The situation for a quartet like the Mighty Clouds of Joy, Martin insisted, was different. "We need hit records to survive. The average radio station that plays gospel doesn't play quartets. They play choirs. We also have to deal with the fact that there is one James Cleveland and hundreds of quartets.

For us to survive, we've got to have hit records. Without one, we're just another struggling group."[63]

Cleveland's issues with "Mighty High" was about more than sound. There was also an important racial subtext to his critique. To better understand that subtext, it is useful to consider his later commentary on what he perceived as some whites' voyeuristic approach to black gospel. In an interview with writer Viv Broughton, he expressed discomfort with the presence of black gospel in non-church settings where whites constitute the majority: "If they want religious music in the clubs, in the casinos where folks are ten feet away and drinking and gambling, then they should get white singers. . . . But they would not insult the intelligence of white singers by asking them to sing in a club."[64]

To his credit, Cleveland never questioned the religious commitment of the Mighty Clouds of Joy members or any other artists who pursued a path different from his own.[65] Moreover, he was far from a gospel purist.

Indeed, some of his more intriguing musical moments of the 1970s came when he revisited the songbook of major secular stars. Four years after Elvis Presley recorded Mac Davis's "In the Ghetto," Cleveland covered the song. His rendition of Davis's tale of intergenerational poverty won him a Grammy for Best Soul Gospel Performance. A year later, Cleveland struck gold again with his moving reinterpretation of Gladys Knight's 1973 hit "You're the Best Thing That Ever Happened to Me." The song appeared on Cleveland's 1975 album, *Jesus Is the Best Thing That Ever Happened to Me*, one of several collaborations with Reverend Charles Fold of Cincinnati, Ohio. Any other artist might have been uncomfortable testing a Gladys Knight remake on an unsuspecting religious audience, but Cleveland performed the tune with a judicious blend of confidence and humor.

On that same recording, the singer delivered a gut-wrenching rendition of "Can't Nobody Do Me Like Jesus" and a crowd-pleasing medley of "I Stood on the Banks of the Jordan," "Lord Help Me to Hold Out," and "Peace Be Still." Shortly after its release in August 1975, *Jesus Is the Best Thing That Ever Happened to Me* topped *Billboard*'s gospel charts, where it remained in the top ten for more than a year and a half.

Cleveland's Global Influence

Not just popular in the United States, James Cleveland enjoyed a growing following among blacks in other countries, particularly London and South Africa. His admirers ranged from Bazil Meade, the Montserrat-born, England-based founder of the London Community Gospel Choir (LCGC), to South African gospel stars Benjamin Dube and Jabu Hlongwane, one of the founders of the ensemble Joyous Celebration. Looking back at the beginning of his ministry, Bishop John Francis of London vividly remembered his first encounter with

Cleveland's music: "The first album that I had that my father bought me was by James Cleveland and the Southern California Community Choir. It was an incredible album." Unable to contain his excitement after his initial listening, Francis vowed to travel to the United States. "I want to meet this guy!" he remembered thinking. "I want to hear the choir."[66] For Francis and other gospel artists in the larger African diaspora, Cleveland's choirs provided a blueprint from which to construct and build their own unique brand of gospel music.

Increasingly aware of his popularity beyond the United States, Cleveland welcomed the opportunity to perform in other countries. Over his recording career, he made several trips to Europe and the Middle East.[67] The circumstances surrounding his international travel were as diverse as the institutions soliciting his services. In 1980, for example, the U.S. military sponsored Cleveland's travel to Northampton as part of its efforts to entertain American troops stationed throughout England. Since the 1950s, the State Department had sponsored tours featuring African American entertainers as a way to advance the nation's foreign policy/Cold War agenda and bolster its image internationally; it relied heavily on jazz artists as cultural ambassadors during the 1950s and 1960s.[68] Over time, however, U.S. officials looked beyond the world of jazz for cultural emissaries. The 1966 First World Festival of Negro Arts in Dakar, Senegal, according to Penny Von Eschen, "was a catalyst for the State Department's shift toward a wider range of black music."[69] Increasingly after that historic festival, which featured gospel star Marion Williams, the government turned to soul, blues, and gospel artists to promote its agenda. "Seeing the extraordinary enthusiasm" for Williams at Dakar, "the Department of State got religion" and increased its use of black gospel singers.[70] Of course, these artists' performances and their interactions with audiences in Africa (Williams) and India (Mahalia Jackson in 1971) did not always advance the "color blind universalism" the State Department sought to export to other countries. Instead, their shows often conveyed "an oppositional rather than racially integrated image of American culture."[71]

Notwithstanding this reality, the State Department continued to use African American artists as cultural ambassadors. Thus, when government officials sought Cleveland's services in Northampton, the gospel star added his name to a long list of African American performers who had taken their message overseas with the support of the U.S. government.

Taking advantage of the opportunity to spread his gospel message to a larger audience, Cleveland electrified the crowd with several gospel classics. "They gonna blow yo' minds tonight," Cleveland alerted the crowd as his Southern California Community Choir took the stage.[72] Later captured on the British show *In the Spirit*, Cleveland's performance was a brilliant showcase of American gospel music.

This would not be Cleveland's last trip to England. In the summer of 1985, he collaborated with the London Community Gospel Choir. The LCGC thrived under the leadership of Reverend Bazil Meade, one of Europe's biggest promoters and teachers of American-style gospel music. Several months before Cleveland's arrival, the LCGC had backed up Al Green during his performance at Albert Hall. Taking note of recent events, one local reporter believed the gospel industry was prime for great growth internationally: "There is a new sense of belonging to a global gospel movement, one that links congregations from Seoul to Detroit."[73]

A day before his scheduled concert with the LCGC, Cleveland arrived at Heathrow Airport, where his driver rushed him to a small Methodist church in London's East End. Waiting for him were ninety members of the LCGC, who over the next hour rehearsed two of Cleveland's songs. Very much the perfectionist, Cleveland coached every section of the choir, fine-tuning their parts, and reminding members to be attentive to technique and to the Holy Spirit. "When you're in the Spirit," he demonstratively explained, "it should be like fire—fire shut up in your bones."[74] It was a moment Meade and the LCGC would never forget—a training session with the King of Gospel.

By this time, Cleveland had also made his mark among lovers of gospel music in another important corner of the African diaspora: South Africa. Identified by record company executives as a developing market for black gospel, South Africa was definitely on the radar of several key industry figures, most notably James Bullard of Word Records, Christian music's largest company. Not long after settling into his position as head of Word's black division, Bullard set his sights on increasing the company's international sales. "We're looking at South Africa with Johannesburg our target city," Bullard informed *Billboard* magazine in 1981. This was no easy task given the country's political culture, but he was confident that gospel could thrive there. "There are 20 million blacks there and we want to expose our product [beyond] those who are already gospel fans. We're already being distributed there through a Christian distributor but we're also now looking at secular distribution."[75] Counted among those gospel artists who already had a following in South Africa was James Cleveland, who along with performers like Andraé Crouch created music that resonated deeply among South Africans struggling to navigate their racial and religious identities in an apartheid state. One such listener was Godfrey Bobby Musengwa, a native of Pretoria who fled South Africa in 1987. First encountering Cleveland's music in the early 1980s, Musengwa turned to the gospel legend for spiritual nourishment, as well as for musical inspiration. "We listened to him and many other Christian artists for personal edification," Musengwa recalled. "But it was also for learning new songs for worship and choir."[76] Throughout his high school years and extending into his undergraduate career in Soshanguve, Musengwa leaned on the musical catalog of Cleveland. Several South African artists, most notably Benjamin Dube and Jabu Hlongwane, also incorporated aspects of what Horace Boyer identifies as the "Cleveland style" into their performances. That style includes "half crooning, half preaching the verses," extemporaneous improvisations during the song's vamp, and singing at the extreme of one's natural register.[77] The passion with which South African artists, particularly Hlongwane, perform Cleveland's songs also serves as an important reminder of how the gospel icon's music created space to imagine new possibilities. In other words, Cleveland's art did not need a "clear political line" to have a "political effect" on certain members of society, particularly those facing state-sanctioned violence and racial and economic oppression.[78]

Pressing Ahead in the 1980s

Though not in the best health, Cleveland remained extremely active as both an artist and industry leader during the 1980s. Under his direction, the GMWA was as strong as ever. Its annual conventions drew attendees in the thousands, and aspiring musicians still flocked to these yearly gatherings to catch their big break in the gospel industry. "It's important that we have this type of organization," Cleveland told one journalist. "This is the only way we have to pass down our gospel heritage and train people professionally to work in various fields of gospel music."[79] If African Americans were to protect one of their most treasured art forms, then they would have to take charge and work collectively.

With this in mind, Cleveland revisited the idea of forming a black gospel college. "I would like to see a college erected somewhere on the campus of a black university," the gospel legend told an *Ebony* reporter. The curriculum would center on the "teaching and perpetuation of gospel music."[80] This plan was connected to another one of his institutional dreams: "Gospeland." Cleveland and GMWA officials envisioned Gospeland as a 350-acre complex consisting of eight distinct operations: "Gospeland of America—Entertainment Park[,] Gospel City[,] Gospeland Temple and Amphitheatre[,] Gospeland Hotel and Convention Center[,] Gospeland Television and Recording Productions[,] Gospeland Travel Tours[,] the Gospel House Auditorium[,] and the Gospeland College of America."[81] Opryland, according to Ed Smith, was the source of inspiration for Cleveland. "James and I visited Opryland and he was very impressed," Smith explained. "We had started one time to get a design concept with senior citizens housing, an amusement park, and our ultimate goal was to build a college of music ... with its thrust on gospel and spiritual music ... you know[,] teach the regular thing but specialize in that area."[82] Gospeland never materialized, but through the GMWA's annual conventions and its local chapters Cleveland passed his love and knowledge of the heritage of black gospel music to younger African Americans.

Despite his extensive work with the GMWA, Cleveland remained committed to his art. Every year, he seemed to deliver a hit to gospel radio, providing new material for black church choirs across the nation and joy to his legion of fans.

In fact, one of my most resonant childhood memories involves a maternal aunt who in the 1980s seemed to play one particular record by Cleveland incessantly: *Live at Symphony Hall in Newark, NJ*, one of the finest albums in his discography. The album featured established acts and old-time friends like Dorothy Norwood, an artist Cleveland had known since his days with the Caravans, and newer acts like the New Jersey Mass Choir, a local group who in 1984 received national attention for their involvement in Foreigner's smash hit "I Want to Know What Love Is." *Live at Symphony Hall* was Cleveland's second recording with the New Jersey choir, which had appeared on his 1983 album *Soon I Will Be Done with the Troubles of the World*. Later signed to Light Records, the New Jersey Mass Choir had a contemporary sound that found perfect expression in radio hits like "I'll Tell It," "Hold Up the Light," and "Oh the Blood." They drew inspiration from artists like Andraé Crouch and Walter Hawkins. And yet, they combined with Cleveland to create, arguably, his last great album.

A stellar recording released in 1984, *Live at Symphony Hall* captures Cleveland, his soloists, and the choir in top form. If nothing else, this record proved Cleveland could still bring out the best in himself and others. The standout cuts included "You've Really Been Good to Me," "In Him There Is No Failure," "He That Believeth," and "He'll Never Let You Down." The latter song had been first introduced at the 1982 GMWA convention, where guest soloist Daryl Coley dazzled the audience with his vocal genius. Two years later at the New Jersey recording, Michael Harris filled in for Coley. Listening to the record, one gets a sense of how much Cleveland enjoyed the process of music making and the opportunities for intergenerational exchange. His love for teaching surfaces most strongly on "He That Believeth," a song on which he performs the role of cultural archivist. "Last night," Cleveland reflects as his rhythm section locks in a tight groove, "I went to the rehearsal and I taught the children an old, old-fashioned song, because I like for them to know some of the heritage of gospel music. And I wanted to take them way back and show them that you can take some of the old and some of the new and put it together." Injecting his own unique brand of humor, Cleveland then quips, "I would ask you to join in but don't nobody here know no old songs but me."[83] Cleveland jokingly presented himself as an old relic; however, he was anything but. Cognizant of the personal benefits of intergenerational exchange, he surrounded himself with talented musicians and singers like Daryl Coley, Kurt Carr, and Keith Pringle who kept his music fresh and exciting.

Even as he adapted to new changes, his music still had a blues quality, a deep connection to everyday people navigating the trials and tribulations of daily life. To be sure, Cleveland was a wealthy man who was treated like a deity in some religious circles, but at the same time, his music touched on themes to which many black folks living in Reagan America could relate. Working in what Albert

Murray refers to as the blues idiom, Cleveland confronted, acknowledged, and contended "with the infernal absurdities and ever impending frustrations in the nature of all existence."[84] And yet, there breathed a hope in the music. Loneliness, depression, heartache, and economic difficulties—none of these challenges, according to Cleveland, were too hard for God.

A masterful storyteller, Cleveland used irony and humor to capture the tragicomic reality of life and to make the hard times a bit more bearable for his listeners. Perhaps nowhere was this more apparent than on his 1983 duet with Charles Fold, "This Too, Will Pass." Tackling the subject of sickness during the vamp, Cleveland tells the audience, "Somebody say I got high blood pressure. Well, we came to tell you tonight. I don't care what you got, high blood, low blood, no blood at all. This too, will pass."[85]

Sickness increasingly became a topic in both Cleveland's songs and his life. Late in 1982, the gospel star was admitted into the Daniel Freeman Hospital in Inglewood, California, for treatment related to hypertension and chest pains.[86] Over the next several years, a combination of health ailments slowed down his productivity as an artist and circumscribed his role as president of the GMWA. The gospel music community worked hard to ensure that Cleveland knew that his labor for the genre had not been in vain. On Monday night, October 29, 1990, a star-studded lineup of gospel and secular musicians gathered at Dorothy Chandler Pavilion in Los Angeles to honor Cleveland's career. The list of performers included Andraé and Sandra Crouch, the Hawkins Family, Shirley Caesar, the Caravans, Táta Vega, and Billy Preston, who delivered an amazing rendition of "How Great Thou Art." The declining health of Cleveland, who couldn't perform due to a tracheostomy, was not lost on the attendees. As journalist Chris Willman noted in his review of the concert, "It was a high-spirited, sometimes tearfully emotional scene reminiscent of last year's televised salute to Sammy Davis, who was also present at his tribute but not able to raise his own voice in song."[87]

On February 9, 1991, Cleveland passed away at the age of fifty-nine. "A great soul has passed," mourned Aretha Franklin. "James was probably the most significant factor on me musically in terms of my early piano stylings. Anyone who heard him, you were touched by him. He was a motivator, an innovator."[88] Gospel star Edwin Hawkins agreed: "We have all been influenced by him. . . . We all bought his records as children—that's how we learned to sing gospel music."[89]

Words of praise also came from music critics. The always-poignant Richard Harrington of the *Washington Post* recalled one of Cleveland's performances at the Upper Room Baptist Church in Northeast D.C. Of particular intrigue for Harrington was Cleveland's handling of the choir: "He would lean into the sound, listening for sharps and flats, shaping timbre and texture, fine tuning the timing, focusing the power, showing the choir how to build tension musically and emotionally, how to balance the demands of his imaginative arrangements while remaining responsible to natural and immediate emotion. Cleveland always seemed to be in mid-gesture—part conductor, part cheerleader—his thick fingers poking at the contours of the melody, his arms spread out imploringly, his head turned slightly away to hide the pleasure as the choir came closer to his expectations."[90]

Cleveland, a master teacher in every sense of the term, derived joy from witnessing others blossom into their full artistic selves. "Within everybody," he once said, "there's a well of creativity. There are so many sitting there in the choir that don't even know their own potential. I draw them out, and I get a whole lot of stuff out of them that they're not aware they have."[91] In addition to working to ensure black singers and musicians maximized their potential, Cleveland dedicated his life to preserving and advancing the many forms of gospel music. His institution-building efforts through the GMWA not only enriched the gospel sound but also contributed immensely to the genre's expansion in the United States and throughout the African diaspora.

CHAPTER 2

A Special Kind of Witness

Andraé Crouch, the Growth of Contemporary Christian Music, and the Politics of Race

The first step toward love is a common sharing of a sense of mutual work and value. This cannot be discovered in a vacuum or in a series of artificial or hypothetical relationships. It has to be in a real situation, natural, free. The experience of the common worship of God is such a moment. It is in this connection that American Christianity has betrayed the religion of Jesus almost beyond redemption. Churches have been established for the underprivileged, for the weak, for the poor, on the theory that they prefer to be among themselves. Churches have been established for the Chinese, the Japanese, the Korean, the Mexican, the Filipino, the Italian, and the Negro, with the same theory in mind. The result is that in the one place in which normal, free contacts might be most naturally established—in which the relations of the individual to his God should take priority over conditions of class, race, power, status, wealth, or the like—this place is one of the chief instruments of guaranteeing barriers.

—HOWARD THURMAN, *Jesus and the Disinherited*

Upon my first engagement with the towering theologian Howard Thurman and his thought-provoking writings on religion and racial reconciliation, the musical ministry of Andraé Edward Crouch immediately came to mind. Through his innovative songwriting, arrangements, and production, Crouch opened up new possibilities for the construction of what Thurman refers to as a "common environment for the purpose of providing normal experiences of fellowship" among Christians from diverse socioeconomic and racial backgrounds.[1] In the late 1960s and throughout the 1970s, Crouch stirred the passions of whites and blacks alike with such gospel classics as "The Blood Will Never Lose Its Power," "Through It All," "Jesus Is the Answer," "My Tribute (To God Be the Glory)," "It Won't Be Long," and "Soon and Very Soon." These songs not only formed the building blocks of his amazing career but also helped establish the sonic and lyrical foundations of contemporary Christian music (CCM).[2] Their influence can be heard across a wide spectrum of religious music, from the gospel pop of Amy Grant to the introspective ballads of Marvin Winans. "Crouch was an innovator, a path-finder, a precursor in an industry noted for its conservative, often derivative approach to popular music," gospel historian Robert Darden rightly points out. "He combined gospel and rock, flavored it with jazz and calypso as the mood struck him and the song called for it. . . . He took risks with his art and was very, very funky when he wanted to be."[3]

FIGURE 6. Andraé Crouch at the Dove Awards, January 4, 1977. Photo by Afro-American Newspapers/Gado/Getty Images.

Crouch mastered his art form and in the process achieved massive popularity among white and black Christians. More than any religious artist before or since, he helped bridge some of the racial divides within the Christian music world.[4] In what historian Daniel Rodgers calls the age of fracture, "when imagined collectivities shrank; notions of structure and power thinned out; . . . [and] blends and hybridities were a fact of religious identity," Crouch held the center.[5] At the height of his popularity, his influence was not only profound but also singular.

Thus, when the iconic artist died on January 8, 2015, at Northridge Medical Center in Los Angeles, a profound sense of loss engulfed broad swaths of the Christian world. Counted among the mourners was multiplatinum selling artist Michael W. Smith, a Kenova, West Virginia, native who discovered Crouch's music as a teenager. "I'll never forget hearing Andraé for the first time," remembered Smith; "it was like someone had opened a whole new world of possibilities for me musically. The depth of his influence on Christian music is incalculable. We all owe him."[6]

Similar sentiments echoed from other parts of the world. Not just popular in the United States, Crouch was a global sensation with fans in Europe, Asia, and Africa. "I was introduced to Andraé Crouch's music in the late 60s," remembered Bazil Meade, founding director of the London Community Gospel Choir. "His songs were easy to sing, with beautiful soulful melodies, and became popular in churches throughout the Black community here in the UK." Fortunate to have the opportunity to tour with Crouch, Meade learned a great deal about interracial interaction from the talented musician: "It was a wonderful experience, to watch him minister with great confidence to a mainly White audience, who loved and admired his ministry and music. I learned to be confident when sharing faith—irrespective of the cultural differences of one's audience."[7] Perhaps the most insightful commentary on Crouch's global impact came from Olugu Orji, a Nigerian who first encountered the singer's music as a student at the University of Ife during the 1980s. "With pointed words that bore the unmistakable imprimatur of divinity, he captured the imagination of a generation of famished and frustrated Christians who sought solid outlets for the holy impulses that coursed within them." Crouch's engaging style, according to Orji, "compelled you to make a robust response to the burning issues of the moment. . . . His powerful lyrics and attention-grabbling rhythms . . . dripped modernity while managing to arrest the admiration of older generations."[8]

As Crouch's popularity grew, his influence extended beyond religious circles. A highly sought-after arranger with keen pop instincts, Crouch collaborated with Quincy Jones, the Commodores, Michael Jackson, and Madonna, among other secular stars. The gifted songwriter also had his songs covered by the likes of Elvis Presley ("I've Got Confidence") and Paul Simon ("Jesus Is the Answer"). Even after Crouch's popularity as a solo artist waned during the 1980s, he remained in demand as a writer and arranger. Considered by many in Hollywood as the "go-to person" for the gospel sound, Crouch composed "Maybe God is Tryin' to Tell You Somethin'," for the classic film *The Color Purple* as well as the opening theme song ("Shine on Me") for the 1980s sitcom *Amen*. As scholar Melinda Weeks rightly notes, "Crouch's career embodies the musical, social, and cultural 'integration' of modern gospel music reflective of the social realities of the 1960s and 1970s."[9]

As one of gospel's most daring musicians, Crouch frequently clashed with gospel purists who felt both his art and his public persona were too Hollywood. His partnerships with secular musicians and his appearances on shows like *Saturday Night Live* struck some as "too worldly" for a gospel artist. Crouch respected the history of gospel music and those pioneering artists who contributed to its growth, but he refused to live in the past. "I'm not trying to preserve a gospel sound," he once sounded off to critics; "I'm trying to preach the word of God and his principles."[10] Crouch's unwillingness to subscribe to conventional ideas about what gospel musicians could and could not do endeared him to several of his colleagues, most notably James Cleveland. Even when Cleveland disagreed with Crouch's musical choices, he respected his willingness to move in new directions. "There is no musical form that Andraé Crouch doesn't embrace," Cleveland admiringly observed. "He can be Dixieland, jazz, soulful, he can be extremely traditional if he wants to be. Wherever his creativity leads him, he goes there. He never allows himself to get boxed in."[11]

Beginnings: Southern California and the Making of a Gospel Pioneer

The seeds of Crouch's adventurous approach to music were sown in his Southern California home, where he and his twin sister, Sandra, developed their love for God and the arts. The Crouch twins were born on July 1, 1942, to Catherine and Benjamin Crouch. A native of Dallas, Texas, Benjamin Crouch studied at Wilberforce University in Ohio and then the Bible Institute of Los Angeles (or BIOLA). Settling down in 1939, Crouch married the LA native Catherine Dorothea Hodnett. The early years of the Crouches' marriage coincided with a period of profound change for Los Angeles, which experienced a dramatic increase in its African American population during and immediately after World War II. New economic opportunities significantly altered the demographic profile of the city, which in 1920 had a black population of only 15,000. Unlike the northern cities of Chicago, Cleveland, Pittsburgh, Gary, and New York, Los Angeles would not experience its "Great Migration" until World War II. According to historian Paul Robinson, "In the wake of Executive Order 8802 [banning discrimination in war-related work], hundreds of thousands of blacks migrated to Los Angeles to work in the newly opened defense industries." Most of the newcomers found employment, but the standard of living in the racially divided city was a source of disappointment for many. "Subsequent overcrowding in Los Angeles's 'Black Belts,'" Robinson explains, "caused the housing crisis to become the number-one issue facing Los Angeles's black community during this time."[12]

Like many African Americans who called Los Angeles home during the 1940s, Benjamin Crouch focused his attention on work, family, and church. The devoted father of three juggled his family responsibilities with the demands of running a small dry-cleaning business. He also carved out time to engage in evangelical work within and beyond his church. Committed to spreading the gospel, Crouch belonged to Emmanuel Church of God in Christ, where he participated in its outreach ministries at local jails, schools, and hospitals. Emmanuel thrived under the leadership of Crouch's uncle Bishop Samuel Crouch, a high-ranking official in the Church of God in Christ (COGIC) who assisted greatly in the denomination's West Coast expansion. During his career, Bishop Crouch presided over COGIC's home and foreign mission department, held the position of first assistant presiding bishop, and served on the board of directors of the World Pentecostal Conference. Heavily involved in the promotion of gospel music in its early stages of development, he helped advance the career of the noted gospel performer Arizona Dranes and facilitated her signing with OKeh Records in the 1920s.[13] Their relationship stretched back to his days in Fort Worth, where he first encountered the brilliant pianist whose distinctive style influenced many gospel musicians. On his journey from Texas to California, Bishop Crouch brought with him an unwavering love for the sacred songs of the black church.

Benjamin Crouch appreciated his uncle's tutelage, but also recognized God's calling on his own life. In 1951, he formed his own church, Christ Memorial Church of God in Christ, in San Fernando Valley. Convincing his children to support his endeavors proved easy for Crouch. As Andraé Crouch later reflected, "I loved church so much I never wanted to miss a chance to go."[14] Immersed in the day-to-day activities of the church as a young boy, Crouch began to exhibit an intense love for music. At the age of fourteen, he wrote one of his most famous compositions, "The Blood Will Never Lose Its Power."

Although Crouch occasionally battled with feelings of self-doubt, due in no small part to his dyslexia and tendency to stutter in public, he began collaborating with other talented young musicians. One of his collaborators was the gifted organist Billy Preston, with whom Crouch formed the group the Church of God in Christ Singers (primarily known as the COGICS) in 1960. The COGICS consisted of Crouch and his sister, Sandra, Preston, Blinky Williams, Frankie Spring, Edna Wright (a future lead singer for the Honeycombs), and Gloria Jones (who like Sandra Crouch later worked at Motown). The COGICS disbanded after Preston landed a job with the soul legend Ray Charles, but Crouch reserved a special place in his heart for the group: "The COGICS were a bunch of spirit-filled kids. I often think of the meetings and services where we sang and what an impact we had on people. God really used us."[15] Crouch soon discovered another group through which to hone his talent and build his ministry: the Disciples. Formed by Crouch in 1965, the group included Ruben Fernandez, Perry Morgan, and Billy Thedford. Their energetic performances created quite a buzz in Los Angeles and surrounding areas.

Signing with Light Records

Word of the Disciples' strong musicianship and expanding following soon reached Ralph Carmichael, a respected jazz arranger turned record executive who founded Light Records in 1966. Carmichael scheduled a meeting with Crouch, and the two men bonded immediately: "After the usual amenities, we began exchanging ideas about music—its trends, its potential, and how it can be used to get kids with the gospel of Christ. I soon discovered that under his mild manner and warm smile, Andraé was a guy with a very serious purpose that had reached 'do or die' proportions."[16] Impressed by Crouch's vision and talent, Carmichael signed the Disciples to a one-record deal. Unbeknownst to Carmichael and Crouch, their partnership would exceed the terms of the contract. Crouch, as both an artist and talent recruiter, would help transform the label into a major player in gospel music. Along with producing some of the industry's best-selling and most innovative records, he secured the label such talented artists as Walter Hawkins in the mid-1970s and the Detroit gospel quartet the Winans in the early 1980s.

Shortly after signing with Light, Crouch released his debut, *Take the Message Everywhere*. The record consists of six originals and five covers, which range from the gospel classic "Precious Lord, Take My Hand" to the pop standard "Without a Song." Much like Crouch, *Take the Message Everywhere* defies easy categorization. Though deeply rooted in the biblical messages of the New Testament, the record draws rhythmic and vocal inspiration from the "California sound" of the Beach Boys, the Fifth Dimension, and the Mamas and the Papas. Crouch also drew inspiration from Detroit's soul scene. His appreciation for Motown is especially apparent on "I've Got It." On this song, Crouch returns to his COGIC upbringing with a commanding testimony on the power of the Holy Ghost. With vivid detail and great fervor, Crouch recounts the Day of Pentecost, when the Holy Spirit filled the disciples and granted them the power to speak in tongues. Though Crouch is listed as the song's sole composer, its rhythms borrow from the Capitols' 1966 hit, "Cool Jerk," which featured members of Motown's studio band, the Funk Brothers.

Though attentive to various trends in popular music, Crouch never allowed his influences to suffocate his own voice. His deep respect for the talent of others coexisted with an equal appreciation for the singularity of his own gifts. Those gifts surfaced most strongly on "The Blood Will Never Lose Its Power." An eclectic mix of Southern Baptist, contemporary gospel, and country, "The Blood" has a straightforward, no-frills quality. Clocking in at two minutes and thirty-eight seconds, it consists of two verses and one chorus. Against the backdrop of a beautiful melody, Crouch and the Disciples sing about Jesus's death at Calvary and the transformative power of his blood, which, the singers remind listeners, "will never lose its power."[17]

Having fulfilled his one-album obligation with Light, Crouch fielded offers from other record companies, most notably A&M, Columbia, Liberty, and Mercury. After much deliberation, Crouch signed with Liberty. One of his singles for the label was "Christian People," which received a fair amount of airplay and even garnered Crouch his first Grammy nomination.[18] The song's modest success in the secular world, according to Crouch, stemmed from its "Motownish, pop sound."[19] Enthused by the public's response to Crouch, Liberty wanted the singer to duplicate the sound of "Christian People." This ultimately created tension between label executives and the adventurous Crouch, a daring musician whose aesthetic tastes were quite diverse. Notwithstanding his affection for Motown, Crouch had other musical interests he wanted to pursue and did not want to water down his message: "I believed that if I continued with Liberty I'd have to compromise my testimony, to sacrifice my songs that really ministered to people. I really had to battle the turmoil in my heart. I prayed and fasted, and the Lord told me He wanted me to minister, so I just rebuked the whole thought of any type of 'top-40' songs and asked to be released from the contract."[20]

Liberty granted Crouch's release, enabling him to renew his partnership with Carmichael. Light Records, Crouch firmly believed, would nurture his artistic and spiritual development. "With them," the singer noted, "we weren't required to compromise our commitment to the Lord, and we've sold thousands of records since then."[21]

With his label situation in order, Crouch released *Keep on Singin'* in 1971.[22] Like its predecessor, *Take the Message Everywhere, Keep on Singin'* had a distinctive voice, a groove and message of its own. It was traditional and contemporary, reverent yet forward-thinking. Standouts on the record included the praise and worship staples "Take a Little Time" and "My Tribute (To God Be the Glory)" and the guitar-heavy "I've Got Confidence," which Elvis Presley covered a couple of years later. Crouch was the mastermind behind *Keep on Singin'*, though the contributions of the other Disciples should not be overlooked. Doubling as a bassist and vocalist for the group, Billy Thedford handled the lead vocals on "My Tribute." Tenor Perry Morgan led the soulful opener, "I Don't Know Why Jesus

Loved Me." And while not an "official" Disciple, singer Tramaine Davis (soon to be Hawkins) turned in a strong performance on "I'm Coming Home, Dear Lord," a song that delves into the themes of brokenness, repentance, and spiritual rebirth. Another valuable player, Crouch's sister, Sandra, provided background vocals and percussion throughout the album.

Crouch remained on the cutting edge of gospel music with his third release, aptly titled *Soulfully*. On this recording, he experimented with many of the sonic innovations taking place in mainstream black music. The rhythmic textures of psychedelic soul pervade "Satisfied" and "Leave the Devil Alone," which additionally incorporates the brassy sound of Memphis soul. *Soulfully* also included two of Crouch's most famous songs, "Through It All" and "It Won't Be Long." "It Won't Be Long" opens with the sounds of an electric sitar, climaxes with Crouch's dramatic reading of John 3:2, and concludes with the ringing of a church bell. Here, he urges listeners to prepare for Christ's imminent return.

With the success of his first three records, Crouch was in high demand as a performer. Venues for his live shows ranged from the famous Gazzarri's nightclub on Sunset Boulevard to New York's Carnegie Hall. Crouch and the Disciples also appeared on a variety of television programs, including the *Tonight Show* with Johnny Carson. Tapped into the evangelical circuit, the group's performance schedule also included Ralph Wilkerson's Melodyland, Oral Roberts's talk show, the *Pat Boone Family Show*, the Assemblies of God's Evangel College, and Bethel College in St. Paul, Minnesota. Since Crouch's ongoing search for spiritual clarity and direction instilled within him a deep concern for young adults fleshing out their relationship with God and organized religion, he very much welcomed the opportunity to perform on college campuses. A testament to his broad appeal, his college tour stops included the conservative Baylor University, the liberal University of California at Berkeley, and the historically black college Bluefield State.[23]

Crouch and the Disciples captivated their audiences with their spirited performances and stylish attire. Taking their sartorial cues from the world of rock, funk, and soul, the band sported bellbottoms, colorful shirts, platform shoes, long hair, and afros. For many concertgoers, Crouch's live shows were life-changing events.

More than forty years after attending his first Disciples concert, gospel legend Marvin Winans still remembered every detail of that experience: Crouch's command at the piano, the band's intensity and camaraderie, the crowd participation, and the racial demographics of the audience. "We went to a concert in Detroit at the Ford Auditorium and my life was changed," Winans recalled in a speech at the Rock and Roll Hall of Fame. "When I walked in that auditorium, it was the first time I had ever saw a black man singing with a predominantly white audience going crazy. And I knew that's what I wanted to do with the rest of my life."[24]

Winans's surprise at Crouch's popularity among white Christians was understandable. While many of its artists preached the equality of all people before God, the gospel industry had always been fractured along racial lines. Of course, this reflected larger dynamics within American Christianity. Granted, during the civil rights movement, several activists made efforts to address the racism within the body of Christ, but these efforts had minimal impact on the religious landscape.[25] As Dr. Martin Luther King Jr. perceptively noted four days before his death, "We must face the sad fact that at eleven o'clock on Sunday morning

FIGURE 7. Andraé Crouch on Oral Roberts's *Christmas Is Love* TV special, December 21, 1975. Photo courtesy of Photofest.

when we stand to sing 'In Christ there is no East or West,' we stand in the most segregated hour of America."[26] This racial divide did not and has not escaped the gospel industry. And yet, during the 1970s, Crouch found a place on black gospel and white Christian stations.

A Match Made in Heaven? Andraé Crouch and the Jesus Movement

A key factor in Crouch's crossover success was his superstar status among thousands of whites identified with the Jesus movement. Originating in San Francisco during the 1967 Summer of Love, the Jesus movement revitalized American evangelicalism with its emphasis on young people developing a personal relationship with Jesus; its adoption of certain aspects of 1960s counterculture, particularly hippie fashion; and its premillennial biblical interpretations. The movement quickly expanded beyond its Haight-Ashbury roots into the Southern California area and then throughout the United States. Often identified as "Jesus People," the movement's supporters were linked through a dense network of communes, coffeehouses, traveling troupes, and churches. Fueling the movement's growth, according to historian Larry Eskridge, was its "thriving material culture." Much of its early impact, Eskridge notes,

> stemmed from an inherent cultural-visual dissonance: Encountering long-haired, jeans-clad, sandal-wearing, countercultural-looking youth being baptized or engaging in Pentecostal-style worship was, for Americans in the late 1960s and early 1970s, literally a sight to behold. The Jesus People added to this initial visibility a penchant for visually reinforcing their Christian commitment through the use of artwork and a wide variety of buttons, decals, stickers, posters, T-shirts, and a new evangelical liking for crosses and religious jewelry. With the help of an enterprising network of evangelical organizations, publicists, and entrepreneurs eager to capitalize spiritually, emotionally, and financially from the Jesus movement, they would create an iconic universe that contributed to the movement's overall growth and vitality.[27]

That iconic universe came into sharper focus for many Americans in the summer of 1971, when *Time* magazine ran a cover story on the Jesus Revolution. The article detailed a Jesus-loving youth culture, composed of idealistic women and men often living in communal houses and spreading the message of Jesus on street corners across the nation. "There is an uncommon morning freshness to this movement, a buoyant atmosphere of hope and love," stated the article. Their love, according to *Time*, "seemed more sincere than a slogan, deeper than the fast-fading sentiments of the flower children; what startles the outsider is the extraordinary sense of joy that they are able to communicate." To understand their joy, one had to begin with their particular approach to religion. "Their lives," *Time* further detailed, revolved "around an intense personal relationship" with Jesus "and the belief that such a relationship should condition every human life."[28]

No longer a secret to mainstream America, the Jesus movement received coverage from both the secular and the religious press, including *Life*, the *Wall Street Journal*, *Christianity Today*, and *Campus Life*. The movement also increased its visibility and popularity through a variety of public events, ranging from Billy Graham–sponsored crusades to outdoor Christian rock concerts. As Shawn Young notes in his book *Gray Sabbath*, this was a religious revolution that masterfully used the tools of popular culture. "Evangelicals have often puzzled over how to appropriately accommodate culture. After all, if it is not done properly, ministers of the Christian message risk harming their ability to properly shepherd the faithful. But the Jesus Movement created a new way to engage. Then with the rise of Christian concerts and enigmatic Jesus music festivals, young people were finally able to experience community events with other like-minded fans of rock 'n' roll, something yet-to-be added to the Sunday morning gathering."[29]

No event drew more attention than the Campus Crusade for Christ–sponsored EXPLO '72, held in Dallas, Texas, from June 12 to June 17. The brainchild of Campus Crusade for Christ founder Bill Bright, the EXPLO brought together tens of thousands of young people from across the country for training seminars, rallies, nightly revivals, and music.[30] Swarms of curious onlookers headed for downtown Dallas, hoping to get a glimpse of the people some derisively referred to as "Jesus Freaks." On the last day of the gathering, 180,000 people assembled for a concert featuring an eclectic group of artists. Topping the list of performers were Johnny Cash, Kris Kristofferson, and Andraé Crouch, who put the raucous crowd in a state of religious ecstasy with a mind-blowing version of "Satisfied."[31]

As the closing event of EXPLO '72 made clear, Crouch was hugely popular among white Christians, particularly those affiliated with the Jesus movement. His pop melodies, along with his introspective lyrics, appealed to numbers of young women and men seeking spiritual meaning and fulfillment in what many viewed as a disconnected world. "Dissident Christianity," according to historian Doug Rossinow, "led young white people toward a stance of severe dissatisfaction with their contemporary culture, particularly with the same aspects of American life that later drew the new left's ire."[32] Feelings of spiritual emptiness, frustration with what many viewed as society's crass materialism, and the persistence of various forms of social injustice led them on a search for meaning, authenticity, and community. Not all but many found affirmation in the music of Crouch, whose lyrics touched on themes of existential anguish and social alienation.

Tempting as it might be to present Crouch as a musician who transcended the color line, such a representation would be an inaccurate portrait of the complex politics of race, religion, and culture in 1970s America. Even among Jesus movement supporters, tension often surfaced around the issue of race and cultural difference. "The ideal of integration was honored among Jesus People," David Stowe notes, "but in reality, the movement remained predominantly white."[33] More specifically, some whites had trouble seeing African Americans as coworkers in the kingdom of God. In their view, African Americans "were more properly the object of missionary work than fellow laborers in the vineyard of the Holy Spirit."[34] White Christians' subtle and overt racism did not escape the notice of the perceptive Crouch, who refused to ignore the hardcore reality of racial prejudice within American Protestantism in general and Christian music in particular. On the road, he frequently picked up on whites' discomfort with his band, which included not just African Americans but a Mexican American (Ruben Fernandez) as well. On one occasion Crouch confronted, rather humorously, the crowd's racism:

> One night as the Disciples were introduced on stage before a concert in Texas I sensed an "uptight feeling" among the audience. But the Lord told me to let them know I was aware of the color of my skin and I didn't worry about it. "We're happy to be here tonight," I said. "We're not here to go to school with you or anything like that. We come here in the name of Jesus. I'm proud to tell you we don't have tails and that we don't bite. We're just coming to tell you a story and we will be gone tomorrow."[35]

Despite his encounters with racism, Crouch enjoyed performing, meeting new people, and traveling throughout the United States. The adventurous musician also liked his time outside the country. After the release of *Keep on Singin'*, Crouch and the Disciples performed shows in the Philippines, Norway, Sweden, Guam, Tokyo, and Saigon. As he noted in 1972, "We cover a lot of miles throughout the United States every year, but more and more I feel a pull to reach out internationally. A couple of years ago, we had our first taste of overseas work, and I saw something there I'll never forget as we looked into the faces of people hungry to hear the gospel."[36]

Crouch loved the intimacy of worship service, the coming together of different people for a common purpose, and the forging of community through live music and collective participation. Within the sacred space of a Disciples concert, women and men of diverse backgrounds not only could connect with God but also could reimagine themselves and the possibilities of Christian community.

Perhaps nowhere was the power of Crouch's concerts more beautifully captured than on his 1973 record, *"Live" at Carnegie Hall*. To accommodate the thousands of fans who arrived (with and without tickets) at Carnegie, Crouch gave an early concert at nearby Calvary Baptist Church and then dashed off to the legendary New York hall for his scheduled performance. On that magical night, Crouch and the Disciples opened with riveting takes on "I Don't Know

Why" and "You Don't Know What You're Missing." Always attuned to crowd dynamics, Crouch acknowledged the audience's diversity during his opening interlude. To loosen up the crowd, Crouch jokingly referred to his fans' different styles of worship (and perhaps their uneasiness with each other): "For those of you from the First Church of the Frigidaire, you don't have to do nothing. But if you come from the other side of the tracks and you know what goes on the other side . . . we want you to clap your hands and join in with us."[37]

A very audible section of the crowd erupted in laughter as Crouch proceeded with one of the most memorable shows of his career. Without missing a beat, he led the Disciples through his impressive catalog of hits. The enthused audience responded with shouts of joy, tears, foot stomping, hand clapping, and spirited dancing as the Disciples effortlessly moved from devotional tunes like "Hallelujah" and "Jesus Is the Answer" to the soulful "Can't Nobody Do Me Like Jesus." On the latter song, bassist Billy Thedford and drummer Bill Maxwell lay down an incredibly funky groove as guitarist Hadley Hockensmith gives a nod to the blues. Anything but a passive observer, background singer and percussionist Sandra Crouch adds to the raucous number with her fervent tambourine playing. In complete control throughout the night, Crouch ended the concert with a crowd favorite, "It Won't Be Long," which included an altar call. Upon its release in 1973, *"Live" at Carnegie Hall* raced to the top of the gospel charts, enjoying great success among white and black fans.[38]

The hardworking Crouch was also promoting another recently released album: *Just Andraé* (1972). Everything about the record—from the artwork to its title—underscored Light's desire to further exploit Crouch's celebrity status in the CCM world. The album's front cover featured a beautiful photo of Crouch, stylishly attired in an orange shirt and blue-jean jacket. Looking away from the camera, Crouch appears to be engaged in deep thought. The back cover included liner notes from Crouch's mother and father, as well as a childhood picture of Crouch and his sister, Sandra. *Just Andraé's* content was as intriguing as its packaging. On the eclectic recording, Crouch plunged into the world of country music with "God Loves the Country People," then ventured left with the psychedelic sound and trippy lyrics of "Lullaby of the Deceived."

Showing no signs of concern about the possibility of overexposure, Light and its distributor, Word Records, flooded the Christian market with Crouch material. Moving beyond the world of music, Word released Crouch's autobiography, *Through It All*, in 1974. Coauthored with Nina Ball, the autobiography documents the singer's early life, his thoughts on music and religion, and his efforts to negotiate his newfound fame. In this text, Crouch also provided some of his most insightful analyses of racial and cultural diversity within the body of Christ. By the time of the autobiography's publication, Crouch had traveled around the world, performing in Europe, Asia, and Africa. In several sections of the book, he presents himself as someone who had evolved quite a bit in his own thinking regarding race and culture: "I really had to pray and ask the Lord what to do in different cultural situations. We tried to meet different people on their terms, to learn of their customs. . . . What moves one group may not move another, but God can deal with us all."[39]

The publication of *Through It All* testified to the marketing machine that drove American evangelicalism during the 1970s, producing everything from records to comic books. And for many young people immersed in the Christian marketplace, Andraé Crouch was everywhere.

New Directions

Even with his many commitments, Crouch still met his label's insatiable demand for new product. In 1975, he put the finishing touches on *Take Me Back*. The record marked the beginning of his long-term relationship with some of the secular world's most skilled musicians: Joe Sample, Larry Carlton, Wilton Felder, and Ernie Watts. Songs like "Praises" and "Tell Them" leaned toward the contemporary Christian market, while "I'll Still Love You" and "Oh Savior" seemed perfectly tailored for mainstream soul radio. No song was more powerful than the title track, "Take Me Back," which featured Danniebelle Hall on lead vocals. On this song, we find Crouch seeking inner peace and spiritual renewal. His introspective lyrics carry the weight of the emotional fatigue brought about by his hectic tour schedule, demanding studio sessions, and the pressures of superstardom:

> I feel that I'm so far from you Lord
> But still I hear you calling me
> . . . .
> I must confess, Lord I've been blessed
> *But yet my soul's not satisfied*[40]

Coproduced by Crouch and Bill Maxwell and engineered by Bill Taylor, Chuck Johnson, and Tom Trefethen, *Take Me Back* had a polished yet soulful sound that provided a template for 1980s contemporary gospel groups like the Winans, Nicholas, and Commissioned. Selling well in the black gospel and Christian music markets, *Take Me Back* garnered Crouch his first Grammy award in 1975.

Instead of reveling in his accomplishments, Crouch pushed his art to new heights with his 1976 release, *This Is Another Day*. Opening with the disco-tinged "Perfect Peace," the album boasts a stellar cast of musicians, including many who had performed on *Take Me Back*. Danniebelle Hall delivers powerful performances on "My Peace I Leave with You" and "Soon and Very Soon." The latter song became a staple at black churches across the nation. Ending with a passionate, outro performance by elders in Crouch's home church, Christ Memorial, "Soon and Very Soon" incorporates the stylistic elements of both contemporary and traditional gospel music.

With this record, Crouch also embraced more abstract lyrics. Direct references to God or Jesus are few. In fact, songs like "Quiet Times" and "Perfect Peace" foreshadowed the "lyrical ambiguity" found in the works of later gospel artists like BeBe and CeCe Winans. Insisting his music still pertained to God and his spiritual journey, Crouch defended his right to pursue different compositional styles and embrace more abstract lyrics.

Popular beyond the gospel world, *This Is Another Day* spent several weeks on *Billboard*'s soul charts, becoming Crouch's first Top 40 R&B record. Crouch also experienced increased play from black gospel radio stations due to the popularity of "Soon and Very Soon."

None of these developments altered Crouch's status among white Christians. Even as the Jesus movement faded into oblivion during the second half of the 1970s, Crouch remained a fan favorite in the CCM world. The "colorful ethnic mix" of Crouch's audience intrigued many within the music industry, including journalist Hollie West of the *Washington Post*. Three days after attending a Crouch concert at Constitution Hall, West pondered the "attraction of this Afro-American singer for young people from a variety of religious faiths and ethnic backgrounds." In West's view, the personal and musical factors contributing to Crouch's widespread appeal included his "congenial temperament," his theological mixture of "love, salvation, and the second coming," his incorporation of dominant trends in popular music, and his "non-threatening" demeanor.[41]

One overlooked factor in Crouch's success was his refusal to elevate one form of Christian worship or doctrine above another. The church, he believed, was too rigid, too judgmental. "We spend too much time questioning everybody's credibility," Crouch pointed out.

> How have you been baptized, in the name of the Father, Son, and Holy Ghost, or in the name of Jesus? Can you wear earrings, or can you wear jewelry in your church? Are tongues of God or of the devil? What day do you go to church on, Saturday or Sunday? Can you eat pork or can you eat any meat? How do you comb your hair? Can you cut your hair or are you not supposed to cut your hair? Do you drink water when you fast? Can Christian ladies wear pants as men do? Can Christians be possessed by demons or not?[42]

The divisive potential of denominationally based doctrine troubled Crouch, a musician whose followers included Baptists, Methodists, Lutherans, Presbyterians, Mennonites, Episcopalians, Seventh-day Adventists, and charismatic Pentecostals, among others. Within Crouch's circle of followers were individuals with varying levels of involvement in organized religion. There were Bible-quoting, Bible-carrying Christians who had spent their entire lives in the church, and there were those who had only recently become born again. The former group, in Crouch's opinion, sometimes played a "holier-than-thou super-spiritual role," especially if "they have received the charismatic gifts." Even though he described himself as a "Holy Spirit pusher" and an opponent of those "puttin' down the Charismatic renewal," Crouch had issues with charismatics who presented themselves as on a higher spiritual plane than others.[43] Though deeply appreciative of his COGIC upbringing, he recognized the variety of Christian religious practices and expressions. That recognition manifested strongly in his music, particularly his 1978 recording, *Live in London*, a foundational record in the praise and worship genre. Songs like "You Don't Have to Jump No Pews," "I Surrender All," "Praise God, Praise God," and "Hallelujah" were sonic manifestations of Crouch's ecumenical vision forged through a spiritual bond with his diverse community of followers. As such, *Live in London* deserves close examination not only as a critical record in Crouch's expansive catalog but as part of a larger effort to reconstruct and reimagine Christian community.

Live in London

Though praise and worship music defies easy categorization, ethnomusicologist Birgitta Johnson's expansive definition of the genre is particularly useful here. Praise and worship songs, according to Johnson, are typically "highly and intentionally participatory with an emphasis on call-and-response and unison singing. Lyrically driven, with special emphasis on personal as well as corporate praise, adoration, reverence, and worship of God. Stylistically diverse, incorporating musical characteristics identified with rock, folk, gospel (southern and black traditions), Latin, world music, rap, country, and pop genres. Melodically uncomplicated for easy retention . . . [and] highly repetitive lyrics with spiritual messages that encourage ecstatic or highly personal encounters with God."[44] No record in Crouch's discography better illustrates his contributions to the praise and worship genre than *Live in London*. There's no grandstanding or showboating among the singers and musicians. The devotional lyrics exalt the majesty and greatness of God, and the simple melodies invite audience participation. Through his reserved demeanor, devotional lyrics, and straightforward melodies, Crouch focuses his audience's attention on God rather than on the vocalists or the band members. Once again, the scholarly interventions of Johnson are important in understanding why praise and worship worked so well for Crouch. In her study of black megachurches in Los Angeles, Johnson argues that praise and worship enabled leaders to manage more effectively the diversity and growing scale of their congregations. The genre, she maintains, "establishes order, encourages intimacy, and musically reinforces a sense of community and the sacred among the thousands of congregants who attend weekly services."[45] The unifying power of praise and worship echoes throughout Crouch's *Live in London* recording, which was also a rewarding experience for nonbelievers in attendance.

"This gospel invasion of the Odeon was a triumph," Cliff White of *New Musical Express* wrote. "I wasn't saved but I'd be more than willing to take a second course of instruction. . . . Purely on a musical level it was superb in parts and rarely less than entertaining the rest of the time." Karl Dallas of *Melody Maker* was equally moved: "I entered the hall on New Year's Day feeling as out of place as a Jew at a National Front rally, but I left feeling blessed. Anyone who can do that, in those conditions, has got to be a special kind of witness, and that's what Andraé Crouch and the Disciples are—something really special."[46] Special indeed. Down in Baylor, Texas, Robert Darden marveled at the record, its sound, its packaging, and its ambition, saying, "I played it as often as I played my Black Sabbath and Wilson Pickett LPs."[47]

Crouch's ability to connect with such a diverse group of music lovers caught the attention of several record labels seeking to break into the gospel market. One of those labels was Warner Brothers, which signed Crouch to a four-year deal in 1979. Crouch's yearlong negotiation with Warner yielded an arrangement favorable to both parties: he would produce one set of records for Light and another set for Warner Brothers. Convinced that Crouch had the potential to sell well beyond the Christian industry, Warner planned to target his material to the R&B market. Despite the marketing strategy, Crouch assured his fans that his sound and message would remain the same.[48]

On the heels of his new deal, Crouch released his ninth record for Light: *I'll Be Thinking of You*. The album's standout cuts included "Jesus Is Lord," "I'll Be Thinking of You," "I've Got the Best," and "Lookin' for You." "I'll Be Thinking of You" featured a guest appearance by Stevie Wonder, whose harmonica solo pairs nicely with Kristle Murden's sultry vocals. Wonder was not the only pop star involved in the recording. Earth, Wind, and Fire's Philip Bailey lends his amazing vocals on "I've Got the Best," a hybrid of R&B and CCM. Soon to launch his own career in Christian music, Bailey provides a preview of things to come for his secular fans.

Crouch's release of *I'll Be Thinking of You* marked a fitting end to the 1970s, a decade in which he composed classic material, performed in sold-out arenas, and garnered some of the industry's biggest awards. The acclaimed singer even had an issue of Al Hartley's Spire Christian Comics dedicated solely to his career in CCM. In the issue, titled *On the Road with Andraé Crouch*, the singer picks up two hitchhikers and tells them the story of his meteoric rise to superstardom. He also shares with them the peace and joy that comes with Christian salvation.

Crouch's inclusion in Spire Christian Comics spoke to his deep connection to the cultural world of evangelicalism.

Successful in a variety of markets, Crouch stood at the top of both the black gospel world and CCM. His music touched the hearts of Christians of different races and denominations, while his musicianship earned him the respect of some of the industry's biggest pop stars.

Crouch's unrivaled stature in the religious world was apparent at the 1980 Grammy Awards, where he and the Mighty Clouds of Joy delivered a spirited performance of his most recent hit, "Jesus Is Lord." That same night, rock star Bob Dylan performed his own gospel hit, "Gotta Serve Somebody," for which he received his first solo Grammy. Dylan's performance, as well as that by Crouch and the Mighty Clouds of Joy, was part of the show's efforts to highlight the history and vitality of gospel music. As the awards host, Kenny Rogers, informed the audience, "Gospel music is the root of all of our music."[49] Celebrating not just the genre's roots but its evolution as well, the organizers for the Grammy telecast decided to include a couple of the gospel categories in the television broadcast of the awards. To loud applause, Crouch collected a Grammy in the category of Best Contemporary Soul Album for *I'll Be Thinking of You*.

As Crouch ventured more into the mainstream, he found himself under greater scrutiny from gospel insiders. Consider, for example, the controversy over his appearance on the variety show *Saturday Night Live* in 1980. The May 24 episode featured Buck Henry as its host and musical appearances from Andrew Gold and Andraé Crouch. Finding *SNL* "too controversial," James Cleveland had declined an invitation from the program's producers to perform on the popular show. His reasoning was simple: the show had never been supportive of gospel music, and his brief appearance would not be beneficial to the genre's advancement. When asked to comment on Crouch's decision to appear on the program, Cleveland applauded his colleague's performance but remained steadfast in his opinion about *SNL*. "Andraé went on and I think he did a very good job for gospel music. I enjoyed Andraé's performance—but I don't think it did anything for the cause."[50] Not one to pull punches, Cleveland had issues with mainstream shows that featured black gospel music for brief segments but avoided in-depth engagement with the totality of the African American religious experience: "What are they trying to prove on a show of that caliber to have a religious side after they've been as risqué as they could be? Then to turn around and end the show with a gospel song. There had been no other mention of religion, spiritual quality, or anything on the entire show, so they were, in essence, presenting Andraé as a performer, not as a religious personality. I mean they gave him time to sing . . . but he's about more than singing."[51]

There was no general consensus regarding Crouch's appearance on *SNL*. "I got hate mail from being on 'Saturday Night Live,'" the singer revealed, "and I got 'God bless you, Andraé, we're with you 1,000 percent.'" Though respectful of his good friend James Cleveland, Crouch defended his right to take his music anywhere. The church, he insisted, could not confine itself to "safe" religious spaces. Rather, Christians had a responsibility to "go unto the highways and byways."[52]

With that mandate in mind, Crouch concentrated his energies on finishing his debut recording for Warner Brothers, *Don't Give Up*. His deal with one of the industry's biggest labels had generated tremendous buzz, and he was confident that the final product would live up to the hype. So, too, was Warner Brothers. Up-front about their objectives, label executives planned to market Crouch's music to R&B radio stations. Two things worked to their advantage: Crouch was a proven star familiar to most in the industry, and the label did not need to spend a considerable amount of time or money tweaking his music for a more general audience. When attempting to cross over, gospel artists frequently update their sound or turn to established producers in the secular world for assistance. Such moves were unnecessary for Crouch, who already possessed a sophisticated sound and had long partnered with some of the most skilled musicians in soul, jazz, and rock.

Crouch's hectic tour schedule put him behind the targeted release date, but the long-awaited *Don't Give Up* finally hit the market in 1981. The opener, "Waiting for the Son," the hard-grooving "Handwriting on Wall," and the snappy "Hollywood Scene" stand out as some of his best work from the 1980s. To realize his artistic vision, Crouch enlisted the help of some of the industry's finest musicians: Joe Sample, Greg Phillinganes, Louis Johnson, Jerry Peters, Steve Porcaro, Bill Maxwell, and Alex Acuña. To those who argued his stellar lineup was solely for marketing purposes, Crouch shot back, "I was looking for the skill and the sound."[53] This attentiveness to sound, he argued, should not be interpreted as a turn away from his religious message. As he explained to *Los Angeles Times* writer Dennis Hunt, "Every song I've written takes you through the scriptures and reinforces the Word of God. I give people a beautiful message, I do it with pop, rock, funk, jazz, disco or anything that will make it appealing." Instead of apologizing for his approach, Crouch encouraged his fellow gospel artists to follow his lead and pay more attention to the quality of their music: "It is a pity that a lot of great messages have been wasted because they have been paired with bad music. That's what's wrong with a lot of traditional church music. That's why most of it bores me."[54]

Beyond the problem of boredom, Crouch also had issues with the insularity of the church world. Still upset about the criticism he endured for appearing on *Saturday Night Live*, Crouch questioned whether his critics within the church understood their responsibilities as Christians: "The Bible says for us to go into the world and preach the gospel. So, what do all those good church people think that means? To keep pouring water in an ocean? The ocean already has plenty of water. We need to pour some of that precious water on some dry spots."[55]

Crouch hoped his latest release, *Don't Give Up*, would reach a wider market, but this would not be the case. Much to Crouch's chagrin, the label selected "Start All Over Again" as the lead single. Upon hearing Warner Brothers' selection, Crouch was admittedly "turned off with the choice." Label executives assured him of the wisdom of their strategy and predicted strong sales for the next singles. "They just wanted my audience to know that I'm still gospel before they release the next single so people won't be saying 'did you hear that song by Andraé, boy's he's out there,'" Crouch stated. Tom Draper, vice president of Warner Brothers' black division, confirmed Crouch's account, reiterating the company's desire to not "create a gap" between Crouch's gospel and pop audience. A safe, first single, he argued, would enable the company to quickly move "in other directions."[56] But Warner Brothers' strategy backfired as the subpar lead single not only failed to gain traction on R&B radio but also gave potential buyers a poor perception of the overall quality of *Don't Give Up*. To make matters worse, the label lacked experience in the gospel market and struggled to distribute the record to Christian bookstores. The record's lackluster sales provided Crouch and other gospel musicians with an important lesson on the challenges involved in switching from a gospel label to a secular one.

Don't Give Up was not the only disappointment for Crouch in 1982. *Finally*, his release for Light Records, fell short of the superb musicianship found on *Take Me Back* and *This Is Another Day*. Though *Finally* featured two of Crouch's more popular compositions, "We Need to Hear from You" and "We Are Not Ashamed," *Washington Post* journalist Richard Harrington dismissed the record as derivative and unimaginative: "In trying to achieve contemporary flavor Crouch falls into stylistic ruts."[57]

Low sales and poor reviews were not Crouch's only worries. His decision to perform in South Africa in 1982 angered several activists in the United States calling for musicians to boycott the country. Insisting that his appearance uplifted the spirits of black South Africans, Crouch positioned himself as a "minister" who was simply fulfilling his evangelical mission. Those who refused to perform in South Africa, Crouch argued, "do not have black people in mind. One guy came up to me and said, 'Please tell the American blacks not to boycott because you are the only ones to keep us together and singing in the midst of everything happening.'" Claiming that his music was popular among black South Africans, Crouch derided the boycott as "stupid."[58] His cavalier attitude and dismissive comments elicited a strong critique from historian William Seraile, who took to the pages of the *New York Amsterdam News*: "Andraé Crouch thinks of himself as a minister delivering a message to South Africa. The only message perceived by many, including this writer, is that Andraé Crouch is at best a cool, opportunistic, greedy tool of the racist regime of the Union of South Africa." Calling Crouch a "poor student of history," Seraile pointed out how South Africa's "racist regime is using entertainers such as Crouch to make the progressive people in the world think that changes are coming with the next sunrise."[59] Granted, the issue was far more complex, given Crouch's popularity among some activists in South Africa who derived spiritual sustenance from the singer as they battled against the apartheid system. Yet, Crouch's public handling of the situation left much to be desired.

By far, Crouch's biggest challenge of the year came on November 12, when he was arrested on drug charges after a Los Angeles Police Department officer allegedly found a vial containing 0.08 grams of cocaine in his car.[60] Many of the major black and white newspapers—the *New York Times*, the *Chicago Tribune*, and the *Baltimore Afro-American*—covered the arrest.[61] Crouch proclaimed his innocence and the authorities later dropped the possession charge due to the small amount of cocaine in question, but in the eyes of many in the gospel industry the music star had become too immersed in the Hollywood scene.[62] To his critics, Crouch's highly publicized arrest—which he argued stemmed from the racist politics of the LAPD—was further evidence of his misdirection.

A determined Crouch continued to record and perform, but the 1980s was a decade of ups and downs for the star. The emergence of new gospel and Christian stars dimmed his light somewhat but did not render him irrelevant. In 1986, for example, he found himself back in the national spotlight with the release of the film *The Color Purple*, which featured his song "Maybe God Is Tryin' to Tell You Something." His longtime friend Quincy Jones requested his assistance with the film's score. "Quincy was short on time—since it was June and Steven Spielberg started shooting in July. Well, just before I was to leave for a few days on the road, he called and asked me to work on it. I said, 'Wow! When do you need these songs?' He said, 'Today.'" A stunned Crouch immediately went to work, looking over the script, rounding up longtime collaborators, and fleshing out a few ideas on his piano. He cranked out fifteen tunes in twenty-four hours. The short time frame proved challenging but exhilarating for Crouch: "I had just been ordering records from different companies to build up my collection of the old great gospel singers, people like Rosetta Tharp[e] and the rest, so I was really prepared to re-create the sound they wanted long before I knew I'd be working on 'The Color Purple.'"[63] A desperate Jones found a gem in Crouch's moving tune "Maybe God Is Tryin' to Tell You Somethin.'"

The song appears at a pivotal point in the film when the character Shug leads patrons from Harpo's juke joint to her father's church, where she powers through "Maybe God Is Tryin' to Tell You Somethin.'" The voice we hear actually belongs to Táta Vega, who was also featured on the Academy Award–nominated song

"Miss Celie's Blues (Sister)." "Maybe God Is Tryin' to Tell You Something" opens with the lead vocalist and the choir (which consisted of some older members from Crouch's father's church) exchanging a series of "yes Lord"s as the pianist rumbles for dramatic effect. The music then assumes the down-home feel of the black church as Vega's powerful voice works wonders on Crouch's confessional lyrics. With great precision and raw power, she wails, "I was so blind, I was so lost, until you spoke to me."[64] The song goes into overdrive at the 2:45 mark as the singers and musicians swing into a full gospel shout. Shaping one of the most discussed scenes in the film, Crouch demonstrated his rare ability to capture the many dimensions of the gospel sound.

A year after contributing to the film score of *The Color Purple*, Crouch wrote the theme song to *Amen*, a sitcom centered on the fictive character Ernest Frye, a deacon at First Community Church of Philadelphia who balances his church responsibilities with his career as a mediocre lawyer. The show provided viewers with a look into the inner workings of the black church and a perspective on what happens among church leaders Monday through Saturday. Written by Crouch, the show's theme song, "Shine on Me," featured the songstress Vanessa Bell Armstrong, who in 1983 released her debut recording, *Peace Be Still*. The song captures Armstrong and Crouch in full command of their art form as the singer races through her signature runs over Crouch's spirited music.

Working behind the scenes more than ever before, Crouch also collaborated with Michael Jackson on "Man in the Mirror" (1987) and Madonna on "Like a Prayer" (1988). These songs functioned as vehicles through which Jackson and Madonna presented themselves as not just entertainers but transcendent figures whose cultural work possessed a deeper spiritual dimension and purpose. In each of these cases, Crouch's primary responsibility was to infuse certain aspects of the gospel aesthetic into the music (and the accompanying visual rendering). "Far more than anything Madonna sings," Jim Cullen writes in his analysis of "Like a Prayer," "it is the choir supporting her under the direction of Andraé Crouch, that gives the song its expressive power. More than that: It's an important manifestation of its essentially American character." The song's religiosity and moral power, Cullen maintains, had more to do with Crouch's presence than Madonna's. "The gospel tradition he represents is the wellspring of American popular music, and when musicians seek to give their work a particular kind of credibility and power, they access it regularly."[65] This also holds true for Crouch's work with Michael Jackson. A powerful artist who exuded spirituality not just with his music but also with his presence, Crouch appeared alongside Jackson during the pop star's legendary performance of "Man in the Mirror" at the 1988 Grammy Awards.[66] As part of what Michael Eric Dyson described as Jackson's "festive choreography of religious reality," Crouch played the role of attentive deacon, encouraging the King of Pop during his moments of spiritual ecstasy.[67]

On the studio version of "Man in the Mirror," which appeared on Jackson's *Bad* album, Crouch's choir sang background vocals alongside his protégés the Winans. The appearance of the Winans and Crouch together was apropos. Crouch had brought the Detroit-based quartet to Light Records in 1980.[68] Five years later, the Winans joined Crouch at Warner Brothers, where they signed with Quincy Jones's imprint, Qwest. In many ways, the Winans' move from Light to Warner Brothers symbolized how much the Detroit quartet had followed in Crouch's footsteps—not just in terms of their career decisions but also in their musical choices as singer-songwriters. "Andraé Crouch," lead singer Marvin Winans later noted, had an "indelible impact on the way we write, the way we do harmonies, chords, structure."[69] Of course, the Winans were not the only gospel act that bore the imprint of Crouch's influence. His songwriting and production informed the work of such gospel acts as Richard Smallwood, Fred Hammond, Israel Houghton, Smokie Norful, Donnie McClurkin, and CeCe Winans, along with white contemporary Christian musicians like Amy Grant, Michael W. Smith, and Steven Curtis Chapman. His pioneering work in the world of contemporary Christian music also blazed a path for African American performers like Larnelle Harris, Leon Patillo, and Ron Kenoly, who achieved remarkable success with predominantly white audiences. In addition to integrating the world of CCM, Crouch created a body of work that would become foundational for praise and worship music, a genre that transformed the black gospel sound and continues to do so. What Thomas Dorsey was to the gospel world in the 1930s and 1940s, Crouch was to the world of contemporary Christian music in the 1970s and 1980s. At the height of his success, he redefined the sonic, spiritual, and even social possibilities of American religious music. To be sure, the gospel/CCM industry claimed its share of immensely talented and influential musicians during the post–civil rights era, but Andraé Crouch was in a class by himself.

CHAPTER 3

Hold My Mule

Shirley Caesar and the Gospel of the New South

There is nowhere in the USA quite like America's South; there is no place more difficult to fully understand or fully capture.... The people who walk that land, both black and white, wear masks and more masks, then masks beneath those masks. They are tricksters and shape-shifters, magicians and carnival barkers, able to metamorphize right before your eyes into good old boys, respectable lawyers, polite society types, brilliant scholars, great musicians, history makers, and everything's-gonna-be-all-right Maya Angelou look-alikes—when in fact nothing's gonna be all right.

—JAMES MCBRIDE, *Kill 'Em and Leave: Searching for James Brown and the American Soul*

If one thing doesn't work you shift and you do something else. If a fast song doesn't work, you use a slow one.... I change every time I get up to sing.... I take everything into consideration, what's going on around me, and I adjust my music for my audience. Yes indeed, I did it last night. Almost every time you hear me sing I do it.... Like for an example, the song my sister (Ann) sings "You can depend on Jesus." I'll say ... in a sing-song fashion "Gonna be alright, gonna be, gonna be alright, everything's gonna be alright." Really what I'm waiting for, I'm waiting for the musicians to get into a pocket; by the time they get into that pocket, phone Aunt Jane. I'll give you a quarter if she ain't home.

—SHIRLEY CAESAR in Brooksie Eugene Harrington, "Shirley Caesar: A Woman of Words"

Thirty years into her recording career, the Grammy Award–winning artist Shirley Caesar showed no signs of slowing down. In 1988, Caesar returned to her traditional gospel roots with the release of her critically acclaimed record, *Live . . . in Chicago*, which dominated the gospel charts for nearly eight months. It featured the hit single "Hold My Mule," a sermonette centered on the fictive character

Shouting John, an eighty-six-year-old farmer who, in the words of Caesar, had joined "a dead church" controlled by ministers who frowned upon his expressive style of worship. To no avail, church leaders had repeatedly attempted to subdue John during his extended "praise breaks" by grabbing his limbs or forcing him to return to his seat. Their efforts always failed miserably. Frustrated by John's refusal to discipline his religious fervor, a small group of church officials traveled to the elder's home to chastise him for his behavior. Upon their arrival, they find John ("and a beat-up old mule") plowing in the field. The proud farmer approaches his guests and then listens to their complaints. Showing no compassion for the elder, the church leaders deliver an ultimatum to John: "If you don't stop shouting, if you don't stop dancing, we're going to put you out of our church."[1] John's demonstrative religiosity had crossed a dangerous line.

If church officials expected John to give in to their demands after their threat of disfellowship, they were in for a major disappointment. When granted the opportunity to speak, John details his many blessings: his ownership of land, his good health, and his trouble-free children. "Not one time have I been to the courthouse," he proudly informs his guests; "not one time have I been to the cemetery. But you don't want me to dance in your church?" The act of recounting his blessings leads John to make the following declaration to the delegation: "Well put me out, I can't hold my peace."[2] A spiritually ecstatic John then proceeds to shout and dance all over his property.

On this popular sermonette, which decades after its release still plays on gospel radio stations across the country, Shirley Caesar demonstrates both her unrivaled skills as a storyteller and her ability to capture the class tensions gripping black America during the post–civil rights era. She also gives voice to older black women and men still tied to the economies and cultural rhythms of the rural South. Caesar's attentiveness to the cultural richness and diversity of black America combined with her singularity as a performer and songwriter have enabled her to connect with multiple generations of gospel fans. One would be hard-pressed to find a gospel artist who has enjoyed her level of success for a longer period of time. First working with the famous Caravans from the late 1950s to the mid-1960s, then striking out on her own to become one of gospel music's most successful performers, Caesar boasts an incredibly impressive discography that captures her remarkable range as an artist. Her hits include sermonettes ("Don't Throw Your Mama Away," "Praying Slave Lady," and "Hold My Mule"), traditional hymns ("Don't Be Afraid" and "Jordan River"), soulful tunes ("Put Your Hand in the Hand"), and country ballads ("No Charge"). Her career is a marvel, and quite frankly trying to convey the brilliance of her artistry can be frustratingly difficult—not just because of her prodigious output but also because of the diversity of her work. Soul, funk, disco, and country—all of these genres have seeped into her music at one time or another. As a recording artist,

Caesar has been at the cutting edge of both traditional and contemporary gospel music, refusing to allow anyone or anything to stifle her creativity.

Onstage, Caesar has also been in the vanguard of the art form, dazzling fans and critics alike with her legendary live performances. In her prime, her concerts featured spirited preaching, extended "praise breaks" during which she danced across the stage or down the aisles, and reworked versions of her most popular songs and sermonettes that captured her gift of improvisation. "I like to compare Shirley's performance to the well-known structure of a short story," writes Brooksie Eugene Harrington. "She gives you the introduction, the rising action, the climax, and the falling action. . . . Shirley knows what she is doing, and . . . she does it in such a meticulous manner that she carries her audience right along with the flow of the waters as she reaches the zenith of her concert."[3] Caesar's mastery as a performer was the by-product of her brilliant fusion of various traditions, modalities, and styles. One tradition was the black sermonic tradition. The "old-time Negro preacher," James Weldon Johnson writes in his classic 1927 text, *God's Trombones*,

> was a master of all the modes of eloquence. He often possessed a voice that was a marvelous instrument, a voice he could modulate from a sepulchral whisper to a crashing thunder clap. His discourse was generally kept at a high pitch of fervency, but occasionally he dropped into colloquialisms and, less often, into humor. He preached a personal and anthropomorphic God, a sure-enough heaven and a red-hot hell. His imagination was bold and unfettered. He had the power to sweep his hearers before him; and so himself was often swept away. At such times his language was not prose but poetry.[4]

Like the classic black preachers before her, Caesar transformed her sermonettes, particularly tunes like "Praying Slave Lady" and "Hold My Mule," into high art.

None of Caesar's success was by chance. Every move was a calculated one. Upon her departure from the Caravans in 1966, she signed with House of Beauty (HOB) Records. HOB and Caesar's partnership yielded some of her biggest hits and most critically acclaimed recordings. Then in 1977, the singer signed with Roadshow, a small secular label whose roster included the bands Enchantment and B. T. Express. Three years later, Caesar inked a deal with the Christian entertainment powerhouse Word Records, which for the first twenty-five years of its existence confined itself primarily to the white Christian market. As a testament to her commercial appeal, Caesar was high on the priority list of all three companies. Word, Roadshow, and HOB envisioned Caesar as a transcendent artist who could help them break into new markets and increase their profit margins considerably. Moreover, label executives regarded Caesar as a versatile performer whose expansive talent allowed her to thrive in a variety of musical settings. Such was the case in the early 1980s, when Word paired Caesar with country producer Tony Brown for her first three records on the label. Her Nashville sessions included some of the industry's most respected musicians and were carefully planned to generate the most commercially viable product. These sessions were radically different from those during her earlier days with the Caravans. "When I recorded with the Caravans," Caesar remembered, "the production budgets were always very meager. There weren't any allocations to hire musicians. Often we borrowed musicians from local churches. At best we had a drummer, a bass, a lead guitarist, and an organ player. We couldn't afford to pay for studio time for more than one day, so we would record ten to twelve songs in one session. If we made mistakes, the producer overlooked them. If the altos came in late or the sopranos didn't sing the song as rehearsed, it was ignored because the budget would not allow rerecording."[5]

With more than six decades of experience as a gospel singer and traveling evangelist, Caesar has witnessed, contributed to, and benefited from some of the major transformations within the Christian music industry. Thus, tracing the arc of her career provides significant insight into a variety of issues, including but not limited to the growing impact of funk and soul music on the gospel sound, the efforts of major white Christian labels to claim a bigger share of the black gospel market, the rise of Nashville as an important geographical center of the black gospel industry, and the struggle of African American religious artists to address some of the major political and social problems affecting their local communities and the larger world. As one of the gospel industry's most popular performers, Caesar used her platform to advance the art form and build what religious studies scholar Cheryl Sanders calls "prophetic community": the "exercising of one's individual gifts of ministry and leadership toward the end of empowering congregations to hear the voice of God and speak the word of God in conversation with the deepest concerns of the people and communities one is called to serve."[6]

In explaining her political activism, particularly her decision to run for a seat on the city council in her hometown of Durham, North Carolina, in 1987, Caesar noted, "I not only care about what happens inside the church; I'm equally concerned about what happens in society at large. In my opinion, if the church doesn't influence society, it has failed to live out God's commission."[7] With this goal in mind, Caesar campaigned on a platform emphasizing full employment, quality housing for low-income residents, improvements to the downtown area without sacrificing the needs of the black poor, environmental protections, and quality public schools. As Caesar ventured into new territory in her public life, her campaign was hardly surprising to gospel fans and industry insiders who had followed her career. The socially engaged artist had never shied away from political issues and themes in her music, as Cheryl Gilkes perceptively notes in her analysis:

Not only does Shirley Caesar make beautiful music, for which she reaps accolades and awards, but also her music, much of which she composes, provides an important narrative or "thick description" of the situations of black people in America and a prophetic critique of the social conditions that challenge black and poor people. Alongside of this description and critique, Shirley Caesar also challenges black people's treatment of one another, particularly across class lines; in the process she illustrates the complexities and complications of class and family issues among black people. Throughout her career, her music has proclaimed God's option for the poor and qualifies as a liberationist discourse.[8]

Caesar provided a model for other women navigating the complex gender politics of both the music industry and the African American church. Her public persona ranged from pious woman mindful of the gender proscriptions of her Holiness background to civic-minded activist committed to improving the lives of the most disadvantaged, particularly those from her hometown of Durham. In her interviews, which in the early part of her career often focused on her single status (Caesar did not marry until her late thirties), she presented herself as somewhat

FIGURE 8. Shirley Caesar performing in *Gospel*, a 1983 documentary film directed by David Leivick and Frederick A. Ritzenberg. Photo courtesy of Photofest.

of a traditionalist on gender issues. "I don't consider myself a liberated woman," the singer told an *Ebony* reporter in 1977. "If I had a man, I would be dependent on him." In that same interview, however, she shared with readers her deep love for her work, her financial autonomy, her extensive community involvement, and her general contentment with her single status.[9] Though she distanced herself from certain labels—as did many other African American women at the time—she was very much in control of her personal and professional life.[10] To prove this point and perhaps provide a visual counterpoint to a few of Caesar's statements, *Ebony* included an image of Caesar confidently occupying the driver's seat of her custom-made tour bus, which she occasionally drove when on the road with her band. Self-made and self-fashioned, Caesar demanded that her art and her life be understood on no one's terms but her own. This was about control, but it was also about self-preservation.

The Parable of My Being: Coming of Age in Durham

"The course of my life cannot be explained in simple human terms," Caesar once wrote. "From the beginning I believe I was destined to fulfill God's purpose and plan for my existence. There is no other explanation. With so much working against me—a semi-invalid mother, a deceased father, low-self-esteem resulting from having been called degrading names as a child, and living in a society plagued by racism, sexism, and segregation—I wasn't supposed to make it." Success, let alone superstardom, was not in the cards—so she assumed. "I should have never escaped the impoverishment that surrounded me. But by God's mercy I did. So here I am still running, still singing, still preaching."[11]

The tenth of twelve children, Shirley Ann Caesar was born in 1938 to James and Hallie Caesar in Durham, North Carolina. The Caesars lived in a modest house on Chautauqua Avenue, located in the city's historic Hayti neighborhood.[12] Southwest of downtown, Hayti was the residential, commercial, and cultural center of black Durham. By the time of Shirley Caesar's birth, Hayti was well known among African Americans not just in North Carolina but throughout the nation. As one historian explains, the district enjoyed a "national reputation as a bustling neighborhood with active black commerce, political activism, higher education, and entertainment. Separated from Durham's downtown by unsightly coal yards and railroad tracks, Hayti's residents met most of their needs along the main thoroughfares of their neighborhood. There black florists, pharmacists, auto mechanics, barbers, dry cleaners, grocers, tailors, restaurateurs, hoteliers, morticians, and other businesses catered to them."[13] Not too far from Hayti, several prominent black businesses, including John Merrick's North Carolina Mutual Insurance Company and Richard Fitzgerald and James Shepard's Mechanics and Farmers Bank, flourished on Parrish Street. With such bustling commercial activity, Durham was regarded by some African Americans as the "Capital of the Black Bourgeoisie." "It is a city of fine homes, exquisite churches, and middle-class respectability," the noted sociologist E. Franklin Frazier opined in his essay for Alain Locke's seminal anthology *The New Negro*. "It is not the place where men write and dream; but a place where black men calculate and work. No longer can men say that the Negro is lazy and shiftless and a consumer. He has gone to work. He is a producer. He is respectable. He has a middle class."[14]

The Bull City most certainly had a visible black middle class; however, the vast majority of African Americans in Durham were working-class people. Like many African Americans in the Hayti district, Shirley Caesar's parents worked as tobacco stemmers at Liggett and Myers. Hallie and Jim Caesar brought with them a fair amount of experience in the tobacco industry. A native of North Wilkesboro, North Carolina, Hallie Caesar had previously worked at R. J. Reynolds in Winston-Salem, where she met her future husband, Jim. The couple fell in love, married in 1923, and relocated to Durham three years later. "I got a job in the tobacco factory," Hallie Caesar remembered, "and worked there for thirteen years full-time. . . . The factories paid a little more here in Durham. When we came here, I thought 8 cents a pound was great, because in Winston we would get 5 cents and 6 cents a pound." Changes in the industry, particularly the phasing out of stemmers, coupled with health issues, compelled Hallie Caesar to leave Liggett in 1939. "When I left the factory, I went home. Raising the children was a full-time job."[15]

Together with her husband, Hallie Caesar instilled within her children the values of hard work and self-respect. The couple also stressed the importance of family and God. "In our family," Shirley Caesar remembered, "attending church was not an option—it was an obligation."[16] The family first belonged to Fisher Memorial United Holy Church and then later joined Mount Calvary Holy Church, which was pastored by Frizelle Yelverton. Under the leadership of Yelverton, young Shirley learned the major tenets of the Mount Calvary Holy Church of America, which on the eve of the Great Depression splintered away from the United Holy Church of America.[17] The Mount Calvary denomination's founder and first bishop was Brumfield Johnson, a North Carolina native who in 1928 held a series of revivals in Winston-Salem. These revivals led to the formation of Mount Calvary Holy Church of America, which had a strong base in North Carolina. Mount Calvary placed heavy emphasis on sanctification, pious living, and Pentecostal Holy Spirit baptism—though it did not promote speaking in tongues as the *only* evidence of spirit indwelling. Such teachings would be an important anchor in the religious life of Shirley Caesar.

Another significant anchor for her was gospel music: "Gospel music has always been a viable part of my life. It was the first music I heard as an infant, and the only music that was sung in our household. My mother could always be heard humming a song of praise or singing a hymn."[18] The Caesar children's love for gospel came not just from their mother but from their father as well. Jim Caesar was one of the most respected gospel singers in North Carolina. He, along with three other workers employed at Liggett and Myers, created the Just Come Four Quartet, a talented group that deepened the local community's appreciation for quartet music. "Quartet singing wasn't too popular when I first came to Durham," Hallie Caesar recalled, "but later on there was a lot of them out there." Among the most popular was the Just Come Four Quartet, which thrived on Jim Caesar's powerful singing. "Throughout the Carolinas and southern states," Shirley Caesar proudly boasted, "he was noted for his anointed and energetic style of singing. . . . I'm told he could electrify and magnetize an audience like no one else could."[19] When not attending Mount Calvary or working at Liggett and Myers, Jim Caesar toured with his group, spreading the gospel and earning additional money to support his large family.

The Caesar family suffered a major blow when Jim died unexpectedly in 1945. "My father's sudden death meant intense economic hardship for the family," Caesar somberly recounted. "My mother, who was a semi-invalid, did the very best to provide for us. Although physically challenged, she was by no means a weak lady. But her handicapped foot made it impossible for her to work in a full-time job. Thankfully, as my brothers and sisters grew older they got jobs to help supplement our income. We struggled but at least we struggled together as a family."[20]

Financial hardships notwithstanding, Caesar excelled in the classroom and thrived in Durham's culturally rich black community. One of her elementary teachers, Charlie T. Roach, remembered Caesar as a stellar student and exceptional leader. "I met Shirley in 1950 when she was 11 years old as my sixth-grade student in a class of 34 at W. G. Pearson Elementary School. She was well-mannered, sweet disposition, charming personality, disciplined, and a pleasure to teach." Years after teaching Caesar, Roach still remembered, quite vividly, her contributions to his class's daily devotion period. "We practiced 15 minutes morning devotion daily before class time. The class rotated leadership alphabetically. The students enjoyed Shirley's leadership so much that they voted her to lead daily. Several teachers from other classes stood at our door in the hallway to hear Shirley sing. . . . They knew she was for real!!!"[21]

School was not the only place where Caesar showed great promise as a vocalist. Heavily involved at Mount Calvary, she participated in the junior choir and worked hard to attract the attention of the congregation: "I made sure my contralto voice was heard loud and clear." On those special occasions when she had a solo, Caesar performed with an intensity that belied her age. "I sang as though my very life depended on the projection of that song."[22] Caesar's talents soon caught the attention of gospel lovers outside her church. With her mother's permission, "Baby Shirley," as she was billed on concert advertisements, started traveling with local ministers and singers, most notably Leroy Johnson and Thelma Bumpass and the Royalettes.

Traveling on the road cut into Caesar's study time, but her grades at Hillside High were strong enough to enroll at nearby North Carolina Central College. Founded in 1909 by Dr. James Edward Shepard, North Carolina Central emerged from its modest beginnings as the National Religious Training School to become one of the shining intellectual gems of the Tar Heel State. Economic hardships plagued the school during its early years, but in 1923 its fortunes improved when it became a state institution and changed its name to Durham State Normal School. Led by Shepard until his death in 1948, the school continued to grow under the leadership of its second president, Dr. Alfonso Elder. Like others from her neighborhood, Caesar looked at the college with great pride and felt it a privilege to attend the historically black institution.

This did not mean that her time at Central was easy. Her family's strained financial situation along with her passion for gospel music compounded the typical challenges of college life. On the eve of her sophomore year, Caesar pondered whether to remain at Central or devote herself fully to pursuing her gospel dreams. As had always been the case for Caesar, her family's limited resources concerned her greatly. "I knew my mother didn't have the money to pay for my tuition or buy my books and beyond that I knew that, given our financial situation, the chance of me completing college was almost nonexistent."[23] Caesar's decision regarding school became a lot easier after she attended a concert in Kinston, where she secured an unconventional audition with Albertina Walker's Caravans.

Sweeping the City: Shirley Caesar
and the Caravans

A major force in the gospel world, the Caravans had evolved from their roots in Robert Anderson's Good Shepherd Singers to become one of the industry's most beloved groups. Vocally, the Caravans were in a league of their own. "As an ensemble," Robert Marovich explains, "the Caravans pounced on vocal lines with church-wrecking power and precision, filling each lyric line and the pause between them with intense emotional conviction. Their tight, intense harmonies, dynamic ebbs and flows, and staccato attack of the verses were straight out of the church."[24] The group thrived under the leadership of Albertina Walker, who brought a host of talented singers and musicians to the group: Bessie and Gloria Griffin, Johneron Davis, Cassietta George, Dorothy Norwood, Inez Andrews, James Herndon, James Cleveland, and Shirley Caesar.

An avid fan of the Caravans, Caesar was determined to capture Walker's attention during one of the group's visits to North Carolina. Since she wasn't on the official program, she arranged for someone to request "a solo from Shirley Caesar." When the request was made, Caesar rushed to the stage and delivered a rousing performance that convinced Walker to add the talented youngster to the group.

Caesar's impact on the Caravans was immediate and profound. On such classic tunes as "I Won't Be Back," "No Coward Soldier," "I Feel Good," and "A Place Like That," she mesmerized listeners with her signature contralto, sermonic phrasing, and commanding delivery. Her talent was boundless. Not just an amazing vocalist, Caesar was also a first-rate entertainer who wowed concertgoers with her passionate preaching and dancing. Moving across the stage and down the aisles, Caesar brought the spiritual energy and worship style of her Holiness church to every performance. "I was full of energy in those days. Backstage in the Apollo, I could run all of the way up all of those stairs and in 30 seconds be on the top floor. I was so active." Moreover, Caesar continued, "I was just very, very charismatic."[25]

Caesar loved performing but found the rigors of touring exhausting. "Those years with the Caravans weren't always easy ones. The schedules we kept and the conditions under which we traveled were very trying. We would pack our bags and all six of us would pile into our Cadillac, sometimes traveling all day to get to a concert that night."[26] Caesar also had to battle unwelcomed advances from male suitors, shady concert promoters who failed to pay performers, and racist Jim Crow laws and customs that made travel problematic for African American entertainers. Despite these difficulties, Caesar appreciated her time with the group. "The Caravans were my mentors, my sisters, my friends, and my family. We disagreed some, cried some, laughed a lot, and poured out our hearts on stage and in churches for the glory of God. I learned from them all and believe even today that I sing a little like each of them. I would like to think that I have a little bit of their styles in my music."[27]

Wanting greater control over her time, her art, and her ministry, Caesar left the Caravans in 1966 and embarked on a solo career. "On my own, I now had the flexibility to coordinate the scheduling of my concerts around my revival dates. Having that freedom was liberating. I no longer felt as if I was failing the Lord."[28]

After carefully weighing her options, Caesar signed with the Scepter-owned label House of Beauty Records. As part of HOB's recruiting efforts, the label offered Caesar a $4,000 signing bonus and pledged to do everything to advance her solo career. Under the direction of John Bowden, HOB aspired to increase its share of the gospel market by signing acts like the Five Blind Boys of Alabama, the Gospel Harmonettes, the Swan Silvertones, and Caesar.[29]

My Testimony: Shirley Caesar's
Tenure with HOB Records

Departing a group as popular as the Caravans carried certain risks, but Caesar's first solo outing, *I'll Go*, proved she was up to the challenge. Anchored by Caesar's stunning contralto and the powerful background vocals of the Institutional Radio Choir of Brooklyn, the music on *I'll Go* reflected the singer's desire to maintain her Caravans audience as well as to reach new markets. Even though Caesar had been in the gospel industry for nearly a decade, *I'll Go* provided her fans with their first glimpse of the person behind the artist. On "Choose Ye This Day" and the title track, "I'll Go," Caesar recounts her family's history, her childhood years, and her father's death at an early age. In both songs, she establishes herself as a battle-tested believer. Throughout her career, Caesar would recount her family's encounters with death and economic hardship as a way to situate herself within the community of the socially disadvantaged as well as to testify to God's deliverance. Another important hallmark of Caesar's music appears on *I'll Go*: her engagement with larger social issues. "Battle Field" and "Choose Ye This Day" reference the Vietnam War and the civil rights struggle, particularly state-sanctioned violence against African American children in political hotbeds like Birmingham.

And then there was "Rapture," a hypnotizing soul number that showcased Caesar's versatility as a vocalist. Though Caesar was unequivocal in her commitment to singing gospel, her performance on "Rapture" confirmed, for many, her potential for great success if she ever decided to enter the pop world.

While willing to engage contemporary sounds and issues, Caesar remained connected to her past, particularly her North Carolina roots. Perhaps nowhere was this connection more apparent than on the record's most powerful cut, "Don't Be Afraid." Caesar's majestic voice captures the religiosity, human warmth, and intimacy of the black church. It conjures up memories of not just the sounds but also the gestures, sights, and smells of Sunday morning.

To reinforce Caesar's deep connection to the church and her Holiness roots, the cover of *I'll Go* featured a picture of the singer in a choir robe. Eyes closed and hands lifted toward heaven, Caesar positions herself as God's servant rather than gospel music entertainer. The image of Caesar was understated, but the music was certainly not. Well aware of the naysayers who questioned the wisdom of her departure from the Caravans, Caesar was happy with the results of her first album. "To me, it was reaffirmation that God indeed keeps His promises."[30]

Caesar's second outing for HOB, *My Testimony*, was equally impressive. It included sermonettes, up-tempo shout songs, and soul-stirring ballads. Caesar composed seven of the twelve songs on the record, which also featured compositions from Cassietta George and James Cleveland. The highlight of the session was her unforgettable performance on "Tear Your Kingdom Down," a haunting number that bears a striking resemblance to "Don't Be Afraid."[31] Singing with great fervor and conviction, Caesar declares war on the devil in no uncertain terms.

Wanting to build on Caesar's momentum, HOB flooded the gospel market with records and singles from the talented songstress. Within months of the appearance of *My Testimony*, the label released *Jordan River*, a record whose title cut adopted the minimalist but powerful approach of "Tear Your Kingdom Down" and "Don't Be Afraid."

Even greater success followed Caesar in 1969 when she released "Don't Drive Your Mama Away," a brilliant sermonette that combined masterful storytelling with strident class critique. "Don't Drive Your Mama Away" tells the story of a mother who has two sons with radically different life trajectories. One son performs well in school, vows to take care of his mother, and eventually becomes a doctor. The other son underperforms in the classroom as a child, has numerous run-ins with the law, and causes his mother much heartache. True to his childhood promise to provide for his family, the "good son" invites his mother to move in with his wife (a schoolteacher) and children and enjoy the benefits of their stable, upper-middle-class life. However, trouble emerges when the daughter-in-law complains about what she perceives as her mother-in-law's negative influence on the children, particularly her country manners and "bad grammar." Siding with his wife, the son informs his mother of his intention to relocate her to a senior citizens' home. En route to the "old folks home," the family runs into the other son, who expresses dismay at the situation and then offers to bring his mother to his house. Though the living accommodations of the "no-good son" pale in comparison to those of his more accomplished sibling, the mother prefers this arrangement to the other possibility: spending her final days among strangers. The sermonette ends on a somewhat triumphant note as the troubled child— who through this kind gesture has now found redemption—and the grateful mother journey down the road toward their new life together.[32] An instant hit, "Don't Drive Your Mama Away" resonated with thousands of African Americans who appreciated Caesar's deft storytelling, as well as her exploration of the class tensions within black communities. "Don't Drive Your Mama Away" also cemented Caesar's status as one of gospel's premier entertainers.

On the road, Caesar generated even greater buzz with her powerful singing, spirited preaching, and joyful dancing.[33] "I cannot do this dead and dry," Caesar once remarked; "I got to move."[34] And move she did. Her live performances received rave reviews from the nation's leading newspapers. *Washington Post* journalist Hollie West showered the singer with praise after her concert at Constitution Hall. Caesar, West marveled, "has the unusual capacity to transform a concert hall into a church-like setting at a moment's notice. . . . In her piercing contralto voice, she performs with the fervor of an evangelist as she preaches the message of her song." The singer's spitfire vocals, passionate preaching, and boundless energy left West spellbound. "Miss Caesar darts back and forth across a stage with such fury that it seems as if she might fall on her face at any time." Fueling Caesar's fire was not just the Holy Spirit but also the energy of her fans: "People were standing in the aisles, clapping their hands and dancing to her fiery rhythm."[35] A perfectionist who fully recognized that working women and men made up the backbone of her audience, she demanded nothing less than the best from her background singers and musicians. On those rare occasions when they missed a beat or played the wrong note, she'd chastise them with a disapproving glance or comment. Simply put, in terms of sheer energy and exactness, she was the closest thing the gospel world had to soul music's greatest bandleader, James Brown.

Caesar's commitment to her art was evident in the high quality of her live shows and her studio productions. A permanent fixture on gospel radio, Caesar won her first Grammy Award in 1971 for her soul-stirring hit "Put Your Hand in the Hand." A year later, she released *Get Up My Brother*. Visually and sonically, *Get Up My Brother* underscores how the cultural politics of the Black Power movement reached far beyond those who identified or positioned themselves as cultural nationalists. The album's cover featured a beautiful portrait of Caesar fashionably attired in a colorful dress. No longer wearing the drab choir robes of the *I'll Go* era, Caesar had a look that reflected the popular styles of the 1970s. As was the case with many black artists, Caesar seemed to be targeting—or at least acknowledging—the soul brothers and sisters in black America.[36]

To tap into gospel's expanding market, as well as the political energy of the times, Caesar also adopted a more contemporary sound on several of the album's cuts, including the title song. With its soulful mix of organ, guitar, Rhodes piano, and drums, "Get Up My Brother" echoes some of the music found on Pastor T. L. Barrett's 1971 record, *Like a Ship . . . (without A Sail)*. The song has a strong Chicago soul vibe, as does Caesar's cover of Curtis Mayfield's protest anthem "People Get Ready."

A versatile artist who could change with the times yet maintain her individuality, Caesar willingly moved beyond her comfort zone to embrace new sounds, techniques, and marketing strategies. At the same time, she refused to abandon her older fans who didn't like their gospel "too worldly." In addition to the more soulful songs, *Get Up My Brother* featured two powerful traditional gospel cuts: "Teach Me Master" and "Nobody but You Lord."

This balancing act continued over the next several years with the release of *The Invitation, Be Careful of the Stones You Throw, Millennial Reign*, and *No Charge*. These four records find Caesar pushing the sonic and lyrical boundaries of gospel. One of her more intriguing turns was her foray into country music, a genre she was quite fond of. "I love listening to country music," she readily admitted. In addition to covering Hank Williams's classic "Be Careful of the Stones You Throw," Caesar scored a major hit with the country song "No Charge," taken from her 1975 album of the same name. "No Charge" relates the story of an exchange between a mother and a son. Written by Harlan Howard and recorded by Melba Montgomery in 1974, the song opens with the narrator describing a scene in which a young boy comes into the kitchen and hands his mother an itemized list of charges for his chores. The enterprising son has a price for everything, from washing the dishes to completing his homework. Taken aback by the son's list, the mother responds with a recounting of her many responsibilities and sacrifices:

> For the nine months I carried you, growing inside me, no charge
> For the nights I sat up with you, doctored you, prayed for you, no charge
> For the time and the tears and the costs through the years, no charge
> *When you add it all up, the full cost of my love is no charge*[37]

Like millions of Americans, Caesar adored Melba Montgomery's version of the song. "It blew me away," she later remembered. "I laid out in the living room on the floor, trying to sing it like a country singer. I couldn't so I just did it my way and it turned out to be the biggest solo record I've ever recorded."[38]

With her incredible range as an artist, Caesar played an important though largely overlooked role in the diversification of the gospel sound during the 1970s. Together with artists like Andraé Crouch, Rance Allen, and the Hawkins Family, Caesar stretched both the lyrical and sonic boundaries of gospel as she not only borrowed from other genres but also addressed larger societal issues.

A New Day: Caesar and Roadshow

Firmly established in her career, Caesar was not afraid to take chances and move in new directions with her sound. Such openness was necessary in an industry where label restructuring, buyouts, and shutdowns could derail the career of even the most successful artists. Few artists understood this more than the business-minded Caesar, who eventually switched from HOB to Roadshow Records: "The year 1975 proved to be a very pivotal one for me. It was the year my recording contract with Hob [HOB] Records ended, and I opted not to re-sign. By my own election, it was almost two years before I finally consented to sign with another label. I needed time to reflect and reevaluate my sense of direction. My primary purpose as a Christian and as a gospel singer has always been to reach as many people as possible with the message of Jesus, regardless of race, gender, demographic location, or socioeconomic status. At Hob Records I didn't feel that purpose was being adequately accomplished."[39]

With the goal of expanding her base, she signed with Roadshow and began preparing for her next record. When Roadshow's president, Fred Frank, and producer Michael Stokes sent Caesar the rhythm tracks to possible songs for her first recording session with the company, the gospel singer assumed she had received the wrong music. "Well, when I got the tape," Caesar recalled, "I said 'wow, this is gutbucket rock and roll! I can't do this.'" Caesar had never been beholden to one particular style, but these tracks were more experimental than her previous material. Losing her fan base and alienating gospel radio programmers were real possibilities in an industry with many artists who fell victim to the crossover chase. And yet, Caesar recognized the need to grow as an artist. "It was a question of knowing where I'd been and then thinking about where I was going. What was perhaps the most important part of my decision about the album was understanding that I was still singing gospel. There was no question of me suddenly becoming a rock/R&B performer!"[40]

Not everyone was so certain after listening to *First Lady*. The music ranged from the disco-tinged "Just a Talk" to the more traditional "Faded Rose" to her funky cover of Stevie Wonder's "Jesus Children of America." "If someone didn't tell you it was a gospel album or you didn't listen carefully, you would never know," wrote M. J. Musik of the *New York Amsterdam News*. "There's disco in 'Jesus Is Coming' and funk in 'Just a Talk.'" All serious music listeners, he insisted, needed to engage the record. "Whether you like gospel music or not, you'll love Shirley Caesar's latest album."[41] Along with generating strong reviews, the album sold more than 200,000 copies, an impressive mark for a gospel recording.

Enthused about the results, Roadshow devoted tremendous money and time into marketing her follow-up release, *From the Heart*. With direction from her producer Michael Stokes, primarily known for his work with the soul group Enchantment, Caesar sampled broadly from the contemporary music scene. The singer offered a soulful version of Diana Ross's "Reach Out and Touch (Somebody's Hand)," gave a nod to the lush sounds of Philadelphia International with "He's Got a Love," and masterfully rode the funky grooves of "Message to the People" and "Heavenly Father."

The material was strong, but Caesar was never comfortable with Roadshow. In addition to feeling as if some of the music was "overproduced," Caesar found the company's crossover efforts unsuccessful, by which she meant not so much lackluster sales (the album had strong sales) but failure to gain traction in the pop market. Despite the company's business strategy and her new sound, Caesar's audience remained predominantly gospel: "While at Roadshow I learned a valuable lesson. Innovative marketing strategies and extensive advertising campaigns are no guarantee that you will expand your market share, particularly if the market you are trying to penetrate is not ready for what you are trying to present."[42]

New Directions with Word Records

These lessons weighed on Caesar's mind after Roadshow's collapse in 1980 made her one of gospel music's most coveted free agents. Once again, she faced the challenge of deciding which company could best advance her career without compromising the integrity of her musical ministry. Ultimately, she decided on Word Records, the biggest label in the Christian entertainment industry. Founded in the early 1950s by Jarrell McCracken, the Waco, Texas–based company had been instrumental in the growth of contemporary Christian music through its record-of-the-month club, its distribution deals with Light and Solid Rock Records, and its impressive roster of artists, including the platinum-selling star Amy Grant.[43] To diversify its market, the label sought to add established African American artists to its roster. Toward this goal, Word formed a black division and appointed as its head gospel industry veteran James Bullard, who had previously worked with Caesar at Roadshow. Impressed by Bullard's track record, Word had aggressively courted the ambitious executive. "They wanted to know if I could make Word number one in black Gospel music," Bullard remembered. "Stan Moser, along with Roland Lundy, Dan Johnson and others at Word[,] said if I was willing to head the new division, they would make the commitment to back it all the way." Hiring Bullard proved a wise decision as he exceeded the company's expectations: "The first eight months we did what Stan projected for the first three years."[44] One important factor in Bullard's success was the company's new signee, Shirley Caesar.

Not long after Caesar's signing, Word sought the services of Tony Brown, who produced Caesar's first three albums for the label. A native of Greensboro, North Carolina, Brown had traveled with his family's gospel group as a child, singing and playing the piano. Short stints with the Stamps Quartet and the Oak Ridge Boys prepared him for his biggest gig: pianist for Elvis Presley's gospel group the Voice. After Presley's death in 1977, Brown linked up with Emmylou Harris as he sharpened his musical skills.

Working out of Nashville's legendary Quadrafonic Sound Studios, located in the heart of Music Row, Brown and Caesar blended their distinctive musical talents to create a satisfying mix of New South gospel. The end result was one of the best records of Caesar's career: *Rejoice*, which was released on Word's subsidiary imprint Myrrh.

The nine-song set opens with the upbeat "Whisper a Prayer," a Caesar-penned tune whose hard-knocking groove draws from country, R&B, and disco. There's a hunger, a palpable urgency, in Caesar's singing—something one might not necessarily expect in a seasoned veteran who had been on the top of the charts for more than twenty years. Her intensity continues on Aaron Wilburn's "Satan,

You're a Liar," a striking tune featuring clashing guitars, drums, and keyboards. Infused with the rhythms of southern rock and the melodrama of country pop, "Satan" pushes Caesar out of her vocal comfort zone.

If you were combing through Caesar's discography for evidence of her musical range, then "Satan" would probably be among your first choices. Not too far behind would be another tune on *Rejoice*: Caesar's cover of Bob Dylan's "Gotta Serve Somebody." Offering her traditional serving of spitfire extemporizations and nuanced phrasing, Caesar exhorts her listeners to come to the side of the Lord.

Later on the record, Caesar rips through "It's in the Book," a bouncy number from the songwriting team of J. L. Wallace, Ken Bell, and Terry Skinner. A dance tune immersed in disco beats, hillbilly rhythms, and light funk, "It's in the Book" lays to rest any doubts about the musical chemistry between Caesar and her Nashville rhythm section. The arrangements are complex, soulful, and swinging. As the drummer and bassist lay down the pulsating groove, Caesar's voice functions as an additional percussive instrument, injecting the song with greater rhythmic complexity.

Caesar's debut for Word was a triumph both for the artist and for the record company. Released in late 1980, *Rejoice* netted impressive sales in the gospel market and had a strong presence on Christian radio. The forty-two-year-old Caesar remained one of the most innovative artists in gospel. Her rendezvous with Nashville country was as bold and fresh as the gospel-funk hybrids emerging from the Clark Sisters and the Winans.

Impressed by Caesar's ability to adapt to the changing times, music journalists gave her Word material extremely high marks. In his enthusiastic review of 1983's *Jesus, I Love Calling Your Name*, Richard Harrington hailed Caesar as "one of the great black singers of our time." Throughout the album, Harrington marveled, "her singing is superb, riding freely over thumping bass lines and earthy choruses alike. Caesar can twist, compress or enhance a lyric a dozen ways without abandoning her central message of affirmation, strength, and enduring faith."[45]

Caesar's first three albums for Myrrh, *Rejoice*, *Go*, and *Jesus, I Love Calling Your Name*, elicited great excitement among fans anxious to see Caesar perform her new material live. "With the release of each of those albums," Caesar later reflected, "I found myself on the road even more. Pastors, promoters, and organizations from all around the country were constantly calling me and the Caesar Singers to come either for concerts or revivals. We were performing in excess of one hundred and fifty concerts per year."[46]

One admirer of Caesar's soul-inspired gospel was Lou Rawls, who frequently invited her to perform for his United Negro College Fund telethon. No stranger to Caesar's mammoth talent, Rawls had known Caesar since her days with the Caravans and regarded her as one of the most brilliant performers of any genre:

I mean when this woman comes out to perform, you can feel the electricity in the room. It's like being in one of those old Baptist churches; you know, where the minister shifts gears on you. You see she does that. She does that in her music. ... The people that have never heard Shirley Caesar and don't know who Shirley Caesar is when they do hear her and see her—they never forget this woman, because this woman strikes you. pow! She hits you right in the heart, because she's sincere and she means what she's doing.[47]

Indeed, Caesar's music connected with people in deep and meaningful ways.

Despite her national profile and extensive tour schedule, Caesar remained firmly grounded in the local politics and cultural activities of her hometown of Durham. Every year, she sponsored the annual Shirley Caesar Evangelistic Crusade, a weeklong event that featured Caesar and other gospel stars. She also hosted a weekly radio show on WSRC that was broadcast throughout the Raleigh-Durham area.

Carving out time to record new material was not easy, but she managed to complete three new albums between 1984 and 1987: *Sailin'*, *Celebration*, and *Christmasing*. Word also released her greatest hits compilation, *Her Very Best*. During this time, Caesar collected three additional Grammy Awards, one for the song "Martin," a tribute to the civil rights leader Dr. Martin Luther King Jr., and two for "Sailin'," her duet with labelmate Al Green. She also returned to

FIGURE 9. Street sign commemorating Shirley Caesar in Durham, North Carolina. Photo by author.

college and earned her degree in business administration with a minor in religion from Shaw University in 1984. Though she never doubted the wisdom of her decision to leave North Carolina Central for a career with the Caravans, Caesar felt incomplete without a college degree. Her desire to finish her education was connected to another passion: politics. Talking and singing about the problems of the world were not enough. She wanted to put herself in a position to effect real, structural change in Durham.

Gotta Serve Somebody: Caesar's Civic Activities in Post–Civil Rights Durham

Three years after receiving her bachelor's degree from Shaw, Caesar ran for a seat on Durham's city council. Noting that she wanted to "focus on the needy, not the greedy," she launched a platform centered around fair housing, programs for the elderly, solving the problem of homelessness, and improving the public school system. The singer received endorsements from the Durham Committee on the Affairs of Black People, the People's Alliance, and the Durham Voters Alliance. Despite her lack of formal political experience, Caesar won an at-large seat, adding councilwoman to her long list of achievements. Election day was a surreal experience for the Durham native. "As the numbers were tallied in my favor, I kept hugging my friends, clapping my hands, and jumping up and down. When all of the precinct results were in, I couldn't believe it. I had won! I couldn't believe we had accomplished what the vote was indicating. I had won election in a southern city by 68 percent of the vote. In fact, African Americans filled all three at-large seats on the council."[48]

After her election, Caesar set her sights on ensuring the city's aggressive urban redevelopment plans addressed the concerns and needs of low-income African American families. "My job is to make sure we focus on affordable housing and not try to push the highest priced housing on people who cannot afford it. We are one with the philosophy of growth but not at the expense of our neighborhoods."[49] In her mind, her civic and religious duties were inextricably linked: "I believe in serving God by serving others." More specifically, she had a deep commitment to Durham. "Durham is where it's at," she once told a local reporter; "this is home."[50] Of course, "home" had experienced great change during the post–civil rights period.

Jim Crow segregation had been dismantled, but racial and economic inequality remained a reality for many African Americans in the Bull City. As historian Jean Bradley Anderson notes, "In the waning decades of the century, a confluence of events and trends enormously increased the complexity of social problems in Durham: urban renewal had displaced many poor families and destroyed low-cost housing; the Vietnam War had left many veterans physically or mentally ill, often addicted to alcohol and drugs, and consequently often homeless." Like other cities across the nation, Durham also felt the sting of deindustrialization. According to Anderson, "The decline of traditional blue-collar jobs in tobacco factories and cotton mills as the economy shifted to biomedical and other research left hundreds of workers jobless and unable to fill jobs requiring an educated and skilled workforce."[51] These problems did not escape the notice of Caesar, who through her political and civic activities hoped to transform the city. Her commitment to the less fortunate won her the respect of thousands of local people. "Shirley is a glorious person in our community," raved one Durham resident.[52]

Live . . . in Chicago: The Making of a Gospel Classic and the Rebirth of a Gospel Legend

Even with her growing political commitments, Caesar remained a force in the gospel world. Her 1988 release, *Live . . . in Chicago*, topped the gospel charts from June 18, 1988, to late February 1989. The record featured one of gospel's hottest acts: Milton Brunson and the Thompson Community Singers. A long admirer of the group, Caesar had collaborated with the "Tommies" in the 1970s and renewed her relationship with the choir in 1987, when she returned to Chicago. Instead of working within the confines of the studio, as she had done for much of her tenure with Word, Caesar opted for a live recording at Brunson's Christ Tabernacle Baptist Church. The church was located on North Central Avenue in the heart of a black community on Chicago's west side. If Caesar was looking for an alternative to the controlled, sometimes sterile atmosphere of the studio, Christ Tabernacle, with its deep connection to the surrounding community, was the ideal place.

The live recording provided a much-needed return of sorts for Caesar. Though they hardly qualified as bad records, her last two outings with Word lacked the innovation and fire of her previous material. Creatively, she was at a standstill. And no one recognized this more than Caesar. "Even though I was winning Grammy Awards and Doves and other accolades, I must admit there was a feeling of discontentment in my spirit. I kept remembering the early years of my career when I would sing a capella—songs like 'Peter, Don't Be Afraid,' 'Teach Me Master, Teach Me,' and 'Satan, We're Going to Tear Your Kingdom Down'—and I missed that old traditional gospel sound. And I believed that many of my older listeners did too."[53]

Working with the Thompson Community Singers provided Caesar with the opportunity to reach a younger fan base, as well as to move outside the studio. "I need to get back to my roots," Caesar pleaded with her record company. "Let me record live with a choir, let me minister, let me be me."[54] In Caesar's view, her music with Word had become too slick, too refined, too predictable. "I have got to be free to improvise, to be creative. That is what I do best. Anything that moves me away from that hurts me more than it helps."[55] Though Caesar presented this record as a return to her roots in traditional gospel, this was the sound of black sacred music moving into the twenty-first century.

On the record's first track, "Never," Caesar floats effortlessly through her verses, then powers through the song's chorus. As the singer testifies to God's faithfulness, she tosses out a series of lines familiar to most gospel listeners: "He'll be your friend, when you're friendless, water, when you thirsty, bread, when you're hungry." With ample support from the Tommies, Caesar works the crowd with her fiery extemporizations. "He's a friend," she clarifies to the audience, "a real friend, he'll walk with you, he'll talk with you, he'll live in you, he'll move in you."[56]

Lowering the pace but not the intensity, Caesar segues into "His Blood," a song she dedicates to the victims of AIDS. Perhaps sensing some tension from the audience, she sternly interjects, "You can say whatever you want, that's a mother's son, a father's boy." Her acknowledgment of the disease's devastating impact on the nation and the African American community marked a welcome departure from the black church's general silence.[57] Predicting a medical cure for the disease within a year, the singer presents the AIDS epidemic as connected to larger social issues. Casting her eye on the "brokenness" engulfing the nation, Caesar calls for spiritual renewal within and beyond the church. As Caesar alternates between singing and preaching, sharing biblical stories of Abraham, Ezekiel, and Jesus, the Tommies melodically repeat the song's refrain: "If you come to him and be sincere / His blood can restore your soul."[58]

The need for spiritual renewal is a recurring theme throughout the album, from the inspirational "Yes Lord, Yes," to the bass-heavy "Born Again." Another dominant theme is the promise of a brighter day for those anchored in God and community. On the duet "Things Are Going to Get Better," Caesar and her former Caravans colleague Albertina Walker encourage their listeners to remain steadfast in their faith. More than twenty years had passed since Walker and Caesar sang as members of the Caravans, but their chemistry was still strong.

All of the aforementioned songs were stellar, but none compared in power or appeal to the night's greatest showstopper: "Hold My Mule."

On this eight-minute sermonette, Caesar introduces the audience at Christ Tabernacle to an elderly man named Shouting John. Against the background of piano trills, bluesy guitar notes, and smoldering drums, Caesar walks her audience through the tale of a brewing conflict between an eighty-six-year-old farmer and his church leaders. Early in the sermonette, she vividly describes church leaders' unsuccessful attempts to subdue the elderly man: "The deacons ran and sat him down; he jumped back up. They tried to hold his legs. His hands were going. When they turned the hands loose, the feet were going!" Working her magic on the crowd, Caesar then shouts: "It's just like fire; it's just like fire shut up in my bones."[59]

Weaving class critique into her narrative, she conveys the church leaders' frustration with John's refusal to oblige the church's politics of respectability. "Doesn't he know we don't act like that in our church?" the status conscious deacons query one another. "Doesn't he know we got dignitaries in our church?" Feeling as if the matter had to be handled outside of Sunday service, the clergymen decide to "go out to John's house."[60]

With the crowd under her spell, Caesar gives a play-by-play account of the church leaders' confrontation with John at his home. "When they got out there," Caesar continues, "they found him and a beat-up mule, plowing in the field." What then follows is a spirited exchange between the leaders and John, who recounts what church folk often refer to as "God's favor." In addition to pointing out his ownership of land, he proudly notes his ability to still "harvest my own crop" at his advanced age. He also speaks of a life free from any entanglements with the legal system. "God gave me all of my children," John testifies, but "not one time have I been to the courthouse, not one time have I been to the cemetery."[61] His point is not to position himself as a member of the privileged elite but as a recipient of God's grace.[62]

If their applauses and shouts are any indication, the audience members at Christ Tabernacle identify strongly with John, a "common man" whose faithfulness to God has been well rewarded. Shifting from preacher to songstress, Caesar closes her story with an image of John rejecting the orders of the church leaders and "dancing all around his place."

Throughout the country, gospel listeners could not get enough of the tale of Shouting John, an everyday man who finished on top. Here was a character who resonated deeply with churchgoing, working-class folks from the South who like John might have been condemned as unsophisticated or uncouth by members of the religious elite. The triumphant John character also appealed to certain members of the African American laboring class whose life trajectories did not fit neatly into popular tales of urban decay, broken homes, and poverty—women and men who had managed like John (only through the grace of God, in their minds) to avoid the traps and pitfalls of America's criminal justice system. Caesar's "Hold My Mule" resonated with African Americans who looked at their lives in totality and felt they had been shown God's favor.

Ironically, Caesar's celebration of Shouting John, an independent black landowner, coincided with the dramatic decline in the number of African American farmers. The same year Caesar released "Hold My Mule," the North Carolina Association of Black Lawyers filed a complaint against the Farmers Home Administration (FMHA) alleging discrimination against African American farmers. In its complaint to the U.S. Commission on Civil Rights, the advocacy group accused the FMHA of racial discrimination: "FMHA's actions have further resulted in a disproportionate number of class members being driven out of farming. Between 1978 and 1982, the total number of black and Indian farmers declined 23.2 percent, compared to 9.8 percent for the white farmers."[63] By 1987, African Americans owned only 2.4 million acres, nearly 10 million less than they did in 1900. Perhaps in Shouting John, African Americans, especially those in the South who had experienced the loss of land or had sold their properties well below their value, found a heroic figure who had managed to maintain one of the race's most treasured yet increasingly elusive assets: land.

Released in the year Caesar celebrated her fiftieth birthday, *Live . . . in Chicago* testified to the enduring power and appeal of her talent. Thanks to the radio hits "Hold My Mule," "Yes Lord, Yes," and "His Blood," *Live . . . in Chicago* dominated the gospel charts for nearly a year. At its peak, according to Caesar, the album was selling on average 25,000 copies a week. In 1989, *Billboard* chose Caesar as its gospel artist of the year and *Live . . . in Chicago* as its gospel record of the year. Caesar's selection was a reflection of the depth of her talent, her commercial appeal, and her singularity as an artist. Here was a musician who had maintained a special place in the hearts of gospel lovers for thirty years—not because of organizational connections or past achievements but because she was still at the forefront of the genre.

Caesar understood and recognized her special gift. "I'm a down-to-earth singer serving a modern God. I'm a southerner, and my roots are in traditional gospel music. I like songs that give a profound message. I'm not saying traditional gospel is the only music. The Lord has all kinds of vehicles to win souls. . . . [And] the Lord is using me in mine."[64]

CHAPTER 4

A Wonderful Change

Walter Hawkins and the
Love Alive Explosion

Every door I've ever walked through was because God
used Walter Hawkins as a key to unlock it.
—KIRK FRANKLIN, *The Gospel Blog*

We didn't set out to be different. We only wanted
to be ourselves. We were interested in incorporating
new musical elements into our sound so that people
would pay attention. We try to keep up with what's
happening musically, to seek out ways to appeal to
people who wouldn't normally come to church.
—EDWIN HAWKINS in Jesse Hamlin, "Good News
for Gospel," *San Francisco Chronicle*

On Sunday night, August 24, 1980, 7,000 gospel fans gathered at the Armory
Starplex in Washington, D.C., to celebrate the second anniversary of the black-
owned radio station WYCB.[1] For its anniversary celebration, the popular station
selected two of gospel's biggest acts as the event's headliners: James Cleveland and
the Hawkins Family. Fresh off the thirteenth annual convention of the Gospel
Music Workshop of America in Philadelphia, Cleveland ignited the audience
with his sanctified brand of gospel music. "I don't know about you," the gospel
singer told the crowd, "but I came to have church tonight."[2] Not to be upstaged
by the King of Gospel, the Hawkins Family brought the spectators to their feet
with "heart-rendering" renditions of "Be Grateful," "He's That Kind of Friend,"
and "Until I Found the Lord." The latter song featured Walter Hawkins, who
delivered a high-powered performance for the enthusiastic audience. Though
the Hawkins Family were immensely talented with several gifted musicians,
Walter was the driving engine behind their most recent success. To be sure,
Edwin Hawkins had been responsible for the crossover smash "Oh Happy Day,"

but by 1980, his brother Walter had emerged as the family's most consistent producer of gospel hits.

Over the course of his storied career, Walter Hawkins gained international recognition for his arranging and production skills, songwriting gifts, and amazing vocals. His broad compositional style ranged from the majestic "Be Grateful" to the gutbucket, bass-and-drum funk of "Until I Found the Lord." Though he emerged in the age of crossover, Hawkins belonged, almost exclusively, to the black church. His records never gained much traction in either the R&B or contemporary Christian music market. And yet, his *Love Alive* series sold in the hundreds of thousands, an indication of his popularity among black gospel music lovers. To this day, his most popular compositions remain embedded in

FIGURE 10. Walter Hawkins performing in 1978. Photo by Harry Naltchayan/*The Washington Post* via Getty Images.

African American religious gatherings and ritualistic practices. Consider how the singing of "Goin' Up Yonder" can transform a funeral into a spirit-filled "homegoing" celebration or how the opening lines of "Be Grateful" can instantaneously redeem a dull, listless Sunday morning service.

While Hawkins never chased secular success, he refused to limit his musical explorations to the gospel world. Conversant with various styles in the black music tradition, Hawkins drew inspiration from rhythm and blues, soul, funk, and even disco. His circle of collaborators included artists ranging from Maurice White of Earth, Wind, and Fire to the disco artist Sylvester James, who also attended Hawkins's church, the Love Center. Hawkins's commitment to artistic excellence was unwavering, but realizing his creative ambitions was not always easy. One of his biggest challenges involved navigating record labels' limited budgets for gospel artists: "We go into the companies with creative thoughts and they (record companies) don't want to spend the dollars."[3]

Notwithstanding these financial challenges, Hawkins successfully tapped into his deep well of creative resources to produce some of the most sonically adventurous recordings in gospel music history. His *Love Alive* series and *Hawkins Family Live* challenged conventional ideas of what black gospel music could and should be, while his production work on Tramaine Hawkins's first two solo records, *Tramaine* and *I Am Determined*, helped crystalize the urban contemporary gospel sound. His daring creativity won him the respect of his gospel peers and some of the most acclaimed musicians in the secular world. Over the years, a wide range of artists sampled Hawkins's songbook, from the pop star Aretha Franklin to avant-garde jazz legend Archie Shepp.

The Making of a Gospel Legend

A native of Oakland, California, Walter Hawkins was born on May 18, 1949, and reared in the working-class neighborhood of Campbell Village (located in the Lower Bottoms of West Oakland). His father, Daniel, worked as a porter and longshoreman on the city's docks to provide for his large family, which included his wife, Mamie Vivian, three daughters (Carol, Feddie, and Lynette), and three sons (Edwin, Daniel, and Walter). Life was anything but easy for working-class families like the Hawkinses during the post–World War II years. As the historian Robert Self explains, "Unemployment and occupational downgrading hit postwar African American communities in Oakland and San Francisco harder than those elsewhere in the United States. After finding employment in manufacturing at a higher rate than African Americans in the country as a whole, Bay Area black workers became casualties of the massive postwar layoffs in the shipyards in equal proportion. By 1950 unemployment among Oakland's

African American workers was 20 percent for both men and women, twice the rate for white workers."[4]

Amid these challenges, the Hawkins family found solace, affirmation, and spiritual guidance in the church. They also found musical training and economic opportunities. Edwin Hawkins attended Ephesian Church of God in Christ, where the renowned E. E. Cleveland served as pastor. Deeply committed to improving the lives of African Americans who called Oakland home, Cleveland was known for his fiery sermons, as well as for his unwavering support for young people. That support became evident to the entire nation in

FIGURE II. Ephesian Church of God in Christ in Berkeley. Photo by author.

April 1968, when Cleveland opened his church's doors for the funeral of Black Panther Bobby Hutton, the seventeen-year-old activist murdered by Oakland police. Some 1,500 locals, along with well-known figures like Marlon Brando, crammed into Ephesian Church to pay their respects to another martyr of the movement. Noting that he was "ashamed" of his generation, Cleveland felt as if young black people had been asked to carry too much political responsibility. "The young men ought to be in school and the old men ought to be doing this work," he declared. The minister then directed his attention to white America, predicting doom for the country if it did not redirect its course. "We need to know that America is on the threshold of destruction," Cleveland raged. "We need to know that she is destroying herself from the inside. We need to know that God is not pleased."[5]

Cleveland's remarks at Hutton's funeral conveyed his deep concern for young black people, whom he had always hoped could find a nurturing space in his church. Young people, he believed, needed a safe space to fortify themselves spiritually and to help them navigate the challenges of black life in Oakland. One way he sought to meet the needs of black teenagers was through Ephesian's vibrant musical programs and youth choirs. To realize his objectives for his music ministry, he relied on the services of Ola Jean Andrews, the director of Ephesian's church choir. Always on the hunt for young talent, Andrews developed a strong relationship with the Hawkins family, particularly brother Edwin. Seeing great potential in the precocious youngster, she encouraged him to move beyond traditional gospel chords and embrace new harmonic structures. As local journalist Reginald Hildebrand tells it, Andrews had a "jazz imbued sense of harmony," and she shared many of her ideas with Edwin Hawkins.[6] Finding support and encouragement at Ephesian, Edwin served as the director of its youth choir. His younger brother Walter eventually became the choir's organist. And musical training was not the only gift the Hawkins brothers received from Ephesian: the church also brought them into contact with Reverend Cleveland's talented granddaughter Tramaine Davis.

Not confined to one church, the Hawkinses' musical ties reached beyond Ephesian. As teenagers, Edwin and Walter Hawkins played for other local churches, including Mount Pilgrim Church of God in Christ, East Oakland Church of God in Christ, and Unity Baptist Church. Their involvement with COGIC and Baptist churches expanded their musical vocabulary, familiarized them with different worship experiences, and introduced them to other Bay Area artists.

The Hawkins brothers' musical development also bore the imprint of their parents' influence. Though a devout member of the Church of God in Christ, Mamie Hawkins lacked the rigidity typically associated with COGIC parents. To be sure, church attendance was mandatory for her children, but Mrs. Hawkins's appreciation for African American culture extended beyond the world of the church, particularly when it came to music. "Music ran in my family," Edwin Hawkins proudly relayed in an interview. "My mother and most of her brothers were musical. . . . One of her brothers was even a jazz musician. So we heard some of that in our home. My mother didn't close any music out just because she was a Christian. She wasn't like some Christians we knew that wouldn't allow jazz to be listened to at home. We listened to it all."[7] Their diverse listening experiences also included country and western, their father's favorite genre.[8]

The Hawkins children also reaped the benefits of the nation's thriving pop music scene. Like millions of other teens, the siblings paid close attention to developments in the pop world. Walter Hawkins loved the music of James Brown, the Supremes, and Stevie Wonder, while Edwin had a strong admiration for Sérgio Mendes and Brasil '66. "We used to do a lot of bossa nova in our music," Walter Hawkins later recalled.[9] The influence of Mendes surfaced in a song that changed the lives of the Hawkinses dramatically: "Oh Happy Day."

Well known in the Bay Area's church circles, the Hawkins Family garnered international attention in 1969 with the crossover hit. The song was initially released on the record *Let Us Go into the House of the Lord*, under the auspices of the Northern California Youth Choir. Organized in the spring of 1967, the choir was the brainchild of Edwin Hawkins and Betty Watson. To raise funds for a trip to Washington, D.C., the choir recorded at Ephesian the eight songs that would appear on the album. Shortly thereafter, a locally based company, Century Records, agreed to release the recording. The choir felt the Tramaine Davis–led song "Joy, Joy" was the strongest cut on the album, but it was the opening number on Side B, "Oh Happy Day," that transformed the Hawkinses' fundraising endeavor into a life-changing event.

I Want to Take You Higher: "Oh Happy Day" and the Gospel Revolution

With its funky backbeat, inspiring vocals from Dorothy Morrison, and Edwin Hawkins's innovative arrangement, "Oh Happy Day" soon landed on the gospel, R&B, and pop charts. The song's major breakthrough came when DJ Abe Kesh of the progressive rock station KSAN-FM added it to his playlist. Then Joe Bostic of New York's WLIB put "Oh Happy Day" in regular rotation. Soon other disc jockeys on the East Coast followed suit. Joe Crane of WNJR of Newark, Jimmy Byrd at Boston's WILD, and Pauline Wells of WSID in Baltimore all gave the uplifting number their stamp of approval. Within months of its release, "Oh Happy Day" was in regular rotation at Top 40 pop stations across the nation. It raced up *Billboard*'s singles charts, peaking at the #4 position. The song's spectacular success resulted in a bidding war for distribution rights, which

Century sold to the most competitive bidder, Buddah Records. Shortly after gaining rights to the song, Buddah reissued *Let Us Go into the House of the Lord* with the Edwin Hawkins Singers as the listed artist rather than the Northern California Youth Choir.

Claiming one of the biggest hits of the year, the Edwin Hawkins Singers toured extensively throughout the United States, appearing on several variety shows (such as the *Dick Cavett Show* and the *Andy Williams Show*) and opening up for some of the biggest names in pop culture.[10] The venues inviting the gospel group ranged from Caesar's Palace in Las Vegas to Continental Baths in New York.

"Oh Happy Day" also achieved great popularity in Europe, where it became a #1 hit in Holland, France, and Germany. The song's fans ranged from pop-crazed teenagers enamored with the song's uplifting lyrics and irresistible chorus to the Beatles' George Harrison, who identified the tune as an inspiration for his 1970 song "My Sweet Lord." On the pages of *Billboard* magazine, writer Ed Ochs wondered if the smash hit might spark a gospel revival on both sides of the Atlantic. "The success of the Edwin Hawkins Singers' 'Oh Happy Day' on the Buddah-distributed Pavilion label may ignite a gospel rush that could not only return rhythm and blues artists to their church roots, but also boost secular artists in the gospel tradition into a larger, more profitable 'pop' picture." Noting how the 1960s, particularly the British invasion, had spawned a blues revival, Ochs suggested the possibility of something similar happening in gospel. "Behind the imminent popular success of the Sweet Inspirations, the fame of Aretha Franklin, and the phenomenon of the Edwin Hawkins Singers lies a gospel revival that could 'discover' James Cleveland as deserving of exclusive praise and awe as Ray Charles, exposing for mass appreciation an art form rich with ethnic tradition, heroes, and excellence."[11] Not simply a novelty hit, "Oh Happy Day" was part of a larger discussion about a potential shift in gospel's status in the larger pop marketplace.

Never before had a gospel song generated so much conversation among music critics. As journalist Daniel Goldberg remarked in *Billboard*'s annual review of the music industry, "No account of gospel in the last few months would be complete without mention of 'Oh Happy Day' which has stirred controversy throughout the black gospel world while capturing the fancy of the general public and becoming gospel's first RIAA [Recording Industry Association of America] certified million-dollar record."[12]

Frequently lost in conversations about the national and international appeal of the song was how much it embodied the spirit of the times in the Bay Area. Looking back at the success of "Oh Happy Day," Henry Delton Williams, a longtime Oakland resident and noted fashion designer, remembered fondly how the song captured the political moment. "That was during the time of the Panthers, Martin Luther King, the Vietnam war. And all the hippies found out that their parents had lied to them about this, that, and the other. And everybody's exploring. Then comes 'Oh Happy Day.' Ed didn't plan on that. It just seemed to be perfect for that period."[13]

That a family from the Bay Area would be responsible for revolutionizing the gospel sound seemed appropriate given the regional trends in pop music. The area claimed several of rock's hottest young groups, most notably the Grateful Dead, Creedence Clearwater Revival, Moby Grape, and Jefferson Airplane. It also had a thriving soul scene. In 1967, Sly and the Family Stone released their debut album, *A Whole New Thing.* Over the next four years, Sly and his band transformed the sonic landscape of popular music with hits such as "Dance to the Music," "Stand!," "Family Affair," "Thank You (Falettinme Be Mice Elf Agin)," "Hot Fun in the Summertime," "I Want to Take You Higher," and "Everyday People." The Hawkinses were no stranger to Sly and his family's talent. Walter's future wife, Tramaine Davis, had been in the gospel group the Heavenly Tones with Sly's sister Vaetta Stewart during their high school years. The Hawkinses also followed the careers of other Bay Area groups like the Chambers Brothers (whose massive hit "Time Has Come Today" assumed anthem status in 1968), Tower of Power (who, along with members of Earth, Wind, and Fire, appeared on the 1980 recording *Hawkins Family Live*), and Marvin Holmes and the Uptights.

Immersed in the Bay Area's music scene, Walter and Edwin Hawkins soaked up the many sounds and vibes of the late 1960s. The locale's influence on their musical ideas is apparent in Edwin's 1969 release, *The Hebrew Boys*, an underappreciated gem in the family's discography that hints at new developments in the field of contemporary gospel. On this record, Edwin's arrangements are magnificent and Walter's vocal contributions are phenomenal. Yet even though he loved working with his older brother, Walter Hawkins eventually found the Edwin Hawkins Singers too restrictive. This had less to do with the talent of the group and more to do with the frenzy surrounding "Oh Happy Day." In a strange way, the pop smash had been both a blessing and a curse. On the one hand, the Edwin Hawkins Singers had become an internationally known act blessed with the opportunity to bring its Christian message to the larger world. The group released six records in its first three years with Buddah: *Let Us Go into the House of the Lord, Peace Is 'Blowin' in the Wind,' He's a Friend of Mine, Live at the Concertgebouw in Amsterdam, More Happy Days,* and *Children (Get Together).* On the other hand, the Edwin Hawkins Singers endured constant criticism from fellow Christians. "We started to get ridicule from the church community. We even had a few ministers and pastors trying to get a petition to get the song off the secular radio," Edwin Hawkins sadly remembered. "That kind of confused me a bit. I was very disillusioned."[14]

For Walter Hawkins, the song presented more issues than just criticism from the church. The success of "Oh Happy Day" kept the Hawkins Family on the road from the late 1960s to the early 1970s, but he yearned for something more, both musically and personally. "The main reason I left the Edwin Hawkins Singers was to make my own statement. I did a nightclub act, but it wasn't very gratifying. Sometimes, it takes those kinds of things to know how you really feel. It took that experience to know what was really within me."[15] On his journey to self-discovery, he signed with the San Francisco–based label Fantasy Records in 1972. His debut recording, *Do Your Best*, was inspirational music with a San Francisco psychedelic soul twist. At first listen, one can hear the influence of his coproducers, Tom Fogerty of Creedence Clearwater Revival and Merl Saunders. The record featured several intriguing cuts—"It Pays," "MacArthur Park," and "Will You Be There," a song later covered by Tramaine Hawkins and Daryl Coley. But if Fantasy expected an "Oh Happy Day" result from any of these songs, the label was in for a major disappointment. By all accounts, the record didn't move many units. Still, *Do Your Best* (along with Walter Hawkins's contributions on Merl Saunders's solo recordings) offers important insight into Hawkins's maturation as an artist.

The busy Hawkins was also steeped in preparation for the ministry. In 1972, his grandfather-in-law E. E. Cleveland ordained him after a period of extensive training and mentorship. Shortly thereafter, Hawkins created the Love Center Church, which initially held services at a small storefront at 8411 MacArthur Boulevard in Oakland. Love Center welcomed young and old, white and black, heterosexuals, gays, and lesbians. It was an eclectic mix of Christians seeking a stronger relationship with God, fellowship, and a sense of belonging. Counted among those who would join the church was disco star Sylvester, an openly gay man who remained close to the Hawkins family until his death in 1988.[16] A spirit of inclusivity undergirded Hawkins's theology, his vision for Love Center, and his music: "The message of God is the same always, but the language and the manner of preaching it changes. . . . Jesus could deal with anybody from the leaders of His time to the beggars and the prostitute he met at the well."[17]

A Brand New Thing:
The *Love Alive* Series

Even with his ministerial responsibilities, Hawkins remained committed to his music. His solo career stalled in the early 1970s, but by the end of the decade, Hawkins had solidified his status as one of the most innovative musicians in the gospel field. His critically acclaimed 1975 release, *Love Alive*, set the world on fire with its special blend of Pentecostal gospel, R&B, jazz, and soul-drenched funk. The album's success was a testament not just to Hawkins's amazing talent but also to his network of supportive family and friends. Unattached to a record label, Hawkins borrowed $1,500 from his mother-in-law, Lois "The Pie Queen" Davis (owner of one of the most popular restaurants in the Bay Area), to finance a live performance at Ephesian Church. "It was just a dream I had," Hawkins later recalled; "I wanted to do a live recording."[18] A tape of the performance eventually reached gospel superstar Andraé Crouch. "Because of being on the road so much," Crouch later recalled, "I seldom get a chance to listen at length to the music of the people I love and enjoy, but when I heard the cassette of a portion of what went on at the recording in the Ephesian Church in Berkeley, I laughed and I cried because of the fresh touch and the new anointing of Walter Hawkins and his family." Crouch was shocked not just at the music but at Hawkins's free agent status as well. "Hearing a tape of this quality, I assumed that it must have already been committed to a recording company. I was wrong!"[19] An enthused Crouch immediately contacted Ralph Carmichael, the president of Light Records, and convinced him to release the live recording.

This proved to be one of Carmichael's smartest investments, as *Love Alive* sold in the hundreds of thousands. The recording did much more than catapult Walter Hawkins to superstardom in the gospel world; it also redefined the sonic properties of contemporary gospel. *Love Alive* revealed Hawkins's unerring eye for talent, his willingness to absorb the varied rhythms of the African and Latin diaspora, and his insistence on pushing the sonic boundaries of gospel beyond the comfort zone of the genre's traditionalists. His funds might have been limited, but he had an abundance of ideas and talent.

Several of Hawkins's family members contributed to the record. However, the undisputed star of the show was his wife, Tramaine Hawkins. In fact, the two most popular songs on *Love Alive*, "Changed" and "Goin' Up Yonder," featured her on lead. On the moving song "Changed," she provided a primer for her peers and the next generation of gospel vocalists. Her stunning soprano soars over the choir as she delivers her message with great conviction and grace. Tramaine's voice is elegant and gentle, but hardly gutless. There's an undeniable power in her vocals, especially after the pace of the song intensifies around the halfway point. Over the next few minutes, she testifies to the transformative power of salvation: "I'm not what I want to be, I'm not what I used to be."[20] Her vocal flights are a pure joy and a technical wonder, but they are always done in service of the song and its message.

Songwriter Walter Hawkins had a brilliant interpreter in Tramaine, who delivered another amazing performance on the now gospel standard "Goin' Up Yonder." The song opens with what is now one of the most familiar melodies in gospel music. Organist Daniel Hawkins and pianist Edwin Hawkins hold down the groove for fifty seconds before Tramaine Hawkins interjects her angelic voice into the mix. "If you want to know," she sings in an elongated rhythm, "where I'm going? Where I'm going, soon." Careful to stretch out each syllable, she repeats the verse with only a slight change to the first line. Then comes the refrain that Hawkins and the choir will evoke throughout the course of the ten-minute song:

> I'm goin' up yonder
> I'm goin' up yonder
> I'm goin' up yonder to be with my Lord.[21]

Much like "Changed," "Goin' Up Yonder" has a reprise in which Hawkins elicits enormous excitement from the crowd. Functioning as both preacher and singer, she moves beyond her natural vocal register as the audience shouts words of encouragement. "As God gives me grace," she sings with the perfect combination of restraint and passion, "I've got to run, I've got to run, I've got to run and run on and run on and run on and run on and run on . . ." Every word seems to blend together as the crowd anticipates her closing moment. "Until I see Jesus," Hawkins repeats twice before belting "Until I see my Savior face to face."[22] The song's tempo then quickens during the last minute and a half as Hawkins and the choir end on a triumphant note.

With "Goin' Up Yonder," Walter Hawkins created a song that was innovative yet easily adaptable to worship service. Its melodic notes and chord changes did not take long for choir directors and musicians to learn. Moreover, a lead vocalist did not necessarily have to possess Tramaine Hawkins's range to capture the spirit of the song. "Goin' Up Yonder" became a crucial part of worship services at black churches across the nation. The song was also a mainstay on gospel radio.

Thanks to the success of "Goin Up Yonder" and "Changed" as well as other standout cuts like "God Is" and "I Love the Lord," Walter Hawkins was in heavy demand. His concerts routinely sold out, and Love Alive flew off the record shelves of mom-and-pop record stores across the country.

Tremendous pressure was on Hawkins to duplicate the success of Love Alive, and he didn't disappoint. Hawkins raised his stature in the gospel world even more with the release of Love Alive II. Recorded at Oakland's Center of Hope Community Church in 1978, Love Alive II boasted the stunning opener "Come by Here, Good Lord," Tramaine Hawkins's scorching ballad "He's That Kind of Friend," Edwin and Walter's duet "I'm Goin' Away," and Lynette Hawkins's solo number, "Right On." The record also included the sonic masterpiece "Be Grateful." In the song's opening seconds, pianist Edwin Hawkins introduces the gorgeous melody, which his brother Daniel quickly echoes on organ. At the one-minute mark, the choir adds another layer of sonic coloring with the simple yet powerful refrain "Be grateful." Then enters Lynette Hawkins. Her powerful voice conveys the dignity of a people who have learned to smile amid the tears:

God has not promised me sunshine
That's not the way it's going to be
But a little rain
Mixed with God's sunshine
A little pain
Makes me appreciate the good times.[23]

The lyrics occasion critical reflection, not just about one's personal situation but about the African American odyssey in the United States as well. Nothing is explicitly political about "Be Grateful," but for many who invest theological meaning in the trials and triumphs of African Americans, it captures some of the essence of the black struggle.

Open to a variety of interpretations, "Be Grateful" was much more than a brilliant song on a seminal album; it was a monumental moment in gospel music history. It was a game changer, an inspired work of art that foreshadowed and spurred future developments in contemporary gospel music. Listening closely to the song, one can hear elements of the choral arrangements and lush production later found in the works of Richard Smallwood, Thomas Whitfield, Milton Brunson and the Thompson Community Choir, and Donald Lawrence.

On *Love Alive II*, Walter Hawkins, the choir, the featured soloists, and the band brought the fire from beginning to end. A rare gospel record without filler, *Love Alive II* didn't have one bad song in the bunch. Of the accompanying musicians who brought their own influences and styles to bear on the recording, Joel Smith (the son of Walter's sister Feddie) deserves special attention. One of gospel's most skilled sidemen, Smith played the drums during the live concert and then laid down the bass lines during the postproduction process. On the ultra-funky "Right On" and "Until I Found the Lord," he demonstrates how gospel music could move away from the conventional 2/4 beat without losing its spirit. Smith's spectacular drumming gives listeners a sense of the artistic freedom Hawkins provided his band. It also reveals the musician's deep respect for his craft. Over the years, Smith had carefully studied drummers like Steve Gadd, Billy Cobham, Harvey Mason, and Bill Maxwell. Of these master teachers shaping Smith's sound, no one was more important than Maxwell. "We used to be on bills together, so I watched Bill a lot and was able to see him in different situations. I love seeing what other people do and check out their techniques and the way they contribute to the music," Joel Smith said. Though he admired Maxwell and other innovative drummers in gospel, jazz, and R&B, Smith recognized the importance of developing his own style: "I never wanted to get lost in the shuffle when it came to my identity. The only thing that stands true is what naturally comes out of you."[24]

What came out of Smith on Hawkins's *Love Alive II* was breathtaking. A multi-instrumentalist, Smith would be remembered as much for his bass work as for his drumming. On "Right On," Smith's thumping bass beautifully complements the scorching vocals of Lynette Hawkins. He also turns in a masterful performance on "Until I Found the Lord," a go-to tutorial for aspiring bassists learning to play gospel.

With *Love Alive II*, Walter Hawkins proved that artistic excellence, craft mastery, saving souls, and commercial success were not mutually exclusive pursuits. He also solidified his status as one of gospel's most innovative musicians and proven hitmakers. No longer in the shadow of his older brother Edwin, Hawkins was a bona fide star in the world of gospel. His first *Love Alive* album held the top position on *Billboard*'s gospel albums chart for more than two years. Its follow-up performed equally well, going on to sell more than 300,000 copies, a great achievement for a gospel album lacking crossover success in the R&B and white Christian markets. Two years after its release, *Love Alive II* remained #1 on the gospel charts. Not too far behind was the first installation of the series, which held the #7 position.[25]

Within the gospel world, Hawkins and his choir gained recognition for more than their albums. Their energetic live shows garnered rave reviews from music journalists in both the secular and gospel worlds. The family traveled widely, performing in churches, auditoriums, and large theaters across the country. Fortunate to catch the group on its stop through the nation's capital, Hollie West of the *Washington Post* could hardly contain his excitement at the group's musical talent and spiritual fervor.

> They concentrate on blending traditional gospel concepts with today's music trends—and the result is marvelous. The group has such a dazzling array of soloists that it's hard to single out anyone. If there was a crowd favorite, it was Tramaine Hawkins, Walter's wife, whose magnificent soprano soared on "Goin' Up Yonder" and dipped and moaned on the balladic "Christ Is the Way." Not to be outdone, however, were Shirley Miller and Lynette Hawkins, both contraltos with significantly different approaches. Lynette Hawkins delivered her songs in a robust manner reminiscent of a locomotive speeding through the night. Shirley Miller was just as powerful but more restrained, moving like a cruising limousine.[26]

Touring provided Walter Hawkins with the opportunity to deepen his connection with his growing fan base. It also forced him to confront his changing status within his family. On their tours and in their recordings, the Hawkins Family embraced a democratic structure in which its three vocal powerhouses—Walter, Tramaine, and Lynette—handled lead and background duties. All three had signature songs capable of bringing the house down. Thus, no one individual dominated the spotlight. In fact, on those occasions when Walter Hawkins was fatigued or under the weather, he handed his lead vocal duties to his brother Edwin. This practice, however, did not always sit well with his adoring fans. "At the beginning of (one) tour, I wasn't feeling that good," Hawkins explained in an interview with *Jet*. "So I asked my brother (Edwin) to take the lead roles and I'd just play piano and sing background." Much to his surprise, fans openly expressed their disappointment with Hawkins's background role. "The people don't understand I have ups and downs like they do, and don't always feel 100 percent. They come to see me perform. And that's something I had to grow to understand."[27]

Guide My Way: Walter Hawkins in the 1980s

Hawkins worked hard to fulfill his fans' expectations not just in terms of his live concerts but also in his recordings. A brilliant singer-songwriter with wide-ranging musical interests, Hawkins believed the gospel world deserved his artistic best. He also believed that the sonic boundaries of the art form were fluid. Conversant with various genres in the black music tradition, Hawkins synthesized years of musical study and practice into his ambitious 1980 recording, *Hawkins Family Live*. Featuring the Oakland-based band Tower of Power (TOP), Maurice White of Earth, Wind, and Fire, and key members of the Hawkins Family, the record was a perfect blend of California soul, lite funk, jazz, disco, and contemporary gospel. If nothing else, this record demonstrated Hawkins's commitment to artistic growth. It would have been easy for him to repeat the tried-and-true formulas of the *Love Alive* recordings, but on *Hawkins Family Live*, he broadens his sound through his brilliant use of Tower of Power. Since the late 1960s, the predominantly white band had been a major player on the East Bay music scene. National success, however, didn't come until 1972 with the release of the group's second album, *Bump City*. Thanks to the radio hits "So Very Hard to Go," "What Is Hip?," and "This Time It's Real," TOP's third album, *Tower of Power*, reached gold status, bringing critical acclaim to the band and its lead singer, Lenny Williams. Very much a part of the East Bay scene, Williams had worked with other notable artists in the area, including Sly Stone and the Hawkins Family. Having monitored TOP's rising success, Hawkins reveled in the opportunity to work with the band. The pairing of Hawkins with Tower of Power yielded amazing results on *Hawkins Family Live*. On the disco-tinged "Keep on Fighting," Tramaine and Walter Hawkins put on a vocal clinic while TOP unloads sizzling hot rhythms. The band excels not just on upbeat songs like "Keep on Fighting" and "He'll Be There" but also on the slower-paced tunes, particularly "What Is This" and "Try Christ." Never before had a brass section been featured so prominently in a live gospel recording, but Hawkins's venture into new territory worked extremely well.

Another highlight for the night was the beautiful ballad "Eternal Life," which featured Edwin Hawkins and Maurice White on lead vocals. White takes the song to another level, injecting his own brand of spirituality and mysticism into the music. As a leader, Walter Hawkins created a context in which every contributor could display his or her virtuosity without sacrificing the communal sound.

Though featuring contributions from secular artists like Maurice White and TOP, *Hawkins Family Live* did not cross over into the R&B market. This hardly bothered Hawkins, who understood the dangers of alienating one's gospel base. "A ministry is not viable if there's no room for growth," he readily admitted, "but we don't want to cross over and lose our base." Hawkins's commentary reflected his bittersweet memories of his brother Edwin's experiences with the pop smash "Oh Happy Day." The sting of criticism from the church world lingered long after the song became an international hit. "When we did 'Oh Happy Day,' we thought it was just another gospel record. But when it crossed over, the Christian community felt we no longer belonged to them and the secular market felt we were gospel. We had no base for about five years."[28] Cognizant of the dangers of short-term crossover success, Hawkins worked hard to maintain his popularity in the gospel world, a world that had afforded his family a standard of living he could have never imagined during his childhood years in Oakland.

On a related note, Hawkins had no interest in branching into the white Christian market. Unlike his California counterpart Andraé Crouch, Hawkins did not have a white fan base. Nor was he particularly interested in cultivating one. Crossing over, he believed, required more effort and more politicking than he was willing to put forth. "I will not prostitute myself or compromise just to reach the white market," Hawkins insisted. His stark language should not be read as animus toward whites but rather as a reflection of his unwillingness to water down his art. "I'm always thinking in terms of broadening our market," he admitted. "But I think we're a little too hot, too raw, too wild or whatever for white people."[29] Hawkins's blunt commentary came at an interesting time, when many record executives at Light and its principal distributor, Word, endeavored to expose more black artists to the white market. In fact, throughout the world of CCM, label executives, musicians, and journalists were confronting the genre's race problem. Frances Preston, then president of the predominantly white Gospel Music Association, had recently asserted that facilitating greater interaction among black and white religious artists was one of her organization's major goals for the year.[30] A year before Preston's statement, the genre's main publication, *Contemporary Christian Music* magazine, ran a feature story on Walter, Edwin, and Tramaine Hawkins. The issue opened with a vivid description of a church service at Hawkins's Love Center, detailed the family's unique relationship to black Oakland, charted their rise to superstardom in the gospel world, and sought to convince the magazine's predominantly white readership why the music of Edwin, Walter, and Tramaine deserved a critical hearing. Focusing primarily on his ministry, Walter Hawkins stated in no uncertain terms his deep commitment to the local community. "Oakland is the territory I grew up in," he explained to the writer. "It's a typical black ghetto area—not the real dense area, but we're real close to it. It's around the corner almost. I really like this area for ministry because I feel like I can really relate to these people."[31] As readers quickly discovered, diversifying his audience was not one of his primary concerns. He did not view the grass as greener on the other side of the tracks. Though appreciative of efforts to bring white and black Christians together, Hawkins reveled in his special place among black gospel music lovers. "If I cross over, fine, but I think it's important for our people to feel we belong to them."[32]

Satisfied with his place within the black gospel industry, Hawkins never garnered much traction in the world of white contemporary Christian music. And yet, his albums sold remarkably well and ranked high on *Billboard*'s gospel charts for not just weeks but years. Even during the recession of 1980, a year when many artists saw dramatic declines in album sales and concert tickets, Hawkins's records continued to fly off the shelves.

One record in particular received a considerable amount of attention from gospel fans and critics: his wife's 1979 debut on Light, *Tramaine*. A strikingly beautiful singer with one of the most distinguished voices in music, Tramaine seemed primed for a blockbuster release. In the eyes of Light executives, the statuesque singer with the big voice and charismatic personality had massive crossover potential. Targeting Christian and mainstream record stores, Light aggressively marketed her debut as a major breakthrough in gospel music.

With flawless production from Walter Hawkins, *Tramaine* lived up to the enormous buzz surrounding its release. The eight-song collection is tight and polished, not a misplaced note or song in earshot. Upbeat tunes like "Look at Me" and "Call Me" are full of harmonic and rhythmic surprises, while classic ballads like "Lord I Try" and "Holy One" demonstrate why Tramaine Hawkins remains the gold standard for many gospel vocalists. Cool and cerebral, she avoids histrionics and excessive displays of technique, trusting the strength and singularity of her voice.

And yet the importance of *Tramaine* extends beyond its brilliant display of the singer's vocal prowess. A hugely important record in terms of solidifying the sound of urban contemporary gospel, *Tramaine* picks up where Crouch's *This Is Another Day* left off and elevates the genre to new heights. It has the precision one expects from a studio recording without losing the energy and spontaneity found in a live setting. This reflected Tramaine Hawkins's remarkable skills as a vocalist and interpreter as well as Walter Hawkins's gifts as a producer. On *Tramaine*, Hawkins's production bore the influence of his brief tenure with Fantasy Records, particularly his work with Tom Fogerty and Merl Saunders. One can also hear the influence of his Light colleague Andraé Crouch. On this impressive set, Hawkins proved himself to be a master not just on the stage but also in the studio.

As both a producer and artist, Walter Hawkins was a proven hit-maker for Light Records, which now stood as the undisputed leader in the black contemporary gospel market. The label's roster included Walter and Tramaine Hawkins, Andraé Crouch, Jessy Dixon, and the Winans. To ensure its continued prominence in the field, Light re-signed Walter Hawkins to an eight-album deal in 1982. Under the new deal, Hawkins agreed to produce three albums under the auspices of the Hawkins Family, three albums for his wife, Tramaine, and one album, respectively, for his sister Lynette Hawkins and his cousin Shirley Miller.[33] Yet Hawkins's work with Light Records was only one aspect of his service to the industry and his ministry. Combined with pastoring his growing church, the Love Center, and producing artists not signed with Light, Hawkins also actively participated in his brother Edwin's music and arts seminar. Established in 1979, the Edwin Hawkins Music and Arts Seminar was a weeklong event at which the family and other gospel acts held workshops for aspiring musicians and artists. The seminar grew out of Edwin and Walter Hawkins's desire to assist young African Americans in their artistic development and maturation. "In my travels," Edwin Hawkins explained, "I ran into many talented young folks whose only outlet to sing gospel music was found in the church. There needed to be a way to help further develop their skills and abilities to the glory of God. So I decided to help them find themselves in the arts. I felt it incumbent upon me to marshal the finest artists and musicians to teach the youngsters." Under his leadership, the first seminar was held April 9–14, 1979, at the Golden Gateway Holiday Inn. The workshops drew about 200 young musicians, many of them hoping to follow in the footsteps of the Hawkins Family. Its leaders focused on "songwriting, vocal technique, keyboard technique, painting, drama, interior design, and fashion design."[34] To the delight of attendees, the first seminar also featured an inspiring speech from Jesse Jackson, who showered praise on the Hawkinses for their accomplishments and reinforced the need for the African American community to support its most precious creation, gospel music.[35] Jackson's presence reflected his deep admiration for the Hawkins Family's music, as well as his appreciation for their support of his own political endeavors. In 1978, the Hawkins Family had participated in Jackson's *PUSH? for Excellence* gospel recording, which was released on Myrrh Records. A year later, Jackson returned the favor with his involvement in the arts and music seminar.

As the seminar grew in influence and size, it functioned as an important space in which Walter Hawkins mentored aspiring new artists (such as John P. Kee, Yolanda Adams, and Kevin Bond) while testing out his new musical ideas. Several of those ideas appeared on his highly anticipated *Love Alive III* recording, which included the hit "When the Battle Is Over." The Lawanda Scroggins and Carol King–led song contained all of the ingredients of a Walter Hawkins classic—powerful vocals, innovative choir arrangements, and mesmerizing bass work from Joel Smith. Another standout cut, "There's a War Going On," featured vocals from Lynette Hawkins. Hawkins's vocal intensity matches the urgency of the lyrics, which entreats listeners to prepare themselves for spiritual battle. "We need the armor," the choir sings as Hawkins belts sections of Ephesians 6.

"There's a War Going On" captured the tensions and uncertainties of the political moment. Deindustrialization, unemployment, poverty, drugs, and violence wreaked havoc on many African Americans living in the Bay Area during the Reagan era. Moreover, the AIDS epidemic had a devastating impact on thousands of Oakland and San Francisco residents, including some who attended Hawkins's church. As such, for thousands of black women and men who heard "There's a War Going On," the title and many of the song's lyrics resonated deeply.

Soon to become Hawkins's best-selling recording, *Love Alive III* entered *Billboard*'s gospel albums chart on January 26, 1985. Its release capped a decade of great productivity and commercial success for Walter Hawkins. During this period, he released four groundbreaking projects, produced two Tramaine Hawkins albums, and appeared on several Edwin Hawkins recordings. His music dominated the charts, as well as enlivened Sunday morning services at black churches across the country. Without question, Walter Hawkins's place as one of gospel's greatest artists was secure. With classic records like *Love Alive I, II,* and *III,* he had elevated gospel music to another plateau.

On his ascent to iconic status in the world of black religious music, Hawkins received support and assistance from many talented musicians, including several family members. One of his most valuable contributors was his wife, Tramaine, who was and remains the most brilliant interpreter of his music. A source of great intrigue for fans and journalists, the super-couple graced the cover of popular religious magazines like *CCM Magazine* and *Christian Herald.* In 1985, however, Walter and Tramaine divorced after fourteen years of marriage. Though Walter had played a central role in Tramaine's success, she remained on the cutting edge of contemporary gospel. Her first solo recording without Walter's guidance, *The Search Is Over,* gained her a new legion of fans in the secular marketplace. The lead single, "Fall Down," skyrocketed to the top of the dance charts, and its follow-up, "In the Morning Time," received significant airplay on R&B and gospel radio. Meanwhile, Walter Hawkins rode the success of *Love Alive III* for several months and then returned to the studio to record *Special Gift* in 1987.

A season of change for Hawkins personally and professionally, the late 1980s also marked the end of his relationship with Light Records. *Special Gift* was released on the black-owned label Birthright, while his *Love Alive IV* was released on Malaco.

Increasingly, Hawkins spent more time pastoring his church, Love Center, especially as it became more involved in social service work, particularly around the AIDS epidemic. Late in 1989, the Love Center converted a six-story house (located in the Adams Point neighborhood) into a shelter called the Ark. The shelter provided housing and food for black AIDS victims. One recipient of the Ark's services was Christine Whitty, a young mother infected with the AIDS virus whose downtown apartment had been destroyed during the devastating

FIGURE 12. Love Center Church in Oakland. Photo by author.

earthquake of October 17, 1989. "This place has given me a secure environment which allows me to do what I have to do for me," she told the *San Francisco Chronicle*. Detroit native Gerald Mann, who had been diagnosed with AIDS in 1982, was equally grateful for the Ark. "These people didn't know me, but they opened the doors and let me in. They didn't ask me whether I was straight or gay, they just said come in." Such work, according to Yvette Flunder, then the associate pastor of the Love Center, was the responsibility of the church. "If a church, particularly a black church, is not dealing with AIDS, crack cocaine, and homelessness, they might as well shut down, because they are no more than a social club."[36] Not content with just performing at AIDS benefits, Hawkins put his institutional muscle and influence behind supporting those affected by this devastating health crisis.

A Special Gift: The Musical Legacy of Walter Hawkins

Hawkins's productivity as a recording artist slowed down in the 1990s, but his music remained a part of the sonic landscape of the black church. Not only were his older songs still a part of gospel radio and black church services, but he also added to his legacy with new material. One of his most welcome surprises came in 1990, when he joined his ex-wife, Tramaine, on the moving live recording "Potter's House," for which she received her first Grammy. On the V. Michael McKay–penned tune, Walter and Tramaine mesmerized the crowd with their astonishing vocals and spirited delivery. As the song ends and Walter Hawkins exits the stage, the audience erupts in cheers, reflecting their deep admiration for Tramaine and Walter Hawkins as a musical collective, as well as their understanding of the latter's central role in enriching the gospel sound. The respect displayed on that night was widespread among fans and artists alike.

Even as Walter Hawkins became less of a fixture on the gospel charts and a new generation built on his advances, he was still regarded as one of the genre's most innovative artists. As Kirk Franklin noted after Hawkins's death, "Every door I've ever walked through was because God used Walter Hawkins as a key to unlock it."[37]

CHAPTER 5

Higher Plane

The Gospel According to Al Green

It's you that I want, but Him that I need.
—AL GREEN, *The Belle Album*

February 23, 1983, was a magical day for many musicians gathered at the Shrine Auditorium in Los Angeles for the 25th Annual Grammy Awards. The star-studded event featured performances from Ray Charles, Jerry Lewis, Little Richard, and Count Basie, as well as a hilarious appearance from the nation's hottest young comedian, Eddie Murphy. However, if the night belonged to any one entertainer, it was the soul legend Marvin Gaye. Along with winning two Grammys for his latest release, *Midnight Love*, Gaye delivered a rousing perfor-mance of his hit single "Sexual Healing."

The event was also special for another soul legend: Al Green. Green had achieved international success during the first half of the 1970s with a string of pop hits, but in 1980 he left the secular world for a career in gospel. Over the next decade, Green padded his already impressive catalog of hit singles and albums with several critically acclaimed gospel recordings. Two of those gospel additions were Green's *Higher Plane* and *Precious Lord*, for which he received two Grammys in 1983.

Upon his departure from the pop world, Green became one of gospel's most marketable stars. In his new role, he contributed immensely to the genre's vitality. Together with artists like Shirley Caesar and the Mississippi-based Williams Brothers, Green added a southern flavor to contemporary gospel music with his unique blend of soul, country, and pop.

Green's gospel recordings are not just essential components of his discogra-phy but also important keys to understanding his larger artistic legacy. In fact, it is impossible to separate secular Al from sacred Al, since each persona draws from the cultural rhythms of the New South and the "body-soul dualism" at the heart of black popular music.[1] As we shall see, the singer's most keen observers understood this well. Watching Green perform in London in 1984, journalist

Mick Brown felt as if the core of Green's artistry had remained the same during his transition from pop to gospel. "Green's performance has exchanged one form of transcendence for another, sexual love for spiritual faith, but it is still all about ecstasy. And there is no more ecstatic singer than Al Green."[2] Brown was not alone in his thoughts. "Think of it this way," wrote rock critic Robert Christgau, "he knew that sex was running out of inspiration for him, so he moved on to God as his source of ecstasy—an ecstasy he approaches most readily in what he really lives for, music."[3]

In many ways, Green's gospel performances also represent a continuation of the southern soul tradition he perfected on such classic records as *Al Green Gets Next to You*, *Call Me*, and *The Belle Album*. His turn to sacred music was much more than a case of the prodigal son returning home. Singing gospel enabled him to stretch himself artistically, to embrace fully not just his religious self but his regional self as well.

FIGURE 13. Al Green performing at Full Gospel Tabernacle Church in Memphis on January 8, 1978. Photo by Ebet Roberts/Getty Images.

Ever since his arrival on the pop scene in 1969, Green had proudly embraced his southern roots. "If you really want to know what my earliest influences were," Green mused in his autobiography, "you'd have to go back to the rain on the window, the wind in the corn crop, or the water lapping on the banks of the river. That is music to my ears."[4] The South in general and Arkansas in particular factored significantly in Green's creativity and self-representation. How else can we explain his bold assertion that the "South gonna do it again" in his 1977 song "Georgia Boy"?

Green's southern pride meshed well with new developments in African American culture, particularly the "South's resurgence in African American social memory and public consciousness." As Zandria Robinson points out in *This Ain't Chicago*, the 1960s and 1970s witnessed a shift in how African Americans publicly negotiated their relationship to the South. "Just as the nation had been southernized, black America was undergoing a public, discursive, and demographic southernization. African Americans were turning South, and those who were already South took new pride in their positions as bearers of the cultural and spiritual roots of black America."[5]

For Al Green, taking pride in one's southernness entailed embracing the region's many sonic traditions. Long identified with the Memphis Sound, which by the late 1970s had lost its esteemed place in the world of black pop, Green appreciated gospel's embrace of the South's soulful *and* country sides. Such flexibility was increasingly rare in pop music. As historian Charles Hughes explains, the terms "country" and "soul" as genre signifiers "became internationally recognized shorthand for the distance between white and black."[6] Country music in particular had become "firmly associated with the politics of white backlash that crystallized around opposition to the civil rights movement and catapulted Richard Nixon to the White House in 1968."[7] Hughes's commentary on the racial politics of the industry's marketing of country is quite useful in understanding gospel's appeal for an artist like Green with such a strong regional identity and sound. Gospel provided a space in which Green could not only continue his engagement with the Memphis Sound but also explore the more country-pop elements of the Nashville Sound. Though Green never explicitly spoke of the artistic considerations undergirding his move from secular to sacred music, gospel's stylistic flexibility and its creative benefits were not lost on him. "Gospel goes hand in hand with your religious convictions," Green once observed, "but it can be as creative as any other art form. You can do your Broadway plays and, as far as I'm concerned, you can do Vegas. You can do the Royal Albert Theater in London or Paul Masson's Winery in San Jose."[8]

Moving from secular to religious music required certain adjustments for Green, but for the most part, he transitioned rather smoothly into the gospel field. His religious recordings sold extremely well, due in no small part to radio hits like "The Lord Will Make a Way," "Jesus Will Fix It," "Everything's Gonna Be Alright," and "Soul Survivor." His gospel albums also received rave reviews from both the mainstream and gospel press. Even after he left the pop world, music journalists and critics like Robert Christgau, Robert Palmer, and Greil Marcus still reviewed his music with the same fervor they had reserved for his earlier material.[9]

On their aesthetic value alone, Green's gospel records deserve a critical hearing. But their importance must also be understood within the larger context of the business history of contemporary gospel music. His signing with Word Records was an integral component of the company's efforts to secure a larger share of the black gospel market. In Green, Word had a respected artist who not only had a proven track record of strong album sales but also was known for his stellar musicianship and his unique perspective on the human condition. That perspective bore the imprint of his journey from a shy boy reared in rural Arkansas to a superstar adored by millions.

Delta Beginnings

A self-described country boy, Albert Greene (with a final *e*) was born on April 13, 1946, on a farm in Dansby, Arkansas. The sixth of ten children of sharecroppers Cora Lee and Robert G. Greene Jr., the young Al developed an intense love for the environment, language, and everyday rhythms of rural life. His family farmed together, worshiped together, and played music together. "Every Greene, young and old," Al Green later remembered, "seemed to have the ability to make a joyful noise. My daddy sang and my mama sang and so did my grandparents on both sides. My brothers and sisters sang, and when it came to be my turn, I sang, too."[10] At the tender age of ten, Al began performing with his brothers when the family moved from Arkansas to Grand Rapids, Michigan. The Greene Brothers, as they were known in gospel circles, had a small following but never gained much traction in the music industry. The enterprising Greene eventually formed his own group, which he initially called Al Greene and the Creations before changing the name to Al Greene and the Soul Makers. The group had their first major break in 1968, when their song "Back Up Train" climbed high on the R&B charts. The Soul Makers' talented lead vocalist, who around this time changed the spelling of his surname from Greene to Green, soon caught the attention of record producer Willie Mitchell. Impressed by Green's vocal talents, Mitchell brought the gifted musician to executives at the Memphis-based label Hi Records.

Finding their first success with *Al Green Gets Next to You*, Green and Mitchell produced a string of hits during the first half of the 1970s. These hits included "Tired of Being Alone," "Let's Stay Together," "Love and Happiness," "You Ought to Be with Me," "I'm Still in Love with You," "Here I Am," "Call Me," and "Take Me to the River," to name few. Green was a ubiquitous presence on pop and R&B radio. He was also very much an "albums artist." Within a three-year span, he released five classics: *Al Green Gets Next to You*, *Let's Stay Together*, *I'm Still in Love with You*, *Call Me*, and *Livin' for You*. Green's albums and singles sold in the millions, yet his music betrayed a rootedness that endeared him to many who believed mainstream African American pop had lost its soul.

Smooth, raw, gritty, melodic, seductive, supple, supernatural—Green's voice was in a league of its own. As one *Rolling Stone* writer noted in 1972, "He can croon, shout, scat, rise to the smoothest falsetto, and throw in the funkiest growls."[11] No single genre could contain Green's vocal genius, so he flirted with soul, country, gospel, the blues, and funk. His vocal agility, along with his supreme intelligence, enabled him to rock the country pop of Willie Nelson ("Funny How Time Slips Away") and Hank Williams ("I'm So Lonesome I Could Cry") as masterfully as the psychedelic soul of Norman Whitfield ("I Can't Get Next to You").

At the height of Green's popularity, many of his biggest hits emerged from his own pen. His impressive songbook included but was not limited to "Let's Stay Together," "Love and Happiness," "Tired of Being Alone," "Simply Beautiful," "Take Me to the River," and "Call Me." Usually fleshing out his ideas in tandem with his rhythm section, Green composed lyrics pivoted around the themes of love, forgiveness, and reconciliation. Taking some of his emotional cues from the late soul legend Otis Redding, Green exhibited a vulnerability at odds with hardened images of black masculinity. On songs like "Let's Stay Together," "I'm Still in Love with You," "God Bless Our Love," and "Your Love Is Like the Morning Sun," he celebrated domestic tranquility and the power of a woman's love. His public persona was one of a devoted, monogamous lover committed to his partner for the long haul. Green's themes of romantic bliss resonated strongly with his female fans. "Your music makes my body smile . . . taking me to a place only my feelings can hear," one adoring admirer wrote. "The way you sing makes me want to do my thing," another fan confessed. "The mere sound of your moan makes a woman's body perform."[12] Green's devotees were moved not just by his records but also by his live performances. In concert, he routinely tossed long-stemmed roses to ecstatic fans whose screams and stage-rushing led to frequent interruptions. Writer Peter Bailey recalled his firsthand experience with Green's "devastating" effects on concert goers:

> A woman sitting behind me kept repeating, "Yes, Mr. Green, yes, yes, yes, yes-sss." Once at Harlem's Apollo Theater, I spent almost the whole show ducking the hefty arms of a soul sister who was flinging them out with abandon during every song. At a Green concert in Atlantic City, a teen-age girl completely broke up into a mass of heaving sobs when he shook her hand while singing the highly

emotional "How Do You Mend a Broken Heart?" At Philharmonic Hall, I could see mature-looking Black women obviously struggling with themselves to be cool. One could almost hear them saying, "Hey, man, I'm too old to be acting like this." Their men, just beamed with pleasure, for it is a known fact that for many brothers, Al Green's records have become a potent weapon in their love rap arsenal.[13]

Clearly, whether in a live or studio setting, Green's velvet funk was warm, inviting, and deeply sensual.

And yet, despite his status as one of the leading sex symbols of the 1970s, Green never abandoned his gospel roots. Several of his records, most notably *Al Green Gets Next to You, Call Me,* and *Belle,* included a gospel song. These songs were as eclectic as the man himself, ranging from the laid-back "God Is Standing By" to the disco burner "I Feel Good." Of his gospel cuts, none was more powerful than "Jesus Is Waiting," the last song on his 1973 album *Call Me.* On the album's stunning closer, Green's agile voice glides over drummer Al Jackson's pulsating rhythms and Willie Mitchell's lush strings to create a heavenly ending for what many regard as his greatest record. The passionate singer offers his listeners what he views as the ultimate gift: salvation. The song's opening moments find Green playing the role of minister, but at the 2:30 mark, he switches positions and seeks to strike his own bargain with God:

> I want you to help me
> And I'll help you,
> Save my soul
> I'll save some for you.

A repentant Green then goes into full confessional mode:

> I've been a fool
> Disregarding your love . . .
> I want to say this evening
> *That I'm sorry.*[14]

As the song fades out, Green's repeated "thank you"s suggests the possibility of some kind of spiritual resolution.

During the 1970s, Green's spiritual journey was also documented in his live performances, including his legendary appearance on the television show *Soul Train.* Created in 1971, Don Cornelius's hour-long variety show drew in young music fans anxious to see and hear their favorite singers, catch the latest dances, and check out the fashion choices of the show's participants. As Christine Acham explains, "During the 1970s *Soul Train* provided a community-forming locus, which allowed the show to cross the country and motivate a convergence of African American cultural expression and empowerment."[15] Typically when a major black artist released a new album, he or she appeared on the show. Al Green was no exception. At the height of his career, Green performed on the popular program several times.

On April 6, 1974, *Soul Train* aired what will go down as one of his greatest performances. Green set the stage ablaze with "Livin' for You," "Here I Am," and "Jesus Is Waiting." Easily the best segment of the show was Green's rendition of "Jesus Is Waiting." Stretching the song's length to seven minutes, Green opens with a narration of the Lord's Prayer as the audience transforms into his congregation. Working the crowd with the ease of a seasoned preacher, Green regularly plays with the song's pace as the rhythm section and blaring horns follow his lead. Just when you feel Green is ready to engage in a prolonged shout, he reverts back to his restrained self. That restraint would finally let loose at the end, when a spirit-possessed Green releases a battery of moans, shrieks, and groans. His contorted body and twisted face provide physical evidence of a transformed man. Without the slightest equivocation, Green had brought the Holy Spirit to *Soul Train*.

Though he had been a born-again Christian since 1973, Green remained firmly planted in the secular world. His 1974 release *Al Green Explores Your Mind* became his fifth consecutive album to climb to the top of the soul charts. It included the R&B hit "Sha-La-La" and the spirit-drenched "Take Me to the River," a song later covered by the Talking Heads. Green's professional life was in order, but his personal affairs would soon become a source of great embarrassment for him. Living a full-fledged bachelor life, Green romanced several women, including a married mother of two named Mary Woodson. Woodson and Green's casual relationship turned deadly on the night of October 18, 1974, when a despondent Woodson brought up the subject of marriage to Green. Not wanting an exclusive relationship with the already married woman, Green reiterated his disinterest in pursuing anything serious. An angry Woodson doused the singer with a pot of scorching grits and then retreated into the bedroom, where she committed suicide. Woodson's suicide, along with Green's severe burns, received national attention as reporters and fans speculated on the circumstances surrounding the tragedy.

The event certainly took a toll on Green's psyche, but he pressed ahead with his career. His label released two Al Green albums (*Al Green's Greatest Hits* and *Al Green Is Love*) in 1975 and then another two (*Full of Fire* and *Have a Good Time*) in 1976. None of these records had the magic of his earlier releases, as evidenced by the lukewarm reviews and subpar album sales.

Something was clearly missing—and no one recognized this more than Green. Talking to journalist David Nathan in 1976, he hinted at the possibility of a career shift: "Right now, I'm planning my lifestyle, the way I want my life to be. There's far more to it than records. I want my own way of living and I want to show people the key to entering into divinity. Yes, people think of me as a sex-symbol. But I want to try and get people to understand the whole basis of life. And it's not really about sex."[16]

Green's search for spiritual clarity found expression on his 1977 release, *Belle*, wherein he sings about God's greatness ("All N All" and "I Feel Good"), the desires of the flesh ("Belle"), and his southern pride ("Georgia Boy"). If not his greatest record, *Belle* was definitely his most complete record since *Call Me*. Taking full artistic control as producer and arranger, Green had amicably parted ways with longtime contributor Willie Mitchell. Fortunately, he had a fine cohort of musicians to assist him in a recording that many critics hailed as his finest in years. While *Belle's* chart performance and sales paled in comparison to earlier hits like *Let's Stay Together*, *I'm Still in Love with You*, and *Call Me*, the record pleased his hardcore fans. *Belle* also inspired some of the most compelling music criticism of the year. Leading the way was Greil Marcus, who believed Green represented the best of the southern soul tradition. In a review published in *Rolling Stone*, Marcus praised *Belle* as a musical masterpiece with deep cultural meaning: "Coming off a violent incident that left a woman dead and his career up in the air, Green turned to Jesus, but unlike almost every other singer, white or black, who'd done the same thing, he didn't proselytize. Instead, wandering through country bars and down southern back roads, he let you share a sense of peace; he even made you feel you'd helped earn it." And nothing pleased Marcus more than "All N All," a song that manages to be both rural and urban, down-home and cosmopolitan at the same time: "Green floats with the music, picking up momentum—but so subtly you don't notice that the song is increasing in force until he breaks the tune open with high, perfectly timed wails so surprising and unfettered he sounds as if he's hitting a note he's been reaching for all his life. I was stunned hearing this: I half-expected Green to start speaking in tongues, but, in a way, he already was." Though devoting much of his review to the songs "All N All" and "Georgia Boy," Marcus praised the entire *Belle* record for carrying "a sense of liberation and purpose deep enough to make the sinner envy the saved."[17]

In his autobiography, Green called *Belle* the most important release of his career. "Musically," he explained, "I was stepping out in faith, walking a tightrope without the old comforting net of Willie and the rest of the crew, but I must say, from the very beginning it felt good. I was long overdue to take a creative chance, and *Belle*, which had a sound that was more layered and textured than anything I'd done before, was a bold step in the right direction."

Working on *Belle* also deepened Green's religious commitments. "Singing songs about Jesus wasn't enough for me. I needed another way to be of service, another way to show Him just how sincere and serious I was."[18] Stepping out in faith, Green purchased a church located in the backwoods of Memphis. "There was nothing special about it," he recalled, "nothing different from a hundred other A-frame churches of worship throughout the South. It looked a little run-down maybe, but nothing a coat of paint and scrub brush couldn't take care of. I pulled the car onto the gravel driveway, past a sign that read FULL GOSPEL TABERNACLE, and shutting off the motor, climbed out and stood with the warm sun at my back and my long shadow stretching to the threshold of God's house."[19] Within a matter of months, this would be Green's church and he would be its pastor.

Full of Fire: The Gospel According to Al

Green's very public rebirth as pastor of Full Gospel Tabernacle was the context in which he left the world of secular music and entered the gospel fold. Now a free agent, Green received significant attention from several Christian labels, including the industry giant Word Records. The company's aggressive courtship of the former pop star proved successful, as Green signed with the label in 1980. Earlier that year, the company had added Shirley Caesar to its subsidiary Myrrh Records. "It is no secret," *Billboard* reported, "that Word has for some time been eager to get into the black gospel area."[20]

With their new partnership, Word and Green found themselves in uncharted territory. The Waco-based label was not familiar with the ins and outs of the black gospel world. This also held true for Green, who had spent the last decade selling pop records. It was unclear whether Green's popularity in the pop world would transfer to the Christian music industry.

Tough under pressure, Green provided the label with what they needed most: a first-rate record with an easily identifiable hit single. Consisting primarily of gospel standards, Green's Word debut, *The Lord Will Make a Way*, was New South gospel at its finest. Even though Green had no songwriting credits, he was very much in creative control. The versatile musician handled the lead vocals and served as the record's lead guitarist, arranger, and producer.

Taking off where the classic *Belle* ended, Green opens his gospel debut with the rocking title cut, "The Lord Will Make a Way." Everything about the song, from the lush strings to the guitar riffs, is classic Memphis soul. If Green had any doubts about leaving the secular world, he shows no signs here. On the opening number and throughout the record, he never seems out of place. Green draws on his deep well of creative talent, as well as on his many influences. The foot-stomping "Saved" finds Green honoring his Delta roots, while "None but the Righteous" bears the imprint of Sam Cooke's profound influence on Green. On the latter song, Green's spirited ad-libs harken back to Bobby Womack and Lou Rawls's legendary vocals on Cooke's soul classic "Bring It on Home to Me."

No one could predict how consumers would respond to Green's first gospel outing. Would the gospel community take his religious turn seriously, or would it dismiss the singer as a washed-up pop star trying to find a new audience? Would secular fans be interested in Green singing about his relationship with the Lord, or would they simply bide their time until he returned to the pop arena? Fortunately, Green had a record company dedicated to his success. Convinced that Green could assist the company in its crossover efforts, Word executives advertised the album heavily in the black gospel market. Their efforts coupled with Green's star appeal generated strong sales for *The Lord Will Make a Way*, which sold 150,000 copies within five months of its release.[21] Much to Green's delight, the title cut was a hit on gospel radio. This was no easy feat, given some uncertainty within the gospel world about Green's commitment to the art form. "No gospel followers trusted me and gospel singers didn't trust me, either," Green later remembered. Not all of this, he believed, was connected to his secular background. "When I came into gospel, I thought there were things to change, things to re-create, things to be reborn. I ran into a brick wall because they don't want gospel to sound any other way."[22]

Not one to back away from criticism, Green pushed ahead with his follow-up, *Higher Plane*. A balanced mix of originals and covers, *Higher Plane* featured Rubin Fairfax on guitar, Larry Lee on bass, Jesse Butler on keys, and Aaron Purdie on drums. The band's irresistible rhythms on the title cut, "Where Love Rules," and "His Name Is Jesus" evoke Green's classic material with Willie Mitchell. And yet, the music never sounds dated. This was partly due to the contributions of Jerry Peters, a studio wizard whose signature string arrangements on *Higher Plane* gave the music a more contemporary edge. Of course, the star of the show remained Al Green, who on this record refuses to follow any rules but his own. His rendition of Curtis Mayfield's "People Get Ready" depoliticizes the civil rights anthem and turns it into a bluesy gospel number. And even though he now performed for the Lord, Green proved unable to turn off the deep sensuality at the heart of his artistry. Perhaps nowhere was this more apparent than on the moving ballad "Spirit Might Come—On and On." Here, Green teases the listener with his extemporaneous testifying, high moans, and ecstatic shouts.

Unlike its predecessor, *Higher Plane* did not have a radio hit. Still, many critics found the latest release superior to *The Lord Will Make a Way*. Strong reviews came from the *New York Times*, the *Village Voice*, and *Rolling Stone*, which praised the record as maybe "the most intimately seductive gospel album ever recorded."[23] Effusive in his praise of Green, Robert Christgau felt as if the singer had found the right groove with his latest release. "Meek and mild, *The Lord Will Make a Way* was Green's sincere attempt to bend to gospel tradition, but on this record it's tradition that bends." The strength of the album, Christgau insisted, lay in its deep grooves. "If there are rhythm sections like this in Heaven (praises be to new drummer Aaron Purdie), the place may be worth a stopover after all."[24]

Love for *Higher Plane* was not universal. Wanting more Al and less Jesus, Andy Gill panned the record in the *New Musical Express*: "Well-meant, devout and honest it may be, but *Higher Plane* just doesn't work." Three things in particular annoyed Gill: the record's overt religiosity, the rhythm section, and Green's vocals. In his view, Green's band was unimaginative and stale: "The rhythms here fall somewhere between the distinctive Mitchell sound and mainstream dim-funk, a bastard, horn-less hybrid which loses out on both counts: too sluggish for disco, too forceful and businesslike for Green."[25] Gill's commentary on Green's vocals was equally harsh. "His voice is a peculiar instrument, capable of great effect through subtlety and restraint, but it doesn't fit redemption songs and celebrations of salvation, so he contents himself with ambling through a mix'n'match series of vocal hints intended to summon up the ghost of former artistry." Another major issue for Gill, who identified himself as a "born-again Zealous Atheist," was the album's strong evangelical overtones. "On earlier albums," Gill explains, "Al's Christianity was present, but in smaller, more concentrated doses, leavened with particularised love and thus bearable. 'My God Is Real,' for instance, spoke of a one-to-one relationship, one man and his god, rather than the general, all-purposes testifying going down on *Higher Plane*."[26]

Gill was not alone in his sentiments. If you watch videos of Green's performances during the 1980s, you will notice some of his pop fans' discomfort with his strong evangelical message. Signs of uneasiness also shot across the faces of quite a few gospel fans, who while happy with the minister's return to the church found his eccentric stage presence and mannerisms a bit much. "Once on stage," Green confided to a reporter, "I have no control. When I get that anointing, that extra something, I can't hold back."[27] The visual evidence of Green's anointing consisted of highly individualized extemporizations filled with his signature laughs, quirky facial expressions, and sensuous body movements.

Navigating the artistry of Green was not always easy, even for critics. "Listening to Al Green's three gospel albums for Myrrh Records is a disorienting experience," Geoffrey Himes confessed in the *Musician*. "The songs are traditional hymns that have been sung in black Protestant churches for decades. But Green, the sexiest soul singer of the 70s, uses the same Memphis musicians, the same steamy syncopation, the same repertoire of husky, shuddering, guttural and squealing vocal come-ons that marked his old hits. The lyrics may direct the listeners' eyes heavenward, but the music causes that devil's zone between the navel and the knees to undulate uncontrollably." Moving beyond his own experiences with Green's studio records, Himes also noted the divide among gospel fans with regard to the singer's live performances. "These shows split gospel audiences right down the middle, as older, more conservative Shirley Ceasar [*sic*] fans would walk out on him, while younger, less inhibited fans would dance in the aisles." The tension in the crowd did not escape Green, who refused to alter his performance. Undeterred by those critics who complained about the screams from female audience members, their desire to touch him in concert, and his willingness to reciprocate their affection, Green vowed to remain connected to his audiences: "I can't explain . . . how you reach out and touch somebody without the extension of your hand."[28]

Even with all of its conservatism, gospel's elasticity as an art form enabled Green to pursue his musical interests on his own terms. It also allowed him to reveal his many sides as both an artist and a man. One of those sides was his proud identity as a southerner with a deep appreciation for the diverse rhythms of the region. Green's exploration of these rhythms continued on his third outing with Word, *Precious Lord*. Cut at the legendary Sound Emporium studio in Nashville, *Precious Lord* moves Green in a different musical direction. The record sounds more Nashville country than Memphis soul. Songs like "Hallelujah" and "Rock of Ages" seem perfectly tailored for Jim and Tammy Faye Bakker's *PTL Club*. This sonic shift was not lost on critic Robert Christgau, who chastised Green for going "sacred" and Nashville on his fans: "Couldn't figure out why I found myself basically unmoved by this exquisitely sung collection of hymns, four of them familiar to me since my days in the First Presbyterian Church of Flushing. Then I realized that the Memphis groove of Al's first two Myrrh albums had somehow turned into rote tent-gospel timekeeping. Then I read the back of the album and learned that it was cut in Nashville, with all that implies."[29]

Nashville had always fascinated Green, and so he jumped at the opportunity to record there. No longer subjected to the sales demands of secular music, Green marched to his own beat. His bold moves continued on his next release, *I'll Rise Again*, a record that swings in multiple musical directions. The album failed to score a major radio hit for Green, but that had more to do with marketing than the quality of the songs. "Ocean Blue (I'll Rise Again)" was magnificent. And "I Know It Was the Blood" had a strong R&B vibe. In music critic Robert Palmer's estimation, *I'll Rise Again* was 1980s pop at its finest. The record, Palmer raved, "does what good pop albums do these days. It warns of coming apocalypse, gives practical advice ('straighten out your life'), questions accepted values and pays tribute to the fickle muses of inspiration and creativity—all in a warmly, melodic, insistently but subtly rhythmic, contemporary style." Palmer was high on the record but harbored doubts about its commercial viability outside the Christian marketplace: "Pop listeners can be creatures of habit. They will listen to a rock group like Talking Heads sing gospel-derived lyrics in a gospel-derived style, or to a gospel-singer-gone pop like Aretha Franklin, but shy away from buying the latest Al Green album because it's a 'gospel record.'"[30]

Palmer was correct. Though Green received strong reviews in the nation's leading magazines, his gospel material did not cross over into the secular market until 1987. That year, he released *Soul Survivor*, which was distributed through the secular label A&M. The record's lead single, "Everything's Gonna Be Alright," reached #22 on *Billboard*'s R&B charts.

To boost sales, A&M released a video for the song. In many ways, the video functions as a celebration of Green, his artistic longevity, his southernness, and the city of Memphis. It features snapshots of historic buildings and cultural landmarks in Memphis, along with the everyday people who give the city its unique character. Tempting as it might be to see Green's video as simply a part of the record company's marketing efforts, it is also useful to view it as an expression of what scholar Zandria Robinson refers to as post-soul southernness. The visuals lend support to Robinson's claims regarding African Americans' "performative investments in southern identity, as everyday identity practice and as commercial product."[31] Though the video had a strong southern vibe, it performed well nationally among African American religious and secular audiences.

Feeling good about the positive response to the video, A&M wanted to ensure Green's latest album had as wide an audience as possible. Fortunately, executives' ideas aligned with Green's own ambitions for the record. When the company sought his input about marketing matters, the singer offered this advice: "We're not going to call it Christian, we're not going to call it secular. We're going to call it Al Green."[32]

Indeed, *Soul Survivor* was a classic Al Green album. It was also one of the best gospel records of the 1980s. Entering *Billboard*'s gospel charts on April 18, 1987, *Soul Survivor* moved quickly to the #1 position. The record stayed on the top of the charts for much of the spring and summer of 1987. The seasoned veteran found a new legion of fans among young gospel lovers enamored with the slick, contemporary sounds of groups like the Winans and Commissioned. The title cut and "Everything's Gonna Be Alright" were by far their favorites. On the other side of the gospel spectrum, older listeners preferred the country backbeat of "Jesus Will Fix It," a tune anchored by Green's signature vocals and underappreciated rhythm guitar.

Uninterested in playing the role of tortured soul genius, Green found salvation, redemption, and even creative license in the artistry of gospel music. Far too often, Green's move to gospel is treated as a form of repentance for Mary Woodson's suicide. The truth of the matter, however, is that Green's sacred turn was also a calculated artistic decision. The world of R&B was changing in good *and* bad ways—and Green's eclectic taste found a perfect match in gospel. At the same time, the gospel community gained a daring artist who through his music disrupted conventional ideas about religion, race, and region.

CHAPTER 6

The Only Thing Right Left in a Wrong World

The Clark Sisters, the Winans, Commissioned, and the Search for Cultural Authority in the 1980s

More and more I feel myself being guided to reach and represent
the current generation, to make a musical vocabulary that
incorporates the past and makes sense of the present.
—ELBERNITA "TWINKIE" CLARK in Carol Cooper,
Pop Culture Considered as an Uphill Bicycle Race:
Selected Critical Essays (1979–2001)

It's not what you're playing, it's what you're saying.
—MARVIN WINANS in Karima A. Haynes,
"The Gospel Controversy: Are the New
Songs Too Jazzy and Too Worldly?"

On Valentine's Day 1985, Washington, D.C., police arrested music legend Stevie Wonder, along with forty-seven other activists, for protesting outside the South African embassy on Massachusetts Avenue.[1] Infuriated by President Ronald Reagan's policy of constructive engagement with the South African government, Wonder was but one voice in a much larger chorus of human rights activists calling for immediate sanctions against P. W. Botha's ruthless regime. Over the course of the year, thousands of women and men participated in countless demonstrations outside the South African embassy. Spirited protests also erupted in other parts of the country, spreading from college campuses to state capitols to local churches.[2] The magnetic energy of the anti-apartheid movement eventually gripped the music industry as various artists spoke out against the South African government and its apartheid system. To lend their support to ongoing protests, several musicians participated in Steven Van Zandt's anti-apartheid anthem, "Sun City." The contributing artists ranged from jazz legend Miles Davis to rocker Keith Richards to poet Gil Scott-Heron, who had been critiquing the apartheid system since the 1970s.

Largely silent during this moment of heightened political tension, much of the Christian music industry observed the anti-apartheid movement from the sidelines. One notable exception was the Grammy Award–winning quartet the Winans.[3] Late in the fall of 1985, the Detroit-based group released a searing critique of apartheid titled "Let My People Go." Nothing on gospel radio compared politically, conceptually, lyrically, or sonically. Funky horn lines and synthesized bass licks modernized a message deeply rooted in Christian biblical texts and African American religious history.[4] Situating the contemporary crisis in South Africa within a broader historical context, the song condemns apartheid as a violation of one of Christianity's most fundamental tenets—the equality of all people before God. Taking a page from the prophet Jeremiah on the song's second verse, lead vocalist Marvin Winans declares God's coming judgment on the unrighteous purveyors of racial oppression:

> Let us pray that they will heed our warning
> For the wrath of God is on its way
> There's still time for change and forgiveness
> *But judgment's drawing closer every day.*[5]

A hallmark of many of the group's compositions had been their scriptural base in the New Testament, but the jeremiad lyrics, sentiments, and overall tone of "Let My People Go" is undeniably rooted in the Old Testament. Soaring over drummer James Gadson's syncopated beats sounds the "voice" of an angry, vengeful God, who minces no words in expressing disdain at South Africa's ruling elite. As the song shifts tempo at the 3:15 mark, God (via his human mouthpiece, Marvin Winans) sternly counsels,

> You better stop
> You can't hide
> I hate evil
> *I hate apartheid*[6]

The Winans' stirring political message failed to gain airplay on white Christian radio stations, even those enamored with the group's previous album, *Tomorrow*. In contrast, African American deejays in the secular world embraced the anti-apartheid anthem and its infectious groove. Entering *Billboard*'s black singles charts on November 6, 1985, "Let My People Go" became the Winans' first Top 40 hit, receiving significant airplay from R&B stations across the country. On the sacred side of black radio, however, the response to the song was decidedly mixed. Contemporary gospel stations played "Let My People Go" incessantly, but despite its roots in the Old Testament, the crossover hit never gained much traction among those radio announcers who perceived the song as outside the boundaries of the gospel tradition.

This stark variation in the gospel community's response to the anti-apartheid song illuminates the creative and political tensions brewing within the gospel industry at the time. Controversy surrounding the direction of gospel music, the beneficiaries of its expansion in the marketplace, and the degree to which the art form adjusted itself to new cultural, technological, and political realities reached a fever pitch by the mid-1980s. Three gospel groups from Detroit—the Winans, the Clark Sisters, and Commissioned—frequently stood at the center of these controversies and debates.[7] Submerging their art in the rhythms and narratives of the postindustrial world, they revolutionized the gospel sound, complicated existing narratives surrounding black urban subjectivity, and suggested ways an increasingly fragmented society could be transformed into a beloved community.

All born and reared in Detroit, the epicenter of urban contemporary gospel music, the members of the Winans, the Clark Sisters, and Commissioned pushed the sonic, theological, and political boundaries of the genre more aggressively than any of their peers. Embracing the techniques, textures, and rhythms of the secular and sacred worlds of black music, they forged a captivating sound with strong emphasis on craft mastery and innovative production techniques. Their bold approach was not confined to the sonic realm. Unafraid to engage controversial issues, these artists put forth a social message that straddled the line between the prophetic Christianity reflected in the message of the Winans' anti-apartheid anthem, "Let My People Go," and an emergent conservatism linked to the teachings of the Moral Majority. On their recordings, strong critiques of structural racism and the social marginality of the poor intermingled with narratives attributing society's purported decline to the breakdown of the nuclear, heterosexual family. Full of political contradictions and ideological tensions, the music of the Winans, the Clark Sisters, and Commissioned reflected the energy and mood of a generation struggling to adjust to a changing world as well as the coexistence of liberal and neo-Pentecostal viewpoints within the black church. These artists' popularity during the 1980s signaled young people's thirst for self-affirmation, self-expression, and transcendence along with their belief that art and religion provided routes to existential freedom, ontological clarity, and spiritual fulfillment.

Individually and collectively, the Clark Sisters, the Winans, and Commissioned played critical roles in establishing the city of Detroit as the undisputed capital of urban contemporary gospel music in the 1980s and early 1990s. Together with Detroiters like Thomas Whitfield, Vanessa Bell Armstrong, BeBe and CeCe Winans, and Witness, they had a strong presence on the radio and the gospel charts and amassed dozens of Stellar, Dove, Grammy, and GMWA Excellence awards. To forge what many would refer to as the Detroit sound, they borrowed from the vocal techniques and musical stylings of artists like Aretha Franklin, Stevie Wonder, and Rance Allen. They also learned from each other. On their journey to developing their own distinctive sound, the men of Commissioned closely studied the Clark Sisters. "That is how we got our vocals," Fred Hammond readily admitted. "We would study them, over and over again, and then we would try to sing that vibe."[8]

Hammond and his Detroit peers also built on the legacy of local gospel musicians who came before them—Harold Smith and the Majestics, the Voices of Tabernacle, Mattie Moss Clark, the Meditation Singers, the Lemon Gospel Chorus (of which the Winans parents, Delores and David, were members), and Charles Nicks. Without question, there was a plethora of talented gospel musicians in Detroit. In fact, one might argue that the surest indicator of a local musician's potential for national success was his or her ability to stand out among the talented artists in the city's gospel circles. "The toughest thing in Detroit gospel is to be known as the best in town," one local writer mused in 1975. "The groups work hard to become known and then they work hard to stay that way." The talent pool was deep in the Motor City, as was local musicians' recognition of gospel's larger importance to African Americans. "Gospel music can't be divorced from the spiritual significance and connotation it has for our people," Charles Nicks explained. "You can joke about any area of black life, until you get into our gospel music. But that's no joke because that's so tied into our religious experience."[9]

Proud Detroiters committed to advancing the city's rich gospel tradition, the Clark Sisters, the Winans, and Commissioned put tremendous emphasis on artistic excellence and innovation. In the shadows of Motown, they engaged in the collective practice of art-making with the goals of commercial success and transforming the larger world. First among these artists to gain national attention was the Clark Sisters. Jacky, Denise, Elbernita ("Twinkie"), Dorinda, and Karen dazzled listeners with their brilliant harmonies, spitfire ad-libs, and remarkable showmanship. Catchy rhythms coupled with mesmerizing vocals rendered their music ideal for sacred and secular settings, making the group a favorite among many longtime gospel lovers, as well as among a substantial number of secular music fans who could not deny their immense talents.

Pure Gold: The Artistry and Commercial Triumph of the Clark Sisters

Under the tutelage of their mother, Mattie Moss Clark, the Clark Sisters developed into a formidable group during the 1970s. A gospel legend, Mattie Moss Clark was born in Selma, Alabama, in 1925. The seventh of nine children born to

Fred and Mattie Moss, young Mattie developed her musical talents as a member of the Holiness Temple Church of Christ in Prayer. Upon her graduation from high school, she attended Selma University, where she studied classical music and choral singing. "I wanted my life to be focused around an orchestra but my mother saw differently. When I was a child, my mother envisioned me directing choirs with unlimited numbers (of people in them) and this is what happened."[10] Like thousands of other young people from the Deep South, Clark migrated to Detroit in the 1940s, linking up with several institutions, including Blessed Martin Spiritual Church, Greater Love Tabernacle Church of God in Christ, and Bailey Temple Church of God in Christ. "I kept moving until I found an area that I wanted to be in; this brought about my being appointed local president of the Church of God in Christ music department of Southwest Michigan under Bishop Bailey. One thing led to another until I was appointed Minister of Music for the national (Church of God in Christ music department)."[11] An innovator often credited with revolutionizing the choir sound by introducing separate parts for sopranos, altos, and tenors (three-part harmony), Clark recorded for Savoy and Sound of Gospel during her career. Committed to advancing gospel as both an art form and a ministry, Clark founded the Clark Conservatory of Music in Detroit in 1979. Though intimately involved in the Gospel Music Workshop of America and very appreciative of its work, she felt as if something was needed on the local level: "I saw too many people that had talent and nobody was helping them."[12] Formally and informally, Clark trained a host of talented youngsters, including artists like Donald Vails, James Moore, Keith Pringle, and Vanessa Bell Armstrong.

As one might expect, Clark's tutelage of her daughters started early. "Mama began training us as children and then we would sing with a choir or make a guest appearance in a church in Detroit," Twinkie Clark remembered. "Then she would train us some more. I began playing when I was 10 and writing when I was 16."[13] Seeing great potential in her daughters, the elder Clark expected nothing but the very best from them. If a musical idea came to her in the middle of the night, she would wake the children up and have them execute her vision. Clark's extensive training paid off. The Clark Sisters released their first record, *Jesus Has a Lot to Give*, in 1973 under their uncle Bill Moss's label, Billesse Records. Three years later, the group signed with Sound of Gospel and released *Unworthy*, their first in several recordings for the Detroit label. Founded by Armen Boladian in 1969, Sound of Gospel was the gospel subsidiary of Westbound Records, which specialized in funk (such as Funkadelic and the Ohio Players). Unlike Westbound, Sound of Gospel depended heavily on the local talent in Detroit. This pool included Thomas Whitfield, Charles Nicks, James Moore, the St. James Choir, the Voices of Tabernacle, Mattie Moss Clark, and the Clark Sisters.

The Clark Sisters' first three records with Sound of Gospel, *Unworthy, Count It All Joy*, and *He Gave Me Nothing to Lose*, didn't move many units but contained several songs ("A Praying Spirit,""Nothing to Lose, All to Gain," and "Everything's Gonna Be Alright," to name a few) that demonstrated the group's remarkable musical gifts. It would take a few years for the sisters to perfect their sound and capture that perfection on record, but they were well on their way to reaching their potential.

The major breakthrough for the Clark Sisters came in 1980, when New Birth released their live album, *Is My Living in Vain*. The record contained several songs that would come to define the Clark Sisters sound: "Is My Living in Vain,""Ha-Ya (Eternal Life),""Pure Gold," and the closer, "Expect Your Miracle." The live set held the top position on the gospel charts for more than a year and moved the group out of their mother's shadow.

If *Is My Living in Vain* testified to the sisters' performative genius in a live setting, their follow-up release, *You Brought the Sunshine*, proved their ability to provide the same quality of musicianship within the confines of the studio. Officially released in 1981, *You Brought the Sunshine* came on the heels of the sisters' live recording as well as two studio solo releases (*Praises Belong to God* and *Power*) from Twinkie Clark. On *You Brought the Sunshine*, the sisters blend their innovative musicianship with their COGIC teachings (see "Endow Me" and "Overdose of the Holy Ghost") to create a record of astonishing beauty and spiritual depth. Their lyrics draw inspiration from the book of Acts, particularly its focus on Holy Spirit baptism, while their lush harmonies and syncopated beats point to their familiarity with the rhythms of disco, jazz, and R&B.

The record's collective genius was soon overshadowed by its smash hit, "You Brought the Sunshine." Influenced by Stevie Wonder's "Master Blaster (Jammin'),""You Brought the Sunshine" topped the dance charts and peaked at #16 on the R&B charts. Its infectious groove moved young churchgoers as well as millions of women and men frequenting the nation's popular dance clubs. To meet the high demand for "You Brought the Sunshine," Sound of Gospel had Elektra Records distribute the single. The 12-inch, which included an extended instrumental, sold more than 200,000 copies in 1983. One had to go back to the Mighty Clouds of Joy's 1976 hit "Mighty High" to find a gospel song with this level of popularity in the secular world. Not only a commercial success, "You Brought the Sunshine" garnered the group critical acclaim from musicians and journalists. "Those girls are baaaddd," noted funkster George Clinton. Critic Barney Hoskyns of *New Musical Express* agreed: "Sunshine is simply heaven on a piece of plastic."[14]

As one might expect, the crossover success of "You Brought the Sunshine" didn't sit well with all of the group's fans. "They don't like you to say disco, they don't like this 12-inch thing," an exasperated Denise Clark complained. "They've told us the beat is too uptempo, as if we are deliberately trying to draw the attention of the sinner."[15] Even their mother, Mattie Moss Clark, faced scrutiny after she joined her daughters on the Grammy Awards in 1983. Feeling as if the group's spirited performance was too worldly, high-ranking officials in the Church of God in Christ chastised Clark (who headed the denomination's music department) and admonished her to exercise more discretion when performing with her daughters.

Notwithstanding the criticism, the Clark Sisters continued to build on the momentum of the crossover hit. To expand their audience, they agreed to appear in the nationally distributed film *Gospel*. Directed by David Leivick and Frederick A. Ritzenberg, *Gospel* featured live performances from some of the biggest stars in the genre: James Cleveland, Shirley Caesar, the Mighty Clouds of Joy, the Hawkins Family, and the Clark Sisters. Filmed in Oakland's Paramount Theatre during the summer of 1982, *Gospel* aimed to recreate for a national audience the experience of a black gospel concert. The Clark Sisters, according to *Los Angeles Times* critic Kristine McKenna, stole the show. "Considered controversial within the gospel world for their frank treatment of such subjects as sex and drugs, the Clark Sisters had everyone on their side this night, and they brought the house down."[16] Equally moved by the performance, director Fred Ritzenberg beamed with excitement when discussing the Clark Sisters: "It seemed that the whole building was going to take off and rise toward heaven. It was a high that I had never experienced before."[17]

Indeed, the Clark Sisters were amazing in *Gospel*. Wearing long chiffon dresses, gospel's hottest quintet performed extended versions of four songs: "Hallelujah," "Is My Living in Vain," "Name It, Claim It," and "Pure Gold." In those songs, Twinkie showcases her prowess as a vocalist and organist, Dorinda takes the crowd to church with her humorous yet powerful preaching, and Karen firmly establishes herself as a vocal powerhouse. On "Hallelujah," the fiery call-and-response exchange between Karen and her sisters electrifies the crowd. The relentless Karen exhorts the audience to dance in the Spirit. "Let me see you wave your hands," she commands as her sisters interject rapid successions of "hallelujah"s. "Let me see you wave your hands, let me see you wave your hands. Can I get a witness?" Nearly three minutes into the song, she descends into the audience and takes her house-wrecking performance to another level. "I had to get down here," she informs the enthused crowd; "I want to get close to my people."[18] The rhythm section stays in the pocket as the group engages in a sanctified shout. It is a sight to behold. Sparkplug Dorinda, who descends into a full praise break, dances in rhythm with the guitarist, an excited Karen runs back and forth down the aisle, Denise bangs on the tambourine with an intensity usually reserved for Sunday service, and Twinkie pounces on the organ with a confident grin on her face.

Last to leave the stage, Twinkie moves her head from side to side, overcome by the Spirit and perhaps the magnitude of the moment. Her elation was understandable. Save their mother, no one had played a bigger role in shaping the group's musical identity. Much of the Clark Sisters' success in the music industry could be traced to the daring artistry of Twinkie, the group's primary composer, arranger, and producer. Her complex layering of electric piano and the Hammond B-3 organ beautifully anchored the spine-chilling voices of her sisters. "In her sisters," one writer raved, "Twinkie has four of gospel's most expressive vocalists, and she's reveled in demanding the most from them."[19] With extensive training from her mother and Howard University's renowned music department, Twinkie possessed the skills, imagination, and cultural confidence to converse with various musical idioms and traditions. Nothing seemed beyond her grasp. Listen to her late 1970s and early 1980s recordings as a solo artist and with her sisters and you will hear echoes of the lyricism and playful dissonance found in Herbie Hancock's *Maiden Voyage*, *Sextant*, and *Man-Child*; the relentless joy in classic Stevie Wonder grooves like "Superstition," "Master Blaster (Jammin')," and "Living for the City"; and shades of the introspective probing present on Keith Jarrett's *Köln*. Twinkie was an artist who managed to be both cerebral and warm, adventurous yet inviting. And despite her genius—or perhaps because of it—she personified the tensions facing black creative artists in the Christian entertainment industry. Spirit and art seemed to be in perpetual struggle. Her influences were wide ranging, but she sometimes struggled to find balance between her creative impulses and her religious commitments. When asked if she listened to "sinful dance music," she responded, "I don't listen but I hear! Having studied at Howard University (DC), I can appreciate all kinds of music, but I don't listen attentively to all kinds of music."[20] Talking to *Village Voice* critic Carol Cooper in 1985, Twinkie readily acknowledged her desire to create "a musical vocabulary that incorporates the past and makes sense of the present."[21] A fearless leader, she insisted on merging the old with the new, harmony with dissonance, and improvisation with contemplative process.

Introducing the Winans

A similar commitment to the creation of a new sonic paradigm fueled Twinkie Clark's childhood friends the Winans brothers, who in the 1970s were known in local music circles as the Testimonials. The quartet—Ronald, Carvin, Marvin, and Michael Winans—released five studio albums and one live recording in the 1980s: *Introducing the Winans, Long Time Comin', Tomorrow, Let My People Go, Decisions*, and *Live at Carnegie Hall*. Their studio projects featured intricate vocal and string arrangements, irresistible hooks and riffs, and an immaculate blend of R&B, gospel, and pop. On the quartet's sessions with Light Records and Qwest/Warner Brothers, they relied on the services of top-notch musicians like Weather Report's Alex Acuña, respected bassist Abraham Laboriel, drummer and producer

Bill Maxwell, and percussionist James Gadson. Listening to the Winans' debut with Light convinced fellow Detroit artist Fred Hammond that production was not something to be taken lightly. Shortly after digesting what he knew would become a gospel classic, Hammond queried his own band, Commissioned, "You mean all we have to do is get a *producer*, and we can sound like that as well?"[22]

The Winans' sound also impressed music critics. Identifying "The Question Is" and "Flyin' Away" as the debut album's best cuts, *Contemporary Christian Music* magazine applauded the production work of Bill Maxwell and Andraé Crouch and celebrated the four brothers for their "tight, mello, co-ol sound."[23] Strong reviews also followed the group's second record, *Long Time Comin',* which like its predecessor blended gospel with modern R&B. The Winans' first two records on Light were very impressive, especially given their meager budget. Looking back at the limited resources provided to the group, producer Bill Maxwell marveled at the high quality of the quartet's first two records, particularly the debut release:

> We barely had any money to do the record. It was done very quickly. We had a band in the studio playing live while they sang. We fixed their vocal parts and did a quick horn session and a couple of guitar sessions—then we mixed the record. It was a very inexpensive album. It's stunning to me now, when I listen to the first two records, they sound the best to me. On the *Tomorrow* album, we had more money and we were trying to be more accessible to radio. We started to delve into the more modern sounds of that time, as opposed to the first two albums, where we used more natural instruments, and they don't show the time period as much. If you put on the *Tomorrow* album, you'll know around what year it was done due to the sound of the synthesizers and drums on the record, because we were dealing with what was more current on the radio back then.[24]

Though Maxwell and Crouch definitely played an important role in the Winans' early success, the group's driving force was principal songwriter and lead vocalist Marvin Winans. Considered by many in the industry to be one of gospel's greatest male vocalists, Winans possessed a velvety smooth tenor with remarkable range and a distinctive tone. His impassioned vocals on "The Question Is," "Trust in God," and "Everything You Touch Is a Song," among other Winans classics, provided a blueprint for other male singers within and beyond gospel. Not just a talented singer, Winans was also an extraordinary writer with a sharp sense of melody, a strong grasp of biblical history, and a vivid imagination that made him one of the genre's most gifted storytellers. "By the time I was thirteen, I had written a hundred songs. They just flowed," Winans remembered. These songs, he believed, were gifts from God. "I don't write them. I live them. I don't try to birth them, I just breathe them."[25]

Cutting loose from tradition in order to create a new gospel aesthetic, Winans and his brothers blazed a path that brought them hundreds of thousands of fans. One group taking notice of their rise was Fred Hammond's band, Commissioned. "They played 'The Question Is' on the radio and I knew they (the Winans) had made it," Hammond recalled. "I knew from that point on, that was something I could reach for."[26]

'Tis So Sweet: Commissioned and the Voice of Young Black Christian America

Signing with Ralph Carmichael's Light Records in 1985, Commissioned consisted of Hammond, Keith Staten, Karl Reid, Michael Brooks, Michael Williams, and Mitchell Jones. Commissioned's genesis can be traced back to three groups in Detroit. "Fred and myself were in a group called Saved," Mitchell Jones remembered. "Keith Staten and Karl Reid were in a group called Sounds of Joy and Michael Williams and Michael Brooks were in a group called Blessed." Well-known in Detroit music circles, the men were familiar not only with each other but also with other gospel acts in the city. "We all really lived around each other," Jones explained. "The Winans and my family went to the same Elementary, Junior High and High Schools and the Clark sisters too. We all grew up in the same area and developed that sound being around each other. I might sing with Daniel Winans, or Marvin Winans might sing with my brother—I guess you might say it's just the Detroit sound."[27] Fate brought Jones, Brooks, Hammond, Staten, Williams, and Reid together in 1982, the year Commissioned officially formed. To help Commissioned reach a larger audience, Mattie Moss Clark placed the band on the program of the Church of God in Christ's annual convocation in Memphis in 1983. A year or so later, the group inked a deal with Light Records, which was happy to sign another group from Detroit. The Winans had sold well for the label, and signing Commissioned ensured Light's continued success within the urban contemporary gospel field.

The group was an immediate hit among black Christian teenagers and young adults. On fan favorites like "Victory," "I'm Going On," "So Good to Know," and "If My People," Commissioned packaged its gospel message with hard-driving beats and New Jack Swing harmonies. A self-contained band, Commissioned was the most aggressive, even if not always successful, in its fusion of gospel, pop, soul, Minneapolis funk, and the rhythmic patterns of hip-hop. Citing Stevie Wonder, the production team of James "Jimmy Jam" Harris and Terry Lewis, and the pop icon Prince as their influences, Commissioned released up-tempo tracks far more edgy than anything found on gospel radio stations during the 1980s. In interviews, Commissioned members made no secret of their desire to compete (sonically) with the hardest, most innovative music in urban America. Their boldness endeared them to many young fans in gospel and made them one of the most popular acts in the genre by the end of the 1980s. "We started playing in very small auditoriums that would seat about 600 to 800, for about a year and a half. Now we are playing in halls from 2000 to 4000," Michael Williams boasted in 1989.[28]

Blessed not only with talent, the group had the backing of a record company deeply committed to their success. Upon the Winans' departure from Light in 1984, label executives invested great hope in Commissioned. Losing the Winans was a major blow for Light, but many within the company thought Commissioned might pick up where the talented quartet left off. The test came in 1985, when Commissioned's debut release, *I'm Going On*, hit record stores. Not just the music but the album's packaging was different from anything in gospel. Stylishly attired in hip, urban fashion, group members had a youthful vibe that separated them from their gospel peers. Their look was more akin to New Edition than to the Jackson Southernaires.

The success of *I'm Going On* further solidified Detroit as the epicenter of urban contemporary gospel. The record also increased anticipation for the sextet's next outing, *Go Tell Somebody*, which appeared in late 1986. Once again, they struck gold among their targeted audience.

Early on, Commissioned established a distinct sound by amplifying the members' background vocals during the mixing process. As Hammond recalls, "I was arguing with my engineer. It was one of our first records and he put the background singers way in the back like all the rest of the singers were doing at that time, and he pushed the lead up, and I took the fader and I pushed the backgrounds up. I told him 'Man, we created these nice vocals and we want people to hear them.' Really, I didn't create [the sound]; I actually got it from The Clark Sisters, and gave it a male spin."[29] Commissioned's vocal techniques and intricate harmonies were a source of enjoyment for the group's many fans, as well as for aspiring musicians like Boyz II Men, Jodeci, Brian McKnight, and Silk, who modeled their harmonizing after the gospel band.

While Commissioned recognized the importance of producing art that would be sonically appealing to young people, the band believed their primary responsibility was to provide a moral compass through which adolescents and young adults could navigate the traumas and joys of everyday life in postindustrial America. Their music tackled such difficult subjects as depression, self-doubt, and fear of failure. Masking pain, disappointment, and frustration with overzealous religiosity or nihilism, they believed, not only betrayed one's responsibility as an artist but also closed oneself off from the possibility of spiritual transcendence. Their honesty appealed to young listeners grappling with existential anguish, crises in faith, and feelings of powerlessness. Through their engagement with the music of Commissioned, young gospel fans encountered many of the theological themes present not only in traditional gospel songs but also in the larger black prophetic tradition: a benevolent God who intervenes on behalf of oppressed people, the equality of all people before God, and the representation of Jesus as a friend in the time of need.

Ordinary Just Won't Do: Confronting the Perils of Postindustrial Detroit and Reagan's America

Anything but detached from social reality, the Winans, the Clark Sisters, and Commissioned absorbed the tensions, struggles, and concerns of the city most responsible for shaping their political outlook: Detroit. All had witnessed first-hand the workings of a black activist Christian community. During the 1960s and 1970s, the city of Detroit claimed several ministers, most notably C. L. Franklin, T. S. Boone, and Albert Cleage, who identified strongly with the black freedom struggle. Boone's King Solomon Baptist Church, the site of Malcolm X's historic "Message to the Grassroots" speech, opened its doors to a variety of political organizations and events, ranging from the Nation of Islam's Savior's Day to the Southern Christian Leadership Conference's annual convention.[30] Widely known for his dynamic preaching, C. L. Franklin was actively involved in the civil rights movement, working closely with Martin Luther King Jr. and the SCLC, as well as addressing key political issues in Detroit. Not too far from Franklin's New Bethel Baptist Church stood the Shrine of the Black Madonna, which thrived under the leadership of Albert Cleage. Very much a part of local black nationalist politics, Cleage also gained notoriety as the author of the widely read text *Black Messiah*.

Extending this tradition of religious activism, the postindustrial black church was anything but an ideological monolith. Within that diverse body, opinions on the most effective ways to assist communities devastated by urban decay, poverty, the drug economy, and an insufficiently resourced public school system varied considerably. One group of ministers, deeply anchored in the ecclesiastical beliefs and moral imperatives of neo-Pentecostalism/charismatic Christianity, stressed the necessity of African Americans improving their conditions through self-help initiatives, moral rehabilitation, and positive confession of God's promise of divine health and prosperity for all faithful Christians. Their alliances with white charismatics like Kenneth Hagin and Pat Robertson put many of them on a political path that diverged significantly from black activist ministers connected to the civil rights establishment. Consider, as a case in point, the career of Detroit cleric Keith Butler. A graduate of Hagin's Rhema Bible Training Center, Butler brought thousands into his Detroit Word of Faith Christian Center with his teachings on the gifts and power of charismata. The outspoken pro-life, limited government, and "traditional family values" proponent also made headway in the world of conservative politics. Butler joined the Republican Party in 1980, served as a GOP precinct chairman in 1984, and five years later became the first Republican on the Detroit city council since World War II. It was his stated goal to "work within the political process to ensure that Judeo-Christian values are instilled in the public policy and public life of this nation." Butler deemed it necessary to challenge much of the "liberal social agenda" that had "destroyed our community": "We need some type of radical change, the time of radical change has come. And some of the people we have in office haven't worked. Many of them have been in office for years and years."[31] Needless to say, Butler's political platform met considerable opposition from other black clergy who might have shared some of his conservative positions on some social issues but found the Republican Party's fiscal policies and perspectives on race detrimental to black people.

Along with providing numerous examples of a politically engaged ministry, Detroit was also the center of intense debates about the future of urban America and the plight of the inner city.[32] A declining tax base, the ravages of deindustrialization, and dramatic population loss plagued the city during the post–civil rights years. The number of jobs in Detroit dipped from 574,225 to 418,725 between 1970 and 1987. If any city symbolized the hard times of the Reagan era and the monumental challenges of the Rust Belt, it was Detroit.

FIGURE 14. Painting of political activists Martin Luther King Jr. and Malcolm X on the back of historic King Solomon Baptist Church in Detroit. Photo by author.

As residents of the Motor City, the Clark Sisters, the Winans, and Commissioned understood the social misery wrought by massive unemployment, poverty, racial discrimination, and political disappointment.[33] Often in their interviews, the singers bitterly recounted the suffering endured by African Americans facing the combined forces of deindustrialization, automation, and racism. On numerous occasions, the Winans brothers shared stories about how their family struggled to survive amid the rapid loss of manufacturing jobs in the city. Their father, David Winans, had firsthand knowledge of the uncertainties of the auto industry. Employed by Ford, General Motors, and Chrysler intermittently between 1950 and 1970, the autoworker remembered being laid off "too many times to count." Twice, the elder Winans had to turn to social services for assistance: "I got up at four in the morning to line up for welfare. We were on it for eleven months before we got out of that mess. It was hard on my pride." Not even the passage of time erased his bitter memories of his experience with the welfare system. "They'd call out loud:'Number six! Winans!' And you'd have to stand up in front of all those people you went to school with who looked like they were saying 'Oh, he's down here too?'"[34]

Even as commercial success enabled the Winans and other artists to escape the economic hardships of their past, they could not ignore the fact that financial difficulties still enveloped many in their former neighborhoods. Nor could they ignore how Detroit's faltering economy, particularly its struggling auto industry, had become a symbol of all that was wrong with the nation's declining rust belt. "U.S. automakers will have to wait another year for a recovery," Warren Brown somberly wrote in the October 5, 1982, edition of the *Washington Post*. "They already have written 1982 off as a disaster."[35] A couple of months later, the newspaper featured another grim story on Detroit. In it, journalist Bill Peterson reported how the city's soup kitchens were crowded for Christmas, serving the area's "new poor": "They lined up along the walls of the room and spilled into the street, waiting for a wholesome looking meal of spaghetti, bread and vegetables and a sack of food to take home. When one chair emptied, two people were ready to fill it."[36] Given these realities, Detroit gospel artists frequently challenged mainstream discourses presenting the United States as a land of opportunity and equality. Echoing some of the sentiments expressed in the working-class blues of Tracy Chapman and Bruce Springsteen, Commissioned, for example, had numerous songs in which the group illuminated the persistence of economic inequality and injustice. On their 1986 recording, *Go Tell Somebody*, the sextet described a political landscape in which "the poor are still oppressed" and "the rich are filled with greed." In similar fashion, Twinkie Clark bemoaned the state of the economy, thumbing her nose at President Ronald Reagan and his trickle-down policies. On the song "I'm in Good Hands," she laments the state of U.S. politics and explicitly questions the public policy agenda of the Reagan administration. Crunching the numbers, she had serious doubts about working people's ability to survive the Reagan revolution.

> When I think about Reaganomics
> It makes me wonder how
> The people will survive living in the city and in the town
> *God's economics beat Reaganomics*[37]

Taking notice of not just domestic issues but international developments as well, gospel artists spoke out against racial apartheid in South Africa along with the United States' financial backing of dictatorial regimes in Latin America and the Middle East. No part of the world was exempt from criticism. Nor were any public figures—political or religious—considered off-limits. Insisting their duties extended beyond providing spiritual nourishment and musical entertainment, young artists also directed their listeners' attention to what they viewed as a major crisis in political and moral leadership. On their popular 1987 song "Right, Left in a Wrong World," the Winans register their disapproval with the Iran-Contra affair as well as with the sex scandals rocking televangelism, particularly Jim and Tammy Faye Bakker's PTL empire. The opening verse brings the listener face to face with a world entangled in a torrent of destructive behavior:

> Well the government seems to be cheating
> Selling arms to the enemy
> And those who supposed to be preaching
> *Are now warring on my TV*[38]

Frustration gripped the Winans, but they embraced neither a politics of despair nor an otherworldly perspective. Not content with simply pointing out the world's wrongs, they shared their opinions on how to correct society's growing problems. Their opinions ranged from liberal to conservative. For instance, demands for more federal spending on education, after-school youth programs, the revitalization of inner-city communities, and solutions for homelessness coexisted with calls for the need to strengthen the family unit.

Consistent with the political tenor of the times, urban contemporary gospel music abounded with culture-of-poverty-influenced narratives bemoaning escalating levels of violence, rising divorce rates, unstable family units, and misguided children lacking "proper" parental guidance and love. Several artists incorporated the sounds of "urban warfare" into their music. On Commissioned's 1987 song "Perilous Times," the piercing sound of gunshots and two men arguing open the track, which provides a tale of rampant violence and social malaise. The proliferation of violent activity was not the only dominant theme; significant attention was also given to another recurring topic in black underclass literature:

the redemption of the black community depended on the strengthening of the black family. If things were to improve, the family unit must be restored.

To substantiate their claims that the "perilous times" of the 1980s stemmed, in part, from the alleged decline of the traditional family unit, many artists conveniently engaged in the politics of historical revision. On their Grammy Award–winning song "Bring Back the Days of Yea and Nay," the Winans sentimentalize the past as a time free of complexity, when everyone recognized and performed their expected roles in heteronormative, patriarchal households.

Increasingly present in songs about the alleged fracturing of the family was the thinly veiled suggestion that communities had been burdened by serious gender transgressions. Take for example Marvin Winans and Twinkie Clark's duet, "Word of God," recorded in 1989 at Shalom Temple in Detroit. The song was featured on Ronald Winans's *Family and Friends* recording, which included several Detroit-based musicians. Transporting the audience to what she presented as a more tranquil and less complicated time, Twinkie reflects on a past in which gender identities and roles were clearly defined. "Why I can even remember when / Women were women and men were men," she sings in the first verse. "But now," Twinkie continues, the crisis in masculinity and femininity has reached a point where one could "hardly tell a her from a him." Ending her verse with an eruptive "we've changed," she conveniently ignores the long history of homosexuality in American and African American culture, especially in the gospel industry, in order to serve her explicitly political goal of influencing the cultural memory of her audience.

Socially conservative ideas, including homophobia, undoubtedly found an outlet in urban contemporary gospel, but so did other more liberal positions. One could never predict the music's direction (politically or sonically), since many of these artists were still in the process of negotiating their own political perspectives and beliefs.

No Cross, No Crown: Urban Contemporary Gospel and Its Critics

As they negotiated their politics, urban contemporary gospel artists also struggled to solidify their place in a genre where change was not always welcomed. Even those artists who in their younger years had been criticized for sounding too secular could be extremely hard on the new wave of gospel musicians. One of the more interesting arguments put forth by traditionalists centered on contemporary gospel's rupture with African Americans' cultural roots. Traditional gospel "tells a more profound story than contemporary music," Shirley Caesar argued. "It's somewhat closer to our roots."[39]

Finding contemporary gospel music too sterile, Albertina Walker believed traditional gospel had more spiritual depth: "I need traditional music to get into my soul." Walker also felt contemporary gospel lacked real sustaining power. "Contemporary gospel is OK. I've got no problems with it," she said. "Trouble is, it don't last long. The music is great and people like it—for a while."[40] Even though Milton Brunson's choir freely incorporated the sounds of funk and jazz into its music, he agreed with Walker. "The contemporary sound is a ballroom beat, when you're sitting there listening to it you never get any spiritual feeling."[41]

This criticism was not limited to artists. Scholar and record producer Anthony Heilbut criticized contemporary artists for their insistence on polishing gospel's rough edges, their move away from the art form's more earthy qualities, and their overemphasis on technique. "The excessive virtuosity defeats its own purposes, whether of expressing spirit or asserting self," Heilbut complained.[42]

Such criticism would not go unanswered. Several musicians railed against writers who failed to recognize the artistic diversity within the gospel genre. Why, they wondered, should black gospel be confined to one sound? Few were more outspoken than Marvin Winans, who also condemned white critics for what he read as their essentialist approach to black sacred music: "White people expect black people to go through all the tomfoolery. The shouting, the dancing, 'Your Arms Too Short to Box with God,' the backwards flips in the *Blues Brothers*. If that's not there, people say, 'That's not gospel.'" So far as Winans was concerned, these public disagreements were not just about music but also about race. "Because of the cultural difference, blacks are pegged in a hole. That's the problem because we're not allowed to be anything other than what you envision us to be. Most of what's successful is 20 folks in a robe running around and screaming."[43]

These debates were deeply connected to a much larger conversation on black representation in the public sphere. Throughout the media, black artists and critics expressed apprehensions about the loss of "tradition" and "community." Consider, for example, Nelson George's seminal text *The Death of Rhythm and Blues*. Charting the history of rhythm and blues from its roots in the race records of the 1920s through the end of the Reagan administration, George lamented the genre's state in the 1980s. African American musicians' desire for crossover riches and acceptance, George insisted, had replaced previous yearnings for artistic innovation and political relevancy. "Something died," the writer bluntly concluded in his assessment of the music coming out of the 1980s.[44] Well into the next decade, this declension narrative continued to shape music criticism on post-soul rhythm and blues.

The jazz world also entertained complex—and at times highly volatile—discussions on the need to return to form or embrace more traditional styles.[45]

Valorization of Wynton Marsalis and other young lions touched off intense deliberations among many jazz critics and historians over the safeguarding, redefining, and mythologizing of "tradition." As Herman Gray demonstrates in *Cultural Moves*, altruistic concerns hardly constituted the sole motive force behind efforts to keep "real," "authentic" jazz alive.[46] Many calls for a return to "the tradition" were rooted as much in market dictates and economic anxieties as in cultural concerns. Transforming tradition into a commodity requires that one draw boundary lines of inclusion and exclusion in order to present one form of expression as purer or more authentic than another.

A similar logic worked in some gospel circles. The 1980s witnessed a growing number of corporations—from McDonald's to Kentucky Fried Chicken—invest in gospel music as part of their outreach and cultural heritage programs. Along with summer festivals, record companies, and radio stations that marketed and profited from traditional gospel artists like Albertina Walker and James Cleveland, these programs presented consumers with the idea that in supporting traditional gospel music, they were sustaining an integral component of African American history and culture. Though in reality, constant change had been the only true tradition in gospel music, conversations about preserving and continuing the legacy of the past proved useful for older artists, including many who, during the 1950s and 1960s, had themselves been criticized for their incorporation of certain instruments (electric guitar, drums, and bass) and arrangements into gospel music. This reality was not lost on Fred Hammond, a student of gospel music history: "They criticized Thomas Dorsey. He was too contemporary, too jazzy. And they criticized Mahalia Jackson. They called her bluesy. It's the same ole thing that's been handed down through the ages."[47]

Of all the criticisms leveled at contemporary gospel artists, suggestions that financial motives drove their art troubled them the most. "I've been offered big bucks to go commercial," Twinkie Clark told the *New York Times* in 1986. "But when I write, I have to write under the inspiration of the Holy Ghost. I can't just sit down and throw anything together. I have dedicated my life to God, and Jesus means more to me than all the money in the world."[48] That Clark felt obliged to defend her commitment to God spoke volumes about the tensions within the gospel industry. No artist pushed the teachings of the Church of God in Christ harder than Clark, who in song after song testified to the transformative power of the Holy Spirit. And yet, at the height of her commercial success, she found herself defending her musical ministry. To make matters worse, traditionalists routinely overstated the financial benefits of performing contemporary gospel music. Like their peers who sung in a more traditional style, contemporary gospel artists were subjected to horrible recording and publishing deals, shady label executives and concert promoters, and cash-strapped fans who lacked the funds to routinely purchase records or concert tickets.

Over time, many urban contemporary artists embraced their outsider status, carving out a space of autonomy in which they could not only advance their careers but also expand the gospel canon in ways beneficial to all. Such was the case for the Winans quartet, which in an effort to reach a larger audience left Light Records and joined Quincy Jones's Qwest Records in 1985.

Decisions: The Winans Strike Gold with Qwest Records

The Winans' departure from Light elicited extensive conversation in industry circles. Would the foursome diverge from their previous sound to sell more records? Would they embrace more ambiguous lyrics to reach those who might appreciate their musicianship but not their Christian message? Would the move to Qwest really advance their career, or would their experience be similar to that of Andraé Crouch, whose time at Warner Brothers had been underwhelming? Their manager, Barry Hankerson, assured gospel journalist Tim A. Smith that the Winans would not change their message. "Qwest felt the sound of the Winans was a sound everyone can enjoy. . . . The material on the album that the group is working on was chosen long before signing with Qwest. If the group had stayed with Light, the same material would have been used. The world is ready to hear something about Christ. It would be foolish for us to compromise." Though Hankerson assured fans that the Winans would not dilute their message, he confirmed the group's desire to reach a larger market. Crossing over into the pop market, he readily admitted, was a goal. "Qwest didn't sign the group to remain in one category. They're going to the mass market, and that's where we want our music to go. We want to take the gospel music message higher. We want our music to be played and listened to all over the world."[49]

Not long after joining Qwest, the Winans released *Let My People Go*. The highly anticipated record had a nice balance of introspective ballads ("Straighten My Life Out" and "Redeemed") and mid-tempo grooves ("Very Real Way" and the anti-apartheid title cut). The group's Qwest debut received a great deal of press—and much to the company's delight, music critics hailed the record a triumph.

A big fan of the lead single, "Let My People Go," Kris Needs of *ZigZag* declared the quartet the hottest thing in gospel. "Gospel fire stoked by a higher plane of musical emotion. The combined force of all four of The Winans is like the Red Sea crashing back down again."[50] On their first outing with Qwest, the brothers from Detroit did not disappoint. Propelled by the single "Let My People Go," the Winans entered *Billboard*'s R&B albums chart for the first time in their career.

The spotlight didn't bother lead singer Marvin Winans, who enjoyed mixing music with politics. Though some of his peers shied away from international issues, Winans appreciated the opportunity to address why he felt so compelled to confront the political situation in South Africa. "There's been a barrage of media attention turned to South Africa," Winans told Kris Needs. "This last 18 months I've been made aware of what was really going on. I met some young people from South Africa in 1984 during the Olympics, who were coloured. They told me how difficult it was there—the blacker you are, the further back you are. There was a lot of attention on things like the sit-in at the South African Embassy and everything." Winans was also moved by political developments in other parts of the world. "Oppression was everywhere—the miners' strike in England going on for months, Northern Ireland, Poland, Central America. The universality to the time was what we were trying to relate." In addition to sharing his political views, Winans was also forthright about his commercial desires for gospel. The art form, he believed, was on the brink of a commercial explosion. "Gospel is starting to come through now," he observed. "For too long it's been treated as the step-child of the music industry. It's not been given the promotion. Now record companies are viewing it as a viable part of the music industry. If we develop the market and give it mass appeal it could come through like Country and Bluegrass."[51]

Winans's confident outlook stemmed in part from the success of his group. With steady radio play and a national tour, the Winans' debut for Qwest reached #1 on the gospel charts. Three of the album singles, "Let My People Go," "Very Real Way" and "Choose Ye," played regularly on contemporary gospel radio stations. And yet, record label executives felt *Let My People Go* underperformed in the Christian market. "It's been a challenging year for us in marketing the Winans," Harold Childs, president of Qwest, explained to *Billboard*. "As everyone knows, we're a pop record company, distributed by WEA. We signed the Winans because they showed strong promise in conquering the pop field. The reaction to their *Let My People Go* album has been great at the pop field but we need to work harder to cash in on their Christian following. Then we can more successfully bridge both areas."[52]

This is exactly what happened with the group's next recording, *Decisions*. The record got off to a strong start with the lead single, "Ain't No Need to Worry," which featured R&B superstar Anita Baker. *Decisions* also featured Michael McDonald on the inspirational "Love Has No Color." To those who questioned the inclusion of pop stars on *Decisions*, Marvin Winans explained,

> When you need to get a certain group to hear your music, then you've got to go get that certain group. If we just wanted gospel people to hear the music, we would have gotten gospel artists. It has proven to be a very prudent and wise decision, both for us and for the artists. We recognize the fact that because we are gospel artists we're only going to be played on so many stations. In order to

change that we needed to get some people to help change that circumstance, not change our music but make sure other people heard us.[53]

At the same time, the Winans attended to the needs of their longtime gospel fans. One song in particular resonated deeply with their followers: the Marvin Winans–penned ballad "Millions." Fusing the new sounds of contemporary gospel with an imaginative take on Judgment Day, "Millions" struck a resonant chord among gospel listeners. On tours and at award shows, this song seemed to always bring the crowd to its feet.

To build on the radio success of *Decisions*, the Winans hit the road to connect with old and new fans. Their concerts elicited tremendous excitement from their followers, as well as from respected journalists like *New York Times* reporter Stephen Holden: "The quartet's rich chromatic harmonies, from which individual voices soar into stately falsetto passages, are delivered with a dynamic control and sweeping sense of line that one rarely hears even in such a vocally virtuosic idiom as gospel." Their polish, Holden admiringly wrote, "comes at no expense of emotional expression."[54] To capture the magnetism of their live shows, the group released *Live at Carnegie Hall* in 1988. Comprising their hit songs from Light and Qwest, *Live at Carnegie Hall* won the group their fourth Grammy.

A year after the release of *Live at Carnegie Hall*, the Winans struck gold with their 1990 record, *Return*. To expand their audience, the Winans drew on the talents of Stevie Wonder, Kenny G (a longtime fan of the group), and Guy's Teddy Riley and Aaron Hall. Impressed by the crossover success of Take 6 and BeBe and CeCe Winans, label executives at Warner Brothers were convinced the Winans could reach a larger audience. Toward this goal, Benny Medina called the group and suggested that they work with Teddy Riley, an immensely talented producer whose clients included his group Guy, Bobby Brown, Keith Sweat, Heavy D, and Michael Jackson. In the late 1980s, Riley had created and popularized a new subgenre in black mainstream music, New Jack Swing. "The formula behind Riley's success," writes music scholar Mark Anthony Neal, "was a conscious effort to layer 'traditional' gospel and soul vocal styles over rhythms closely associated with those found in some forms of hip hop."[55] Very familiar with the Winans' music, Riley infused the stylistic elements of New Jack Swing into *Return*'s biggest hits, "It's Time," "Don't Leave Me," and "A Friend." To his credit, he made sure the group was comfortable with his shifts in their sound. "He was totally open and really willing to listen to us," Michael Winans noted. "He kept telling us to let him know if we didn't like something he wanted to do."[56] The partnership worked wonderfully. The lead single, "It's Time," was a top five hit whose accompanying video played regularly on BET. The song featured a guest appearance from Riley, who rapped on its introduction and the bridge.

Riley was not the only member from Guy who appeared on *Return*. Crooner Aaron Hall delivered a strong performance on the hit single "A Friend." Hall's soulful tenor blended perfectly with the Winans' lush harmonies and Riley's melodic production. To push record sales, Qwest released another Riley-produced single, "Don't Leave Me," a hard-driving groove with a classic New Jack sound.

Moving beyond the traditional marketing outlets available to gospel artists, the Winans appeared on the *Oprah Winfrey Show*, the *Arsenio Hall Show*, *Video Soul*, and numerous secular award shows. With radio-friendly singles and an extensive promotion campaign, the group scored their first and only gold certification with *Return*.

With a healthy dose of sibling rivalry to motivate them, the quartet enjoyed their return to the spotlight in the aftermath of the recent success of their brother and sister BeBe and CeCe. "You don't work hard to be on the bottom," Marvin Winans bluntly noted. "People that try to present a pious attitude only lie to themselves. We want everybody in the world to own a Winans record. We feel that God has equipped us mentally to deal with it. It's very easy to be successful if you keep Jesus in focus."[57] With support from Teddy Riley, one of pop music's biggest hitmakers, the quartet from Detroit had returned in grand fashion and in doing so cemented their status as one of the most important groups in gospel history.

Bringing It Back Home: The Clark Sisters Sign with Word Records

The second half of the 1980s was great for the Winans, but the road was not as smooth for their peers the Clark Sisters. Due to label disputes, four years passed between the release of the group's 1982 *Sincerely* album and its follow-up, *Heart and Soul*. Notwithstanding the absence of new material, the group maintained a relatively high profile in the gospel world. Songs like "Is My Living in Vain," "Expect Your Miracle," "Endow Me," "Name It, Claim It," and "You Brought the Sunshine" were still in rotation on gospel radio stations, while the group's energetic live shows pulled in large crowds.[58]

With the hopes of returning to the top of the charts, the Clark Sisters finally released their studio record *Heart and Soul* in 1986. Like so many of gospel's biggest stars, the group had signed with Word Records and its black division, Rejoice. Still shouldering much of the responsibility for the group's studio material, Twinkie Clark wrote and coproduced (with Norbert Putman) all but two songs on *Heart and Soul*. To keep up with the times, Twinkie embraced a more electronic, digitized sound. "The stuff is so high-tech that if you mess up, it's going to come across," she half-jokingly told *New York Times* reporter Jon Pareles.[59] *Heart and Soul* was a solid record with several radio-friendly cuts, most notably

"Time Out," "He'll Turn Your Scars into Stars," "Jesus Is a Love Song," "Pray for the USA," and "There Is a Balm in Gilead." There's something for everyone: strong ballads, sultry mid-tempos, and hard-driving funk grooves. Though not quite the aesthetic achievement of *Is My Living in Vain* and *You Brought the Sunshine*, it was a step in the right direction for the sisters.

To maintain the momentum, the group released *Conqueror* in 1988 and the live set *Bringing It Back Home* the following year. On *Conqueror*, the group gave a nod to the nation's fastest growing art form, hip-hop, with "Computers Rule the World (but God Is Still in Control)," synthesized a decade of R&B on "The Darkest Hour Is Just before the Day," and updated the Clark Sisters sound with "Jesus Forevermore." Twinkie's superb musicianship prevents the group from falling victim to corny R&B clichés and homogenized, flaccid funk. While remaining true to her creative impulses, Twinkie Clark worked hard to appeal to gospel's wide fan base. "The thing I aim at doing is writing something on the album for everybody. That means young folks, middle folks, and old folks."[60]

But feeling the pressure of trying to please multiple audiences, Twinkie grew weary of her enormous responsibilities as the group's primary songwriter and producer. After the release of the group's 1989 live recording, she left the Clark Sisters to focus more on her personal life and develop her identity outside of the context of the group. *Bringing It Back Home* marked the perfect end of an adventurous decade for the Clark Sisters, a successful yet battle-tested group that had endured their share of criticism from the church and the gospel community. With their releases on Sound of Gospel and Word, the group had not only redefined the gospel sound but provided sonic inspiration for future pop stars like Mariah Carey, Missy Elliott, Xscape, Fantasia, Mary J. Blige, Faith Evans, and Beyoncé.

Ordinary Just Won't Do: Commissioned and the Sounds of New Jack Gospel

Though not as prominent as the Clark Sisters, Commissioned also influenced a younger generation of gospel and secular artists. Every year between 1985 and 1991, the group put a new record in stores. And each release charted new territory in terms of sound while remaining true to the group's core message. Frequently in the shadow of the Winans, Commissioned struggled to gain attention from the mainstream press. But in the eyes of their many diehard fans, they were the best male group in gospel.

As the eighties came to a close, Commissioned ended its four-year stint with Light Records after the release of *Ordinary Just Won't Do* in 1989.[61] The record opened up with the high-energy tune "Back in the Saddle," then segued into the popular title cut. Dabbling once again in the sounds of New Jack Swing, the group turned up the heat with "If My People," an old-fashioned jeremiad modernized by the rhythms of the street. On this record, the members of Commissioned incorporated rap into their verses for the first time. Though some critics viewed the band's sound as a blatant attempt at crossover, Fred Hammond defended his music as an extension of his cultural background and artistry. "I've got a bit of Hawkins and the Winans and Cleveland in me, but there is also Earth, Wind, and Fire and Stevie Wonder and Gladys Knight. That's my musical heritage. That's what I grew up with. My music is cultural."[62]

As Hammond makes clear, the music of Commissioned reflected the sum of all the members' influences, cultural and political. The same can be said of the Winans and the Clark Sisters. These were the children of Detroit, the land of Motown, the birthplace of the Gospel Music Workshop of America, ground zero for the nation's urban crisis, and an epicenter of black religious activism. Very much attuned to the economic hardships and social malaise facing African Americans in their local communities and the nation at large, they believed in the power of faith, prayer, and community. They also believed in the power of artistic expression. In seeking to make sense of a rapidly changing world, their music revealed the complex ideological tensions engulfing black religious publics in the post–civil rights era.

CHAPTER 7

If I Be Lifted

Milton Brunson and the Thompson Community Singers

Praise the Lord with the harp; make music to him
on the ten-stringed lyre. Sing to him a new song;
play skillfully, and shout for joy.
—Psalm 33:2–3 (NIV)

West of Detroit, in the city of Chicago, the predominantly black neighborhood of Austin claimed one of the greatest choirs in gospel music history: the Thompson Community Singers (TCS). The Tommies, as they were affectionately known, scored numerous hits during their fifty-year tenure. Under the leadership of Reverend Milton Brunson, the choir built on the city's rich musical legacy to create a sound like no other in gospel. Dramatic ballads, house-wrecking shouts, and mid-tempo grooves—the Thompson Community Singers mastered them all with the perfect combination of style, individuality, precision, technique, and grace. Their throbbing grooves, infectious chants, melodic hooks, and deeply felt vocals provided a model for gospel musicians and choirs across the country. At the peak of their success, the TCS amassed numerous awards and accolades, as well as several #1 gospel albums.

Organized by Milton Brunson in 1948, the Thompson Community Singers held their first practices in the basement of St. Stephen AME Church. Initially consisting of Brunson and several of his McKinley High School classmates, the choir featured African American youth from various churches and denominations. The decision to draw choir participants from a community rather than from a single church was a new phenomenon that would play a critical role in the development of gospel music in Chicago and throughout the country. Robert Marovich explains: "Because membership in a church choir was reserved for members of that church, community choirs formed to enable people from various churches and denominations, and especially youth, to sing together. Community choirs also offered a positive social outlet for the rising number of Christian teens, an alternative to the rising tide of juvenile delinquency and gang membership."[1] Well known in Chicago, Detroit, and a few other cities on the gospel highway, the TCS did not cut their first album (*Yes, Jesus Loves Me*) until 1963. Six years later, the Tommies scored their first hit with "I'll Trade a Lifetime." Under Brunson's leadership, the Tommies developed into one of the nation's most celebrated choirs, fusing the various styles of black music into their studio recordings and concerts.

A master teacher, Brunson demanded excellence from his choir. Everything had to be tight: the lyrics, the arrangements, the soloists, the choir, and the band. "I believe if you're presenting the King, which is Jesus Christ our Lord, you should do things in the way He would have you to do them; decently and in order," Brunson declared.[2] Brunson's meticulousness reflected his deep love and respect for gospel music, as well as his commitment to improving the lives of young people. The ambitious Brunson envisioned his musical ministry as a form of social work: "I'm here to reach people in trouble, especially teenagers. Today's teenagers are surrounded by gangs, drugs, and despair. They need hope. I'm not here to make money, I'm not here to gain fame. I'm here to reach out a hand."[3] Working with Chicago's youth fueled Brunson's energy, and even though he had children of his own, the success of his choir members gave him great satisfaction: "They go out and become doctors, lawyers, teachers—good, productive people."[4]

Though Brunson was the founder of the Tommies, he relied heavily on the musical talents of others. Over the years, the choir's distinguished list of alums included Jessy Dixon, Percy Bady, Kim McFarland, Ricky Dillard, Ethel Holloway, Steve Huff, Tyrone Block, and Darius Brooks. Thanks to the songwriting and production contributions of Jessy Dixon, the Tommies thrived during the 1960s and 1970s. Songs like "Old Ship of Zion," "I'll Trade a Lifetime," and "I Love to Praise His Name" played on gospel radio nationwide. Dixon's departure in the early 1980s created space for a new crop of talented writers and producers, most notably Darius Brooks and Percy Bady. First linking up with the choir on the 1984 classic *Miracle Live*, Brooks wrote such fan favorites as "Safe in His Arms," "My Mind's Made Up," "For the Good of Them," "I Tried Him and I Know Him," and "God's Got It." Equally impressive were the contributions of Percy Bady, whose hits included "He Cares for You," "There Is Hope," "There Is No Failure," and "He'll Make It Alright."

While Bady, Brooks, and Dixon were steeped in the rhythms and sounds of contemporary gospel, Brunson fashioned himself as a traditionalist. "I don't like contemporary gospel music," he unabashedly told the *Chicago Tribune* in 1992. In his mind, the lyrical ambiguity of many contemporary gospel songs rendered the music spiritually impotent. "Oh they're singing, 'I love you, you love me,' and then they're telling you it's a song about Jesus—but how's a person supposed to know that? I want to sing about the Lord. Everybody else can do whatever they want."[5] Much like his fellow Chicago native James Cleveland, Brunson envisioned himself as a keeper of the gospel tradition forged by Thomas Dorsey, Mahalia Jackson, and Roberta Martin. His views reflected his age as well as his upbringing in the Windy City.

Beginnings

Milton Brunson was born in Chicago on June 28, 1929. His parents, Lawrence and Maude Brunson, were natives of Arkansas who had migrated north with the hopes of securing a better life for themselves and their growing family. The Brunsons, who married in 1916, lived on West 14th Street. Like many of his male neighbors, Lawrence Brunson worked as a factory hand in the local stockyard. The youngest boy in a family of seven, Milton Brunson attended McKinley High School, where he befriended a group of young people who would assist him in the formation of a youth choir. Needing a place to rehearse, Brunson approached Reverend Eugene Thompson about using his church as a site for rehearsal. Thompson agreed. Grateful for the minister's support, Brunson named his choir the Thompson Community Singers.

Over time, the choir became a visible presence on Chicago's gospel scene. On June 18, 1961, the TCS became the first gospel group to sing in Chicago's famed McCormick Place.[6] The choir's profile increased in the coming years. Throughout the 1960s and early 1970s, the Tommies regularly appeared on Sid Ordower's *Jubilee Showcase*, which was broadcast over WLS-TV on Sundays at 8 a.m. Their discipline and talent amazed Ordower: "Here was this neighborhood choir that was singing at a professional level and touring the country, a remarkable development."[7]

The Tommies were extremely talented and had quite a reputation in the local area, although they did not record professionally until 1963. That year, the Chicago-based label Vee-Jay released the choir's debut album, *Yes, Jesus Loves Me*. On this impressive collection, the Tommies covered James Cleveland's "Deep Down in My Heart," offered a unique rendition of "Yes, Jesus Loves Me," and showcased their vocal prowess on "Down by the Riverside." The choir also covered the gospel classic "Old Ship of Zion," a song to which they would return on subsequent albums.

A year later, the TCS released *The Soul of the Thompson Community Singers*. This record featured the talented Jessy Dixon. A native of San Antonio, Texas, Dixon was an immensely gifted writer and musician who in 1959 caught the attention of gospel legend James Cleveland. Not long after meeting Cleveland, Dixon moved to Chicago. In 1965, he became the director of the Thompson Community Singers. Like Brunson, Dixon demanded nothing but the best from his singers and musicians. The Tommies thrived during Dixon's tenure, which is beautifully documented on such classic TCS records as *I'll Trade a Lifetime* and *Joy*.

Dixon's musical contributions and his leadership proved indispensable as Brunson faced the challenge of balancing his responsibilities as the choir's founder and leader with his new ministerial duties. In 1964, a small group of worshippers at Gethsemane Star decided to form their own church, Christ Tabernacle Baptist, and asked Brunson to serve as its pastor. Feeling as if their request aligned with his larger spiritual goals, Brunson accepted their invitation to lead the fledging church.

His ministry at Christ Tabernacle was demanding, but he remained committed to the Tommies. The choir was now a permanent fixture on the local gospel

FIGURE 15. Christ Tabernacle Baptist Church in Chicago. Founded by the Reverend Milton Brunson, Christ Tabernacle was the site of many of the Thompson Community Singers' legendary recordings. Photo by author.

scene and frequently traveled to other parts of the country. Having released their first two records with Vee-Jay, the Tommies moved to the HOB label in the late 1960s. The partnership paid off as the choir scored their first radio hit with "I'll Trade a Lifetime." On the heartfelt tune, Maggie Bell delivers a moving performance with full backing from the choir. "I'll Trade a Lifetime" received play on gospel radio stations across the country, as well as on a few secular stations in Chicago. The album of the same name, which was released in 1968, also boasted such fine cuts as "What a Friend" and "Poor Pilgrim of Sorrow." The Tommies maintained their high quality of musicianship with the release of *No Man Is an Island* in 1969. With outstanding numbers like "Pray on My Child" and "The Holy Ghost Is Here Right Now," *No Man Is an Island* was gospel soul at its finest.

The Tommies' growing stature in the gospel field caught the attention of the *Chicago Tribune*, which in 1970 ran a story on the choir. On the eve of the Tommies' appearance in *Peace: The Possible Dream*, a drama that traced the African American experience from slavery to the Civil Rights Act of 1964, *Tribune* reporter Terri Schultz traveled to Brunson's West Side church to gain a deeper understanding of the ensemble's mission and ambitions. She detailed Brunson's background, his formation of the choir in 1948, and the Tommies' development into one of the city's most respected gospel groups. Noting the choir's recent performances at New York's Apollo Theater, Madison Square Garden, and Carnegie Hall, she informed readers of the Tommies' reputation beyond the Windy City. When asked why the choir didn't garner more attention, Brunson pointed to the sensationalist nature of the local media: "More than four children a week are killed in gangs in Chicago's black communities. That is what the papers feed on. I'm afraid these kids aren't news because they aren't out busting windows."[8]

Under Brunson's guidance, the TCS didn't miss a beat. As the gospel industry entered the 1970s with new stars and new expectations, the Tommies held their own in an increasingly competitive field. Enjoying a relatively stable relationship with HOB, Brunson and the TCS released *Give Me a Clean Heart* and *If Everybody Was Like Jesus* in 1972, *Jesus Is Just Alright* in 1973, *Moods, Images and Reflections* in 1974, and *He's Able to Carry You Through* in 1975. Working in tandem, Brunson and Dixon complemented each other beautifully. Whereas Brunson kept the choir grounded in the evangelical mission of the church, the adventurous Dixon ensured the TCS's continued growth artistically. Onstage, the members enthralled audiences with their passionate singing, taut rhythms, and unparalleled discipline.

The choir's relationship with HOB ended with the release of *He's Able to Carry You Through*, but the Tommies would not be without a contract for long. Joining Nashboro's Creed label, Milton Brunson and the Tommies released *Joy* in 1977 and its follow-up, *To All Generations*, in 1979. *Joy* was at the intersection of R&B-influenced gospel and contemporary Christian music. Songs like "It's My Desire" and "A Heart" would have easily fit on an Andraé Crouch or a Walter Hawkins record. So, too, would the rollicking "I Love to Praise His Name." Written by Jessy Dixon, the song found a home at black churches of various denominations, from Baptist to Church of God in Christ.

Joy had moderate success, but *To All Generations* did not fare as well. It is hard to understand why a record with gems like "God Will Take Care of You," "The Lord Is Blessing Me," "Direct Me," and "Sing until the Power Comes Down" did not make a dent on the gospel charts. Perhaps *To All Generations* experimented too much with the rhythms of disco and funk for the traditional gospel listener. Or maybe the album was a casualty of the record industry slump of 1979. For reasons that are not entirely clear, *To All Generations* would be the Tommies' last release on the Nashboro label.

Fortunately, the talented choir soon found another label home: Word Records. Their 1982 release on Word, *It's Gonna Rain*, paired the soulful sounds of "old-time gospel" with the youthful vibrancy of contemporary gospel. The record featured compositions from Dixon, Calvin Bridges, Jewel Esterling, and Marvin Winans. The Tommies revisited old classics and introduced fans to a new song that would soon become a Sunday morning staple: "It's Gonna Rain." As musicologist Samuel Floyd rightly points out, "It's Gonna Rain" was a brilliant use of "polyphony, call and response phrasing, a walking bass line, tight group harmonies, falsetto-scat vocals, and a jazz/R&B based rhythmic accompaniment."[9] The title cut was an instant classic that was performed at church services across black America.

New Horizons

The choir's sophomore release for Word, *Miracle Live*, was even stronger. It contained at least four songs—"There Is No Way," "Jesus Is a Rock," "Jesus, We're Depending on You," and "He'll Make It Alright"—that became favorites among gospel choirs across the country. Upon its release, *Miracle Live* raced to the top of the gospel charts, becoming the Tommies' first #1 record. It bridged the divide between traditional and contemporary gospel, taking the best of the new and old sounds of black sacred music. Forward-thinking Brunson wanted to ensure his choir had its own distinctive sound. "When you hear Edwin [Hawkins], you know it's him. When you hear my friend up there in Detroit, Thomas Whitfield, you know it's him and when you hear Richard Smallwood, you know it's him. Everybody has an identification. So we felt that we ought to have our own sound. That's what I was trying to do."[10]

With a firm grasp of their artistic vision, the Tommies embarked on their next recording, *There Is Hope*. Disciplined but never predictable, the choir moved seamlessly from power ballads to funk-laced jams. The record opens with "Safe in His Arms," which features Beatrice Gardner on lead vocals. With impeccable execution and heartfelt passion, Gardner and the choir inject deep meaning into every note. The Tommies bring the same level of precision to another standout cut on the record, "Over and Over and Over." Anchored by bassist Steve Huff's sinuous riffs and the horn section's jazzy improvisations, "Over and Over and Over" delivers the funk while channeling the spirit of gospel's hardest rocker, Sister Rosetta Tharpe. On the song's vamp, guitarist Al Willis's ax grinding pairs nicely with his bandmates' propulsive rhythms. A similar intensity marks "There Is No Failure" and "The Holy Ghost," two monster jams full of rhythmic complexity.

If the record's fast-paced tunes reflected the Tommies' immersion in the rhythms of contemporary gospel and R&B, the contemplative "There Is Hope" underscored the choir's concern about the particular challenges facing African Americans in Chicago and other postindustrial cities. Milton Brunson was especially troubled by the violence pervading the inner city. "Back in the 1960s, for example, gangbangers might hit you in the head and rob you. Now they rob you and shoot you dead. Now they're coldhearted. They're caught up with drugs, which makes them crazy. These people have no fear. They can take away a person's life, just like that."[11] Not just violence but unemployment, homelessness, and social decay were topics of discussion in "There Is Hope." This was a narrative of urban crisis and decline. And yet, the resonant voices of the choir and lead singer Percy Bady push us to believe in the promise of a brighter day. This hopeful spirit carries over to another ballad, "Lord, I Believe," an uplifting tune featuring Darius Brooks.

There Is Hope held the #1 position on *Billboard*'s gospel charts from August 9, 1986, until March 21, 1987, when the New Jersey Mass Choir's *Look Up and Live* took over the top spot. By the fall of that year, however, the Tommies reclaimed the top position with their critically acclaimed release *If I Be Lifted*. Considered the choir's best record by many fans and critics, *If I Be Lifted* featured three radio hits: "He Cares for You," "God's Got It," and "Thank You." On "God's Got It," the funk flows freely as Steve Huff's bass lines, Denise Battle's scorching vocals, and the choir's booming voices lock into a tight groove for five glorious minutes. The Kim McFarland–led "Thank You" is equally impressive, as the former member of Walt Whitman and the Soul Children of Chicago makes her presence felt immediately. Not to be outdone, Tina Watson delivers an amazing performance on the opener, "He Cares for You," which stands out as one of the choir's finest moments on record.

For nearly a year, *If I Be Lifted* dominated the gospel charts. And as one might expect, the Tommies were in high demand among gospel concert promoters. On the stage, they were a sight to behold. Stylishly attired in beautiful robes, their appearance was as magnificent as their sound. It was especially hard to keep one's eyes off Tyrone Block, the Tommies' expressive choir director, who moved with unabashed confidence. Working in tandem with Block, band members egged each other on as they engaged in spirited improvisation. Feeding off the energy of the crowd and each other, the Tommies breathed new life into hit songs like "Safe in His Arms," "Lord, I Believe," "The Holy Ghost," "Thank You," and "Over and Over and Over."

On the stage and in the studio, the Tommies were at the top of their game. Not only were they prolific, but they also managed to maintain a high level of musicianship over a span of consecutive releases. Their albums were cohesive, well-sequenced units that were enjoyable from beginning to end.

Showing no signs of slowing down, the Tommies released *Available to You* in 1988. Solid throughout, *Available to You* had three stellar cuts: "Rest for the Weary," "For the Good of Them," and "I'm Available to You." On the whole, the record was a healthy mix of soulful gospel and reflective testifying. As had been the case on the previous record, lead vocalist Kim McFarland turned in an impressive performance. On the hugely popular single "For the Good of Them," her phrasing is as exquisite as her angelic tone, which provides an excellent counterpoint to the choir's thunderous vocals. Not just a gospel radio hit, "For the Good of Them" was a song that many choir directors used to gauge the range of their lead vocalists.

Equally popular, "I'm Available to You" had a ubiquitous presence on gospel radio and at Sunday morning services in Chicago and across black America. Perfect for an altar call, "I'm Available to You" achieves a fully refined and beautifully blended sound with exact intonation and expressive warmth. On the bridge, the TCS's four-part harmony provides orchestral ornamentation yet maintains the traditional call-and-response form of gospel music.

As the 1980s came to a close, the Tommies had much to celebrate. Their records had achieved critical acclaim and commercial success in the gospel world. Moreover, by blending contemporary and traditional gospel, their music provided an example of how to move forward artistically without compromising spiritual integrity.

Moving Forward in the 1990s

With their gifted collection of songwriters and musicians, the Tommies appeared poised to continue their streak of chart-topping records. In 1990, the choir released *Open Our Eyes*, which included the beautiful ballad "I Tried Him and I Know Him." *Open Our Eyes* became the Tommies' fourth consecutive record to top the gospel charts. Their streak of #1 albums continued with the release of *My Mind Is Made Up*. The record's ultrafunky title cut harkened back to earlier jams like "God's Got It" and "Jesus Is a Rock." As the gospel industry continued to grow, the choir was winning new fans and garnering new accolades. After decades in the business, the Tommies won their first Grammy in 1995 for *Through God's Eyes*. It was a well-deserved honor that took on special meaning given Reverend Brunson's declining health. Over a two-year span in the mid-1990s, Brunson suffered three mild strokes. Despite his health challenges, he pressed ahead in his musical ministry as he leaned on his talented cohort of directors and songwriters. In early 1995, the choir released the critically acclaimed recording *Shout*. Unfortunately, the Tommies' run was near its end.

On April 3, 1997, Milton Brunson died at his Oakbrook Terrace home. His death dealt a devastating blow for many Chicagoans, especially those immersed in the city's black religious world. Not just the leader of a popular choir and church, Brunson was a cultural anchor of West Side Chicago. "Growing up on the West Side, everyone knew who Rev. Brunson was, and it was a dream to become a Thompson Community Singer," Kimmley Ellis reflected.[12]

Of course, the Tommies' impact on gospel music reached far beyond Chicago. A sonic bridge between gospel's past and its future, the music of Reverend Milton Brunson and the Thompson Community Singers was the sound of where the art form had been and where it was going.

Along with providing gospel fans with numerous hits, Milton Brunson had also been an active participant in conversations about the genre's direction. Over the years, he had frequently registered his discontent with gospel artists who, in his view, watered down their message in order to cross over into the secular market. Gospel, he believed, could reach "the world" on its own terms. "I don't feel I need R&B sounds to try to capture people to come to church," he once told an *Ebony* reporter.[13] The music, he insisted, had to maintain its singularity. "People are looking for something that is going to give them hope. You can't shake a booty to a gospel song."[14] Brunson's comments occurred at a time when several black gospel artists had crossed over into the mainstream. Moreover, a growing number of secular labels had renewed their interest in gospel as acts like the Winans and Take 6 demonstrated the genre's profitability. The next two chapters explore black gospel artists' quest for crossover success and the internal debates it spawned within the industry.

CHAPTER 8

Through It All

Vanessa Bell Armstrong and the Perils of Crossover

In my opinion, she has the best female voice in the world.
You can't outsing Vanessa Bell Armstrong.
—OPRAH WINFREY, *The Oprah Winfrey Show*, 1986

The year 1982 marked another difficult one for the music industry. Sluggish sales, low inventory, and cash flow problems plagued record companies, major retail outlets, and mom-and-pop stores across the country. Sales plummeted in every genre, resulting in massive cutbacks in artist promotion and marketing. To make matters worse, there was the problem of piracy. Tightened budgets coupled with technological advances led to consumers recording songs from the radio on blank cassettes. These developments created monumental problems for the music industry, which had been singing the blues since 1979. That year, *New York Times* critic John Rockwell declared the golden era of sales over: "The 4 billion-a-year record business, after nearly 25 years of uninterrupted growth, has suddenly run into a period of faltering sales, staff cuts, and general demoralization."[1] To alleviate their financial problems, labels employed a wide range of strategies with the hopes of rebounding from the three-year slump. These included implementing new marketing initiatives, acquiring smaller companies, and laying off employees. Late in the summer of 1982, CBS records fired 300 workers and closed nine of its branch offices.

Not immune to the economic hardships engulfing the nation, Christian music labels also reevaluated their business practices, their marketing schemes, and the scale of their operations. "I think our market is oversaturated with product," complained Roland Lundy, vice president of Word Records. In addition to cutting down their rosters, some record labels eyed new markets. One such company was the Benson Music Group, home to the biggest Christian sensation of 1982, Sandi Patty. To expand and diversify its consumer base, Benson decided to enter the black gospel market by partnering with Onyx Records, which was under the leadership of music veteran Gentry McCreary. Even though the label was new in the game, Onyx was quite confident about its potential for success. This was partly due to one of the company's new signees: Vanessa Bell Armstrong, a vocal powerhouse from Detroit whom many deemed the next

FIGURE 16. Vanessa Bell Armstrong performing during the Allstate Gospel SuperFest 2015 at House of Hope Arena in Chicago. Photo by Raymond Boyd/Getty Images.

Mahalia or Aretha. A year after announcing its signing of Armstrong, Onyx released her debut, *Peace Be Still*.

In the early to mid-1980s, Armstrong had an impressive run as one of gospel's most heralded vocalists. Her first two records, *Peace Be Still* and *Chosen*, sold extremely well in the gospel market, exceeding even her label's expectations. Armstrong's signature cover of James Cleveland's "Peace Be Still," along with hits such as "Nobody but Jesus," "Any Way You Bless Me," and "He's Real," left listeners awestruck, as her impeccable phrasing and jaw-dropping runs put more than a few vocalists in revisionist mode.

Armstrong's star shined brightly in the three years following her debut release, but at the most inopportune time, industry politics stalled the progress of her career. On the heels of her second album, *Chosen*, the financial collapse of her record label left the rising star without a contract. Then in 1987, Armstrong released her first record for the Jive label, a secular company that envisioned crossover success for the talented songstress. Though Armstrong's voice was as strong as ever, the record's R&B sound and ambiguous lyrics left some of her hardcore fans puzzled. Later in her career, Armstrong admitted her own discomfort with some of Jive's decisions: "They were trying to direct me into the secular market, and they just lost me. Fans were wondering, 'What's up, you're going secular?'"[2] In many ways, Armstrong's tenure with Jive Records served as a cautionary tale of the dangers of overt crossover attempts and partnerships with secular labels inexperienced with the Christian market.

Aretha's Sonic Heir

Like many of contemporary gospel's biggest stars, Vanessa Bell Armstrong hailed from Detroit. The second child of Jesse and Mildred Bell, she was born on October 2, 1953. Early in childhood, Vanessa Bell demonstrated a deep passion for music. No artist moved her more than Aretha Franklin, a longtime resident of the Motor City. Franklin occupied a special place in the hearts of native Detroiters, including many musicians with aspirations for a career in the recording industry. Young female singers, in particular, practiced her hits, studied her vocals, and mimicked her mannerisms with the hopes of one day realizing their own dreams. Bell was no exception. "I wanted to be like Aretha Franklin. And so every talent show I went to, I would get up there and sing one of Aretha's songs."[3] Soon the aspiring singer moved out of her idol's shadow and began to develop her own voice. Though her parents had constantly reminded her of God's special calling on her life, it was a school program honoring the life of Dr. Martin Luther King Jr. that gave the teenager greater spiritual clarity: "I sang 'Precious Lord' in the school auditorium after Martin Luther King passed, and that's when all my running from God ceased. It was like I felt the Lord speaking to me, saying 'You know, this is what I want you to sing.' That's when I started giving my heart and soul to the Lord. An overwhelming sensation came over me when I was singing that song. It was like warmth."[4] Upon exiting the stage, she felt spiritually renewed.

Fortunately, Detroit had a community of skilled artists and teachers willing to assist in her artistic development. One such person was Mattie Moss Clark. As she had done for so many artists in the area, Clark exposed Bell to a world beyond Detroit. "Dr. Clark gave me my first break," the singer later remembered. "She took me along with the Southwest Michigan Choir to the Apollo Theater in New York, [where] we appeared with the Mighty Clouds of Joy, Shirley Caesar, James Cleveland."[5]

It was a wonderful experience, but national fame would be delayed for Vanessa Bell, who married and started a family relatively young. Her husband, Samuel Lee Armstrong, worked at a Chevrolet plant in Detroit to support their expanding family. Vanessa Bell Armstrong traveled around the city and surrounding areas singing in churches and talent shows. In her husband's view, she deserved a much bigger stage. With this in mind, he convinced her to attend the 1982 Gospel Music Workshop of America convention in Los Angeles. There, she joined other artists hoping to catch the attention of the many gospel executives roaming the halls for unsigned talent. On the last day of the convention, Armstrong managed to get on the program. Largely unknown but quite experienced, she thrilled the audience with a spirited version of "He Looked beyond My Faults (and Saw My Needs)." "She tore the place up," Samuel Armstrong proudly boasted in 1984.[6]

Chosen: A Star Is Born

After a strong performance at the GMWA, Armstrong had several labels vying for her services. The gifted singer signed with Gentry McCreary's label, Onyx. Few executives in the world of contemporary gospel music had accomplished more than McCreary, the first African American executive at Word Records. A native of Oakland who had served as manager of the Heavenly Tones in the 1960s, McCreary was a savvy promoter who had an unerring eye for talent and a fabulous relationship with black gospel radio. His most groundbreaking work came in the late 1970s and early 1980s, when he served as director of national radio promotions for Light Records.

Taking advantage of the contacts and skills he acquired during his tenure at Light, McCreary worked to build Onyx into a gospel powerhouse. The label's roster would include Armstrong, Richard Smallwood, Danniebelle Hall, Keith Pringle, and Thomas Whitfield, who served as the main producer of Armstrong's first two records. A native of Detroit, Whitfield was more than qualified to guide Armstrong through her first recording. An immensely talented composer, arranger, producer, and pianist, Whitfield was a leading architect of the urban contemporary gospel sound. Some of the most innovative gospel music of any era can be found on his first two records for Sound of Gospel, *Brand New* and *Things That We Believe*. Whitfield's training in jazz and classical music combined with his gospel background resulted in a remarkably fresh sound that earned him the respect of his mentors, his peers, and later generations of gospel performers.

Vanessa Bell Armstrong was no stranger to Whitfield's genius. "Thomas Whitfield and I grew up together. He knew my style and incorporated the music around it." Most importantly, Whitfield let Armstrong's talent take center stage: "I remember him telling me, 'You don't need a glossy production. Your voice is an instrument in itself. You can do more with one word than many people can do with one verse.'"[7] A voice as powerful as Armstrong's has the tendency to overwhelm even the most talented producers, but this was not the case for Whitfield. The two Detroit natives were a perfect match, and their chemistry was evident in the music.

Upon its release in May 1983, Armstrong's debut, *Peace Be Still*, was a major conversation piece among gospel fans and music industry insiders. Much of this had to do with her cover of one of the most iconic songs in gospel music history, James Cleveland's "Peace Be Still." To the millions of gospel fans convinced that Cleveland had had the last word on the song, Vanessa Bell Armstrong would prove otherwise. Within seconds of the song's start, her version distinguishes itself from Cleveland's. With her signature vibrato, Armstrong extends the length of the first verse considerably. On the lines "Carest thou not that we perish / How can thy lie asleep," the singer alters the tonal quality of her voice as she bends note after note. Though the story of Jesus and the disciples crossing the Sea of Galilee is a fascinating one, it's hard not to lose oneself in Armstrong's splendid vocal technique. Throughout the song, she is in full control of her instrument, lowering and increasing its intensity with the precision of a seasoned veteran. Perhaps sensing that the song's message has gotten lost in her vocal acrobatics, Armstrong slows down the pace during the last two minutes. "I'm talking about peace," the singer croons, "in your home, on your job, late in the midnight hour."[8] The softness in her voice suggests the rising star might be ministering to herself in addition to her audience.

Armstrong's vocal magic did not stop with "Peace Be Still." Her cover of Dottie Rambo's "He Looked Beyond My Faults (and Saw My Needs)" is definitive, while her performance of "He's Real," produced by Walter Hawkins, stands out as one of her finest moments on the record. Armstrong's singing proved just as inspiring on *Peace Be Still*'s up-tempo songs, particularly "Labor in Vain" and "Anyway You Bless Me." Her spitfire ad-libs and husky melisma made the latter song a fan favorite.

Peace Be Still generated considerable buzz in the gospel industry. It peaked at #3 on the gospel charts, becoming one of the biggest selling albums of the year. Taking the gospel world by storm, Armstrong received a Grammy nomination for "Peace Be Still." The honor shocked the unassuming star still grappling with her newfound success. "I'll probably be excited when I get there and see all those stars," Armstrong told the *Detroit Free Press*.[9]

Enthused by the overwhelmingly positive reception to Armstrong's first album, Onyx released her follow-up, *Chosen*, in 1984. If the record's title was intended to suggest Armstrong's unique place in the industry, the material lived up to the description. *Chosen*'s burning opener, "What He's Done for Me," finds the singer in excellent form as she stakes her claim as gospel's most daring vocalist. Her brilliance continues on the next tune, "Nobody but Jesus," a soul-stirring ballad as marvelous as "Peace Be Still." A master stylist, Armstrong drew praise from music fans and critics alike. "Her incredible range and depth of feeling echoes early Aretha," journalist Larry McKeithan raved in the *New York Amsterdam News*. "She manages to squeeze out an incredible measure of emotion out of a word, a syllable."[10]

Armstrong's talent did not escape the notice of music veterans. Moved by her first two records, jazz singer Nancy Wilson described the newcomer's voice as "exquisite." "Her riffs and runs seem impossible—she really has the pipes."[11] A singer's singer, Armstrong provided a blueprint for many aspiring musicians who carefully studied her innovative vocal techniques. "When I turned 13," gospel singer Smokie Norful later recalled, "Vanessa Bell Armstrong became like the premier vocalist in my mind. I studied her riffs and her runs on the *Peace Be Still* album. She was such an inspiration for me vocally."[12]

Twenty years after hearing Armstrong's "Peace Be Still" for the first time, scholar Michael Eric Dyson recalled, rather movingly, the song's profound impact on him. One day, Dyson's close friend James Pippin phoned him with the request that he immediately come to his house to hear a young singer who was going to "give Aretha a run for her money." To what he regarded as a ridiculous statement, Dyson quipped, "Look, bro, you don't have to get all hyperbolic." Annoyed but curious, Dyson dashed to his friend's apartment. An anxious Pippin greeted Dyson at the door and then proceeded to play the title cut of Armstrong's debut. The instrumentation at the song's opening left the skeptic Dyson unimpressed, but his emotions switched rather quickly:

> "Master," she began in an understated, clear alto declaration, delaying her next words so we could fix our minds on the meaning of her lyrics as the piano pounded out her deliberate pace. "The temp-ehhhhhhest is ray-ging." Now I had strengthened my posture and leaned in as if to grab every syllable as it spilled through the thinly wired netting of Pippin's stereo speakers. My delighted host

was grinning like a Cheshire cat. The singer slid up the word "tempest" like a plane effortless gliding into air, except she met self-induced sonic turbulence halfway through. But she navigated her voice expertly amidst the deliberate gruffness she evoked to stress the storm she was singing about.

Armstrong's unleashing of what Dyson remembered as "growling, groaning, lacerating syllables in wild succession" put him in a state of spiritual ecstasy: "She rained down such ferocious assurances of divine intervention, that the storm from which she promised God's protection seemed my only refuge." Armstrong, a transfixed Dyson concluded, was "Aretha's sonic daughter, her gospel twin." Their similarities lie not just in pitch, tone, and style, but also in their possession of "a mesmerizing, tantalizing, enthralling gift that demanded notice."[13]

In his own distinctive fashion, Dyson captured the emotional response of many gospel listeners upon their first encounter with Armstrong's voice. Listening to Armstrong for the first time was akin to entering an unknown region, where the sights and sounds are mysterious yet inviting. With songs like "Peace Be Still," "Any Way You Bless Me," "He's Real," and "Nobody but Jesus," Armstrong's impact on the gospel world was immediate and profound.

Unfortunately for the rising star, there were major problems with her label Onyx, which ended its partnership with Benson in late 1984. Only two years after deciding to dive into the black gospel market, Benson retreated back into the predominantly white world of CCM. The company closed its black division and severed its ties with Onyx. In a strange twist of events, Armstrong was now a free agent.

Pressing On

The huge success of *Chosen* and *Peace Be Still* put several labels in a bidding war for Armstrong's services. After careful consideration, Armstrong and her management team decided on Jive Records, a relatively young label under the London-based Zomba Music Group. Founded in 1981 by Clive Calder and Ralph Simon, Jive had a small yet solid lineup of artists, most notably Billy Ocean, Whodini, and Jonathan Butler. Label head Clive Calder recognized Armstrong's talent and vowed to put the absolute best record on the market: "I told Vanessa she's the best female singer I've ever heard and that we'll just keep on recording until we have an album that I'd pay $8 for."[14] Jive and Armstrong's team had intense listening sessions, which also included Armstrong's manager, Barry Hankerson, and one of the record's producers, Marvin Winans. "We sat down and listened to these tunes," Armstrong recalled, "and they just blew us away." Armstrong was excited about the material but anticipated potential backlash from some of her fans: "I don't think the older saints are going to be ready for this." Even still, Armstrong felt confident that she was moving in the right direction. Jive, she proudly noted, "[is] taking me into a broader avenue and I'm ready for it."[15]

Feeling as if Armstrong had massive crossover appeal, Jive appreciated the recent exposure the singer had received as a result of her appearance on the Winans' 1985 release, *Let My People Go*, and on one of television's most popular new programs, the *Oprah Winfrey Show*. A huge fan of the Winans, Oprah Winfrey dedicated an entire episode to gospel music in the spring of 1986. The rising star wanted to share with her expansive audience the art form that had sustained her during good and bad times. In her introductory remarks for the show, Winfrey relayed her deep love for the Winans and their latest recording, *Let My People Go*. That record featured Vanessa Bell Armstrong, who had also become one of the host's favorite singers. When introducing the audience to Armstrong, Winfrey noted that there are singers who can sing, then there are singers "who can saaang." Armstrong, Winfrey explained, fell in the latter category. The studio audience quickly learned why the talk show host held Armstrong in such high esteem. Integrating her signature runs and eruptive growls throughout her performance, Armstrong delivered moving renditions of "Teach Me Oh Lord," "Nobody but Jesus," and "What He's Done for Me." Even without a live band, she brought the energy and spontaneity expected of a live gospel performance.

Not afraid to explore the full range of her artistic gifts, Armstrong also starred in the gospel play *Don't Get God Started*. The play, coproduced by her manager, Barry Hankerson, provided the singer with the opportunity to build her fan base as well as reconnect with loyal followers. During this time, Armstrong also received additional exposure as the lead vocalist on the theme song for the NBC sitcom *Amen*.

Armstrong's high visibility heightened the anticipation for her Jive debut, which the label released in November 1987. Eponymously titled *Vanessa Bell Armstrong*, the eight-track record was a solid outing with strong contributions from producers Loris Holland, Timmy Allen, and her longtime friend from Detroit Marvin Winans. The R&B flavored "You Bring Out the Best in Me" cracked *Billboard*'s top black singles charts, while "Pressing On" held steady on gospel radio. The album also boasted two standout ballads from Winans, "The Denied Stone" and "Always." With the producers' heavy use of synthesizers and drum programming machines, the record's slick, polished sound fit in perfectly with the general trends in contemporary gospel music. But while Armstrong was anxious to build a following in the R&B market, she had no intentions of abandoning the gospel insiders who had promoted her career, particularly gospel radio announcers: "You can't forget where you come from and who helped you out in the beginning and they were faithful to me and I'm going to be faithful to them too."[16]

Upon its release, Armstrong's Jive debut had a strong following in the gospel world and performed relatively well in the R&B market, but the singer's follow-up, *Wonderful One*, confounded many. Her singing was still strong, but the material paled in comparison to her earlier work. One bright spot on the record was her cover of Labi Siffre's anti-apartheid song, "Something Inside So Strong." Several secular radio stations and video outlets put the song in rotation, but this mattered very little in terms of record sales. *Wonderful One*'s weak performance was disappointing in light of the R&B market's growing openness to urban contemporary gospel. In fact, while Jive struggled to translate Armstrong's increased visibility into sales, BeBe and CeCe Winans celebrated the gold certification of their record *Heaven*. Combined with expanding their secular following, the Winans duo maintained their Christian audience (white and black).

No one questioned Armstrong's talent, just her direction. Though she remained one of the industry's most acclaimed live performers, Armstrong's recording career was in a slump, one that even her reunion with Thomas Whitfield, the primary producer of her first two records, failed to end. Her 1993 record, *Something on the Inside*, produced some buzz at its initial release, then fizzled out. Armstrong's rut didn't escape her peers in the music industry, including an emergent talent named John P. Kee, who felt the gifted songstress had been paired with the wrong producers. "I'd hear her and think, why didn't the producer do this or that or how I would do it another way."[17]

The talented Kee would get his chance in 1995, when he served as the producer for her CD *The Secret Is Out*. With the underperforming *Something on the Inside* behind her, Armstrong welcomed her new partnership with Kee, who rushed at the opportunity to produce the album. Not since her earlier work with Whitfield had she had a producer so attentive to detail: "I used to go in the studio, lay down some runs, they'd say how great I was, and we'd all go home. But not John. He's exploring my talent and challenging me all the way."[18]

Though diverse in style and sound, Armstrong's 1995 recording, *The Secret Is Out*, melded well as a unit. The disc featured ballads, mid-tempo grooves, choir-oriented tunes in the vein of John P. Kee's material with the New Life Community Choir, and a jazzy medley of two of her signature songs, "Peace Be Still" and "Nobody but Jesus." Now in her early forties, Armstrong faced the challenge of rebuilding her career. Fortunately, her voice was still a wonder to behold. To be sure, age had thinned her upper register and her squalls lost a bit of their edge. But her supreme intelligence as a vocalist enabled her to make the necessary adjustments. On the record and during her promotion performances, Armstrong was in exceptional form.

Nevertheless, *The Secret Is Out* suffered from poor sales. A disappointed Kee attributed the lack of enthusiasm for the record to poor timing. In the two years between *Something on the Inside* and *The Secret Is Out*, the gospel industry had experienced a generational shift in terms of power and sales. This was largely due to the arrival of Kirk Franklin and the monumental success of his debut, which by 1995 had sold more than one million copies. A straight-ahead gospel album, *Kirk Franklin and the Family* was a "hybrid of high-stepping worship and praise with traditional church music."[19] Franklin's rise coincided with another important stylistic shift: the growing popularity of praise and worship music. This shift was evident in Fred Hammond and Radical for Christ's *The Inner Court* and CeCe Winans's first solo outing, *Alone in His Presence*. These two records differed significantly from the slick urban contemporary gospel songs that had made Hammond and Winans household names in black Christian communities during the 1980s.

Despite the changes in the industry, Vanessa Bell Armstrong looked optimistically toward the future. "I have not reached my peak," she insisted. "I'm still climbing." Her climb would not be an easy one. Though she would continue to record, her popularity never reached her early 1980s level.

While the economics and politics of the record industry might have undermined her career at critical moments, Armstrong's talent and impact ensured her legacy would be long-lasting. One hears her influence in the music of Kim Burrell, Faith Evans, Kelly Price, Mariah Carey, and many others. On a deeper level, she occasioned a critical transformation in how the voice functioned as an instrument in gospel music. Together with the Clark Sisters and Daryl Coley, she helped usher in a new, more vibrant style of singing, one immersed in the gospel tradition yet borrowing heavily from jazz and soul music.

CHAPTER 9

Hold Up the Light

The Crossover Success of BeBe and CeCe Winans

> Despite our Pentecostal upbringing the Winans children were as much a product of our Motown environment as were the kids who lived next door in Detroit. We inhaled the fresh melodies and let the mellow harmonies of the music in the streets run across our minds every time we were in their reach. The only difference was that we left those sounds in the street whenever we crossed the threshold of our home.
>
> —CECE WINANS, *On a Positive Note: Her Joyous Faith, Her Life in Music, and Her Everyday Blessings* (with Renita J. Weems)

The year 1987 was an exciting one for Detroit gospel. Thomas Whitfield, the Winans, Vanessa Bell Armstrong, and Commissioned all released new material. The Queen of Soul, Aretha Franklin, returned to the gospel fold with her double album, *One Lord, One Faith, One Baptism*. And BeBe and CeCe Winans released their first recording with Sparrow Records.

No longer referred to as "the other Winans," BeBe and CeCe established themselves as formidable artists with a commercial appeal that eventually surpassed that of their older and highly successful brothers, the quartet known as the Winans. In their peak years as a duo, the Winans siblings racked up numerous Grammy, Dove, and Stellar Awards, graced the covers of religious and secular magazines, and performed for white, black, and Latinx audiences across the nation. Well-known beyond the gospel community, BeBe and CeCe Winans were intricately connected to the celebrity culture of the black pop world. Their records featured some of the biggest artists in popular music, from their dear friend Whitney Houston to soul balladeer Luther Vandross to rapper-entertainer MC Hammer. In contrast to their older brothers, the duo's crossover story involved much more than their success in pop music. In an industry still deeply divided along racial lines, BeBe and CeCe Winans had a large following among white contemporary Christian music fans. Their polished productions and inspirational lyrics endeared them to teenagers and young adults who rarely ventured into the world of black gospel. To this day, their music still holds a special place in the hearts of CCM fans. A few years back, when *CCM Magazine* ranked the greatest albums in the history of contemporary Christian music, BeBe and CeCe's *Different Lifestyles* was the only album by a black act in the top ten. Its predecessor, *Heaven*, was ranked #37, two slots ahead of Kirk Franklin's *Nu Nation Project*.[1]

More than any other act of the late 1980s and early 1990s, BeBe and CeCe Winans demonstrated the massive crossover potential of black gospel music. Their two best-selling records, *Heaven* and *Different Lifestyles*, were monumental achievements. With its three radio hits, *Heaven* became the first black gospel album to sell 500,000 units since Aretha Franklin's 1972 classic *Amazing Grace*. The historic record featured pop icon Whitney Houston, an avid gospel fan

FIGURE 17. BeBe and CeCe Winans and Whitney Houston backstage at Harlem's Apollo Theater on May 15, 1989. Photo by Jack Vartoogian/Getty Images.

who counted BeBe and CeCe as two of her closest friends. A groundbreaking recording, *Heaven* amassed numerous awards and accolades for the brother and sister duo.[2]

With full marketing and publicity support from their record labels Sparrow and Capitol, BeBe and CeCe maintained their crossover success with their next release, *Different Lifestyles*. Yielding two #1 R&B hits, *Different Lifestyles* moved one million units, one of the few records in gospel history to achieve platinum certification from the RIAA.

No small factor in the group's appeal was the songwriting gifts of BeBe Winans. A self-described humanist, BeBe aspired to create art that reflected much more than his religious identity as a Christian. Unlike most gospel artists, he refused to compartmentalize the sacred and the secular, the flesh and the spirit. "One thing that I've accepted, before I'm a Christian, I'm a human being. When He formed me in my mother's womb, I was a human first, before I was a Christian."[3] This perspective pushed him toward topics rarely explored in gospel: the desire for intimacy, marital discord, depression. A self-confessional songwriter, BeBe spoke openly and honestly about his personal struggles. In doing so, he challenged the idea of religious conversion and Christian salvation as the only solutions to life's many problems. To achieve individual happiness and by extension a beloved community, he argued, Christians had to rethink their relationship not just to God but also to the larger world. If a semblance of heaven on earth was to be achieved—and that was a goal for the optimistic Winans duo—then humans had to create a brotherhood and sisterhood. That is, they had to reconcile themselves to each other.

In creating self-reflective, uplifting music that appealed to millions, BeBe and CeCe Winans drew inspiration from their life experiences. Thus, their art bore the imprint of their upbringing in Detroit, their early work for the televangelism empire PTL, and their ongoing effort to grapple with the question of what it means to be Christian and human in the modern world.

From Motown to PTL

Children of 1960s Detroit, Benjamin (BeBe) and Priscilla (CeCe) Winans grew up in a large family under the guidance of their mother and father, David and Delores Winans. The Winans parents had their seventh and last son, Benjamin, on September 17, 1962. Since only eight years separated BeBe from his eldest brother, David, he developed a strong bond with his older siblings—all boys. He was also close to his younger sisters, Priscilla, Angelique, and Debra. The oldest of the girls, CeCe Winans was born on October 8, 1964. Shy, reserved, and extremely quiet, CeCe adhered closely to her parents' Christian teachings and rarely stepped out of line. Though frequently paired together, CeCe and

BeBe had very different personalities. More outgoing than his younger sister, BeBe learned at an early age the importance of asserting one's voice in a family of twelve. If you wanted a seat at the table or in the car, a solo in the junior choir, or a word with an exhausted parent who had nine other children vying for their attention, then you better speak up and move fast.

Like all of their siblings, BeBe and CeCe Winans centered their lives around family, church, and gospel music. By the time the two reached their adolescent years, there were two singing groups in the family: the Winans and the Winans Part 2. The Winans consisted of brothers Ronald, Marvin, Carvin, and Michael. Winans Part 2 consisted of BeBe and CeCe, their slightly older brother Daniel, and Marvin's then-wife, Vickie. The younger Winans group showed great promise, but a call from Charlotte, North Carolina, would put BeBe and CeCe on a different course.

Family friend and musician Howard McCrary invited the two Winans siblings to audition for Jim and Tammy Faye Bakker's *PTL Club*, a popular religious show looking to hire additional singers. The brainchild of the Bakkers, the *PTL Club* had roots in the *700 Club*, a Christian show Jim Bakker hosted from 1966 to 1974. The *700 Club* was the flagship program for the Portsmouth, Virginia–based Christian Broadcasting Network, which eventually expanded into Atlanta and the Dallas–Fort Worth area. A series of developments led Ted Turner, the owner of WRET-TV, an independent station in Charlotte, to solicit Bakker's services for an open time slot. Enthused about the possibilities at WRET, Bakker struck a deal with Turner and began airing a new show called the *PTL Club*. A year later, the show launched nationally, building a strong following among evangelicals throughout the country. The ambitious Bakker then proceeded to build a Christian satellite network. He purchased 2,300 acres of land in Fort Mill, South Carolina, a small town less than twenty miles south of Charlotte. With the goal of creating a spiritual oasis equipped with everything their Christian fans could ever need or want, the Bakkers built Heritage USA in 1978. The sprawling site included a resort hotel, a campground, a shopping complex, a residential area, a theme park, and a television studio. The Bakkers' vision meshed perfectly with the secular and spiritual desires of many evangelicals. As Emily Johnson explains, "During a historical moment in which more and more Pentecostal believers were climbing into the middle class, the over-the-top experience of Heritage USA helped to reinforce the message of a new Pentecostalism. Far from banning makeup, soda, and leisure activities as their forebears had, this new generation embraced some measure of self-indulgence and they gave it Christian outlets, including a theme park."[4]

Though largely unfamiliar with PTL and the televangelism phenomenon, BeBe and CeCe Winans welcomed the opportunity to advance their careers. With their parents' permission, the duo traveled to Charlotte and auditioned for the show, which did not go as smoothly as expected. The producers loved CeCe but rejected BeBe. Frightened by the idea of their teenage daughter living alone in a city down south, the Winans parents informed PTL that the duo was a package deal. If BeBe was not given a position at the network, then CeCe would have no choice but to decline its offer. Wanting CeCe desperately, the producers at PTL agreed to hire the pair.

Leaving Detroit for this new opportunity in Charlotte was exciting for the teens but also a bit scary. Even though the Bakkers preached a message of racial unity, PTL had a predominantly white staff and audience. "It was awkward and strange there in the beginning, especially for BeBe and me," CeCe later admitted. "It took us a while to get used to being around white people."[5] One especially vexing issue for the pair was the audience's worship style, which CeCe found far too reserved. "Learning to sing in front of white audiences was by far one of the hardest things to adjust to. I'd never sang before such quiet audiences. . . . We could be up on stage singing our hearts out, but the audiences never gave us an ounce of support. Not an 'Amen' in the place. No 'Praise the Lord.' Not even a 'Sing children!' as we might have gotten back in Detroit. Not a whimper of feedback."[6]

Charlotte also posed a unique set of challenges for the two. Whereas Detroit had a population of more than one million, Charlotte had a population of around 320,000 at the time of the siblings' arrival. Unlike Detroit, however, Charlotte was a city on the rise, a shining jewel of the New South's sunbelt economy. Its population expanded at a rate of 26 percent during the 1980s with annexation and in-migration.[7] Like the Winans duo, many blacks moved to the city for greater economic opportunities. Then in 1983, Charlotte elected its first black mayor, Harvey Grant, a positive sign for a city once in the national spotlight for its heated debates around school busing.

Even so, CeCe missed Detroit. "Charlotte was too tame for my northern-city-girl tastes. . . . In Detroit there was electricity in the air, even when just traveling between home, church, and school. People were always milling about. Music was always blasting from some radio or tape deck somewhere. Cars were backed up on the highway." Such energy, she disappointedly observed, was missing in Charlotte. "All the stores in Charlotte closed early. We had to go miles to find a black church. We were starving for color."[8]

Notwithstanding the differences between Charlotte and Detroit, the Winans duo eventually found their groove in the city and, perhaps more importantly, at PTL. With their immense talent and youthful energy, the brother and sister soon developed a close bond with PTL fans, including the silent ones. In the process, the two learned an important lesson about the diversity of religious experiences within the body of Christ. "Singing at PTL expanded our horizons," CeCe recalled. "We learned to accept that our way was not the only way to worship or to sing to God."[9] Over time, BeBe and CeCe led more songs and even became more visible within Charlotte's religious circles. Their success did not escape the notice of the business-minded Bakkers. To capitalize on the siblings' popularity, PTL records released the duo's debut album, *Lord Lift Us Up*.

With assistance from Marvin Winans and producer Bill Maxwell, the duo had access to some of the finest musicians working in gospel. Uneven but impressive, their debut featured the inspirational "Up Where We Belong," Andraé Crouch's "We Are Not Ashamed," the bouncy Marvin Winans–penned tune "The Giver of Life," and several ballads from BeBe. Included in PTL's "thank you" package to contributors who gave money (including life partnerships) to the network, *Lord Lift Us Up*—which could also be purchased in select Christian stores—debuted on *Billboard*'s gospel charts on January 26, 1985. Even with limited distribution, *Lord Lift Us Up* held steady on the charts for more than a year.

Looking back, one can see how PTL provided BeBe and CeCe with more than just an employment opportunity and greater exposure to white Christians. Its abundant life theology and positive thinking approach offered the duo an alternative to the lessons taught in their Pentecostal household and church. It also gave them a touch of the showbiz lifestyle found in Hollywood. As John Wigger notes in his detailed account of the rise and fall of Jim and Tammy Faye Bakker, PTL was a space in which celebrity culture was embraced as a means to advance one's evangelical mission.[10]

Having gained invaluable experience from PTL and the Bakkers, the Winans pair were ready for their next endeavor. The moderate success of their PTL release had caught the attention of several record labels, including Sparrow, which signed the act in 1986. Founded by Billy Ray Hearn, Sparrow was the largest independent Christian label at the time of the duo's signing. Though not particularly known in the black gospel market, the label had recently attracted attention for inking a deal with the pop singer Deniece Williams. Two years after Williams's smash hit "Let's Hear It for the Boy" topped the pop charts, the songstress revisited her sacred roots with *So Glad I Know*. The record won two Grammys and appeared on the gospel, inspirational, pop, and R&B charts. Williams was an immediate beneficiary of Sparrow's new distribution deal with Capitol, a deal that yielded a dramatic increase in the company's sales in the non-Christian market. "Capitol has really done a great deal to improve our sales in the secular marketplace," Hearn informed *Billboard* magazine in 1986. "In the past secular sales have amounted to about 9% of our business. They have increased to 15%."[11]

These developments boded well for Sparrow's new act BeBe and CeCe Winans, who in the opinion of many record executives had enormous crossover potential. Young, gifted, telegenic, and marketable, the duo simply needed to harness their talent into a distinctive sound that would set them apart from their urban contemporary gospel peers. They found the perfect partner in Keith Thomas, a talented musician who would go on to produce hits for superstars like Vanessa Williams and Amy Grant.[12] A native of Atlanta, Thomas had been a staff writer and producer for Word Records during the early 1980s. His clients included some of Christian music's best-selling acts—Carman, the Gaithers, Dion, and Sandi Patty. Experienced in the music industry but a relative new-comer to African American gospel, Thomas found a perfect outlet for his musical ideas in BeBe and CeCe Winans, two singers with powerful voices that could easily adapt to a pop context. Likewise, the duo found a welcoming producer who appreciated their unique talent and their vision for gospel music. "There's a real chemistry with Keith," BeBe explained to journalist Bob Darden. "We talk, he plays the piano. He can interpret our lyrics and do things we never thought about doing."[13]

It was a perfect marriage of musical personalities and sounds, as evident on the duo's first offering for Sparrow, *BeBe and CeCe Winans*. The eponymous record had no traces of the Winans' Pentecostal roots. There were no references to spiritual baptism or the benefits of living a sanctified life, no extended praise breaks. It was slick R&B-influenced gospel that pivoted around the themes of persevering through adversity, God's deep love and concern for each person's well-being, and the healing power of forgiveness. The record opens with the infectious "I.O.U. Me." BeBe's lush baritone blends perfectly with CeCe's sultry alto as they weave in and out of the song's melody with surgical precision. The two also turn in superb performances on "Love Said Not So," a fan favorite featuring their older siblings the Winans, and "Change Your Nature," a melodic tune in which they touch on familiar "urban crisis" themes. Though best when improvising off each other, BeBe and CeCe made sure to establish their own individuality as musicians. CeCe solos on "No Hiding Place," "For Always," and "In Return," while BeBe handles the lead vocals on "Call Me" and "Still in Love with You."

Listening to the record, you can hear the duo's maturity as vocalists. You also notice the producer's attention to detail. This was not a rushed product. "Compared with the three days BeBe and I had spent in the studio years earlier recording the PTL album, months went into making this album. They wouldn't release it until they were sure the sound coming out of the speakers was the same as what they were hearing in their heads."[14]

The care with which the label and the artists approached the recording paid off. With three radio friendly singles, including "I.O.U. Me," which received some airplay on R&B stations, *BeBe and CeCe Winans* expanded the duo's fan base considerably. Not just popular among African Americans, the tandem also dipped into the fan base of artists like Amy Grant, Michael W. Smith, and Steven Curtis Chapman. A testament to their crossover appeal, they even opened for Sandi Patty, one of CCM's biggest hitmakers. While they appreciated the additional exposure from touring with Patty, the duo preferred to hit the road alone. "When you tour with someone of that magnitude, you don't get a good perspective of who you are," BeBe Winans opined.[15]

Touring enabled the duo to connect with fans, but it also forced them to confront their complex relationship with church leaders. Though their audience was primarily gospel music fans, the Winans duo preferred the freedom of more secular venues. "We still get an occasional church," BeBe noted, "but we prefer not to. There's just a freedom we have in an auditorium." Of particular concern for BeBe was the desire of some pastors to censor their material. "I love the pastors we work with, but some disagree with the songs we sing or think some of the songs we sing don't minister in the way they'd like."[16] Not one who absorbed criticism easily, BeBe preferred to avoid confrontation by not dealing with churches or pastors who questioned the duo's religious commitments. As BeBe explained, "I get hurt with that kind of talk. It's a tough industry for someone who is tenderhearted anyway. I don't like to even offend my enemies, so it has been easier to stay away."[17]

BeBe's stance on performing in churches reflected his temperament as well as the duo's growing popularity. Not only did they have one of the hottest records in the Christian music industry, but they were also racking up some of the industry's most coveted awards. Much to BeBe and CeCe's delight, they were nominated for three Dove Awards, winning in the category of Best New Artist. The duo also won in the Best New Artist category at the Stellar Awards. And at the 1988 Grammys, CeCe emerged victorious in the Best Soul Gospel Female Performance category.

As the duo rose to the top of the gospel world, they not only picked up their share of awards but also acquired a very powerful and influential friend, Whitney Houston. Enamored with the duo's sound and inspirational messages, Houston befriended the Winans siblings in 1988. Their talent and spiritual commitments resonated deeply with Houston, who, like them, derived great artistic inspiration and spiritual sustenance from the black church. A native of Newark, New Jersey, Houston honed her skills in her family's church, New Hope Baptist. The gifted singer, whose family, the Drinkards, had roots in gospel, became the breakout star of 1985 when Arista dropped her debut, *Whitney Houston*. Quickly becoming one of the era's biggest stars, Houston released one pop smash after another within a year's time.

Though Houston pursued a career in pop, gospel remained close to her heart. And no gospel act excited her more than BeBe and CeCe Winans, who offered the pop star not just a musical connection but also friendship. Coming off the record-breaking success of her first album, which sold more than 7 million copies, and caught in the whirlwind of promoting her second release (*Whitney*), Houston appreciated the spiritual grounding her relationship with the Winans duo provided: "What I found in BeBe and CeCe was the way I was raised and the way I grew up, and it kind of just made me feel a lot more placed when all this hoopla (newfound fame) was happening."[18] Very public about their friendship, Houston and the Winans twosome were frequently seen at concerts and industry functions together. Their love and affection for each other was transparent and genuine. As BeBe Winans later related, "The main joy with Whitney is there's such a chemistry it's almost as if she was born and raised with us because the energy she gives is the same, the style is the same. It's like 'Wait a minute, was you over at my house sleeping in the basement and didn't tell nobody?'"[19] Always willing to assist her friends, Houston was a huge presence and influence on the duo's next record, *Heaven*.

BeBe and CeCe Strike Gold

Perfectly suited for R&B fans, as well as for contemporary gospel listeners, *Heaven* was a cohesive, eleven-song set with irresistible hooks, catchy melodies, soulful crooning, and heartfelt lyrics. The record yielded three crossover hits, "Heaven," "Lost without You," and "Celebrate New Life." The latter song featured Whitney Houston, who also lent her vocals on "Hold Up the Light." The duo made no attempt to appease gospel purists troubled by their contemporary sound. Sonically, this was an R&B record. And yet, the record's messages reflected their faith. On songs like "Heaven" and "You," the duo extended the offer of Christian salvation to nonbelievers. But as with almost everything they did, BeBe and CeCe spread the gospel on their own terms. Despite their Pentecostal background, the duo stayed clear of fire-and-brimstone proselytizing.

Their approach paid off. The lead single, "Heaven," performed well on R&B stations like KJLH in Los Angeles, WTMP in Tampa, XHRM in San Diego, and WHUR in Washington, D.C. WHUR DJ Mike Archie credited the song's success to its popularity among the black adult contemporary crowd: "This song appeals to upper-demo adults who reacted quickly and went out and purchased the album. Early on, we tested the waters before we dove in. It has been great for a.m. drive, similar in performance to 'Mornin'' by Al Jarreau."[20] Like the album's title cut, "Lost without You" also received strong radio play from R&B stations. With the crossover success of "Heaven" and "Lost Without You," the record was certified gold.

A commercial success, *Heaven* also amassed numerous awards, including two Grammys. At the 1990 Grammys, the Winans siblings won in the categories of Best Gospel Vocal Performance Female and Best Gospel Vocal Performance Male. Few were surprised with the duo's success at the Grammys, but their dominance at the Gospel Music Association's Dove Awards caught some off guard. BeBe and CeCe won Group of the Year, Contemporary Black Gospel Song of the Year, Contemporary Song of the Year, and Contemporary Album of the Year. Once again, the Winans duo represented one of the few African American gospel acts whose success was not relegated to the traditionally black categories.

In the aftermath of *Heaven*'s phenomenal success, BeBe and CeCe Winans toured widely in both the United States and abroad. They also contributed to the music projects of several family members and industry friends. These projects included Ronald Winans's *Family and Friends* recording, Whitney Houston's *I'm Your Baby Tonight*, Take 6's *So Much 2 Say*, and Melba Moore's "Lift Every Voice and Sing." These side projects pleased but hardly satisfied hardcore fans, who clamored for new material from the duo.

Then finally, in the summer of 1991, the duo released their highly anticipated CD *Different Lifestyles*. The record featured three hit singles, "Addictive Love," "I'll Take You There," and "It's O.K." Though *Different Lifestyles* enlisted some of the biggest names in gospel and secular music—Whitney Houston, MC Hammer, Luther Vandross, Mavis Staples, Take 6, and the Winans—the record's success stemmed largely from BeBe and CeCe's unique talents, particularly their strong pop instincts and savvy marketing skills. The duo selected as their first single "Addictive Love," a mid-tempo ballad that sounds more R&B than gospel, more secular than sacred, more blue-light basement soul than Wednesday night prayer service. In the accompanying video, which played frequently on BET's *Video Soul* and *Video Vibrations*, the Winans duo performed against the backdrop of a lush waterfront property. None of the visual reference points for religious music—a church or a gospel choir donned in robes—was present. In fact, if one turned down the volume, you would have never guessed the video was for a gospel song.

With strong backing from Capitol, "Addictive Love" raced up the radio and sales charts. The song held the top position on *Billboard*'s R&B singles chart for two weeks. This was the first but not the last #1 hit for the Winans pair. On the heels of the success of "Addictive Love," the duo released "I'll Take You There," a remake of the Staple Singers' 1971 classic. BeBe and CeCe's version featured soul legend Mavis Staples, who worked her vocal magic on the song's bridge. Once again, the duo struck gold as the song reached the top position on the R&B charts. It was the first and only time a gospel act would have two consecutive #1 songs on *Billboard*'s R&B singles charts. Wanting to move as many units as possible, Capitol squeezed out another top ten hit with "It's O.K.," a dramatic ballad based on BeBe Winans's marital woes. The song documents a couple working through the stages of anger, forgiveness, reconciliation, and healing. On this ballad, there is no division between BeBe's public persona and his private life.

Throughout the record, from the Luther Vandross–arranged "Searching for Love" to the pensive "You Know and I Know," there are moments when there is no resolution in sight, no visible light at the end of the proverbial tunnel. Joy, the duo seem to say, does not always come in the morning. In many ways, such openness about life's enduring heartaches and pains endeared them to listeners wrestling with their own personal issues.

With the success of "Addictive Love," "I'll Take You There," and "It's O.K.," *Different Lifestyles* hit the 1 million sales mark by 1993. The record also secured the twosome a slew of awards—Grammys, Stellars, and Doves—as well as cover stories in several national magazines and newspapers.

The crossover success of *Different Lifestyles* occasioned some interesting debates within and beyond the world of gospel about the genre's direction. As it had often done in the past, *Ebony* magazine provided a space for musicians and fans to weigh in on the state and future of black gospel music. In March 1992, the monthly published the article "The Gospel Controversy: Are the New Songs Too Jazzy and Too Worldly?" In the article, several musicians opined on gospel's direction, the merits of its crossover attempts, and the need for it to maintain its distinctiveness as an art form. Moving away from conversations about lyrics, some traditionalists expressed concern about the music's sonic directions. Frank Williams, of the Mississippi Mass Choir and the Jackson Southernaires, cautioned his peers against abandoning those formal gestures and qualities that separated gospel from other genres. "If you heard B. B. King, people wouldn't have to tell you it's the blues. If you heard Elvis Presley, it's rock 'n roll. Gospel music should be the same way. When people hear it they should know it's gospel music."[21]

In the months after the article's publication, several *Ebony* readers weighed in on the debate over gospel's direction. Sixteen-year-old Tawanda Gray of Baltimore adored the Winans duo and other urban contemporary gospel acts and found their work important to advancing the message of Jesus Christ: "I may not have known Mahalia Jackson or how majestically she sang, but one thing I do know is that young folk are being saved through 'Addictive Love.'" Noting that she understood and sympathized with "how the older saints may feel about contemporary gospel music," she grounded her support of the Winans duo and other younger acts in scripture. "The Bible says to go and teach all nations baptizing them in the name of the Father, Son, and Holy Ghost. So whichever method reaches the unsaved, go for it."

Not in agreement with Gray, Fern Porter of Wellsville, Ohio, wondered whether the sonic quality of the Winans' music prevented them from truly reaching the unsaved. "One day I was listening to BeBe and CeCe's 'Addictive Love,'" she recalled. "My brother, who is not saved, came in and asked me what I was doing listening to that kind of music. I had to explain that it was a gospel song. He then asked 'if it was supposed to be a gospel song why didn't it say anything about God or Jesus?'" Her brother's query pushed her to consider a larger question about the Winans' music: "If the purpose of giving their songs a jazzy beat was to get the message of God to people who don't go to church, how can they do this if those people don't even know the song is a gospel song, because the artist chose to omit the words 'God' or 'Jesus' and replace them with 'Him' or 'You.' Seems to me the artists are defeating the purpose by doing this." Left unaddressed in this reader's insightful remarks was the extent to which the duo's sound also appealed to young kids and teenagers in the church turned off by traditional gospel. As one reader communicated, urban contemporary gospel served as a useful tool in keeping her children firmly rooted in the teachings and message of Christ. "We'd rather have them listen to any form of gospel with gospel lyrics than punk, rock, heavy metal, etc." This parent's reasoning moved some but not others. Believing gospel should be kept in its "pure form," Charles Turner of New Jersey was convinced black sacred music had lost its way. Christians, he argued, must take a stand. "Don't turn our churches into ballrooms. Let us pray in quiet dignity."[22]

Not all criticism of the duo's music emerged from the gospel community. Nor was it all centered on their lyrical ambiguity. Some music critics found the Winans siblings' sound too derivative. Others thought the duo lacked soul. In his review of *Different Lifestyles*, *Washington Post* critic Geoffrey Himes dismissed the twosome's offering as unadventurous pop lacking any real punch. "If you want an example of how syrupy synths and mechanical drum programming can make a pop-gospel album sound gummed up and stiff, check out BeBe and CeCe Winans "Different Lifestyles.""[23] Though much gentler in his review, Edwin Smith of *Rejoice* questioned whether the two were losing their identity:

> All in all, *Different Lifestyles* is good but one wonders if BeBe and CeCe can maintain their originality and uniqueness while producing music that caters to commercial success. Much of the project sounds like they were after the sounds made famous by producers like Jimmy Jam and Terry Lewis, L.A. Reid and Babyface, and Narada Michael Walden. As such one cannot distinguish readily that special something known as the Winans sound. It would be a tragedy for the name that has become legendary in innovating gospel music to become regulated to the rank of those with formula success but no creativity.

In Smith's view, *Different Lifestyles* was a letdown. "This album, for all its attempts at innovation, falls flat in the originality Winans' fans have come to expect."[24]

This was neither the first nor the last critique of their sound. But by this time, the duo had learned to handle critiques from within and outside the church. This was especially the case for BeBe, who was committed to expanding his influence in the music world. Taking advantage of his and CeCe's high profile, BeBe ventured into more production work for other artists. In addition to producing a song ("Jesus Loves Me") on Whitney Houston's *Bodyguard* soundtrack, he produced records for the Clark Sisters, Margaret Bell, and his younger sisters Angie and Debbie.

These side projects, along with a heavy touring schedule, delayed the duo's return to the studio. In fact, three years passed before *Relationships*, the follow-up to *Different Lifestyles*, appeared in stores. Thanks to the singles "If Anything Ever Happened to You" and "Stay with Me," the record sold more than 500,000 units, earning the twosome their third gold certification. But despite fans' excitement about their return, something was missing from the duo. Their television appearances and performances lacked the ebullience and joy so visible in their earlier days. No longer were they the twenty-something artists elated to have a platform most gospel acts could only dream of. Now they were seasoned veterans struggling to balance their love for music, their commitment to their ministry, and the harsh business realities of the record industry.

Wanting to pursue other projects, including a solo record, BeBe Winans felt the act had run its course. Thus, gospel's most successful duo amicably parted ways after the release of *Relationships*. Fortunately for Sparrow Records, CeCe quickly emerged as a formidable solo artist. Her 1995 solo debut, *Alone in His Presence*, sold 1 million copies, despite its dramatic departure from the classic BeBe and CeCe sound. Less R&B and more CCM, *Alone in His Presence* was a foundational record in the expanding praise and worship genre. CeCe's popularity also increased with the release of "Count on Me," her popular duet with Whitney Houston from the *Waiting to Exhale* soundtrack. Moving more toward R&B than gospel, BeBe continued his exploration into more relationship-centered topics with his solo projects, *BeBe Winans* and *Love and Freedom*. Neither record sold as well as his sister's solo releases, but they did produce a couple of moderate radio hits.

Even though BeBe's and CeCe's tenure as solo artists has exceeded their time as a duo, their collective work from 1987 to 1994 had a profound impact on the evolution and development of gospel music. While frequently maligned by gospel traditionalists who felt as if they were too immersed in the sounds and lyrics of R&B, the pair were deeply committed to advancing gospel music as both art and ministry. It was their desire to see the genre expand not just commercially but also sonically and lyrically. As we shall see in the pages ahead, they were not alone in their efforts to take gospel to higher ground. Their vision of a more expansive gospel sound found expression in the work of three artists to which the next two chapters turn: John P. Kee, Take 6, and the Sounds of Blackness.

CHAPTER 10

Outside the County Line

The Southern Soul of John P. Kee

> He was wonderful in the way he employed conscious and
> unconscious art.... He brought into play the full gamut
> of his wonderful voice, a voice—what shall I say?—
> not an organ or trumpet, but rather of a trombone, the
> instrument possessing above all others the power to
> express the wide varied emotions encompassed by the
> human voice and with greater amplitude.
>
> —JAMES WELDON JOHNSON, *God's Trombones*

> South going to do it again.
>
> —AL GREEN, "Georgia Boy"

More than thirty years have passed since my first encounter with the music of
John P. Kee, but the memory of that experience remains fresh in my mind. On
a weekend visit to my aunt's house, where gospel music played from sunup to
sundown, we both found ourselves mesmerized by a new song: Kee's "Wait on
Him." Within seconds of the song's opening verse, my attention shifted from
mildly interested to fully engaged as Kee's powerful voice ripped through the
speakers: "I'm going to run this race, if I go by myself," Kee sang as the choir
roared: "Wait on Jeeee-suuuus." As Kee and the choir riffed off each other, bassist
Andrew Gouche, guitarist Jimmy Hill, and drummers George Clinkscale and
Calvin Livingstone held down the rhythm section. During the extended vamp,
Kee ad-libbed with a ferociousness reminiscent of Joe Ligon of the Mighty
Clouds of Joy: "They that wait on the Lord, shall renew their strength.... They
shall mount up on wings, as eagles. They shall run, not get weary."[1] This was the
sound of Christian faith forged in the crucible of the southern black church.

The release of *Wait on Him* in 1989 marked the beginning of a remarkable
creative run for Kee and his New Life Community Choir (NLCC). Between
1989 and 1996, Kee released hugely popular singles as well as the critically acclaimed records *Wash Me* and *Show Up!* (which was certified gold). Enjoying

widespread radio play, sold-out concerts, and high record sales, Kee won the hearts of thousands of gospel lovers with his signature voice and classic songs. Not since James Cleveland had a male vocalist in the gospel world occupied such a ubiquitous presence on gospel radio. Tunes like "The Storm Is Passing Over," "Lily in the Valley," "Never Shall Forget," "Standing in the Need," "Wait on Him," "Wash Me," and the smash hit "Jesus Is Real" were in constant rotation. These

FIGURE 18. John P. Kee performing at the Indiana Convention Center in Indianapolis. Photo by Michael Hickey/WireImage for Gospel Music Channel.

songs were also part of the repertoire of countless black gospel choirs across the country. Even as the black religious community became increasingly diverse, Kee's music held an esteemed place in a variety of African American churches, from Pentecostal to Baptist.

Especially down south, Kee's blue-collar aesthetic and country home vibe earned a special place in the hearts of gospel music fans, particularly those who saw themselves or their families' history in his work. A proud southerner, Kee frequently transported his listeners to the black South, where women, men, and children cared for and loved each other, where elders shared their wisdom with the young, where the church anchored the social and cultural lives of a striving people. Kee was an artist for whom the South's past and present supplied endless inspiration and material. On both his studio and live recordings, he can be found resurrecting the spirit of his father, honoring the religiosity and deep faith of his grandmother, and reflecting on his life-changing encounters with ordinary southern women and men in the streets of Charlotte, North Carolina. Throughout his discography, the South looms large as an incubator of his cultural, religious, and political sensibilities. Kee's South is neither monolithic nor static but a geography constantly responding to new political forces and new social realities.

Kee's musical engagements with the South reflected larger trends in African American culture. Throughout the region, many southern black artists sought to articulate what literary scholar Thadious Davis refers to as the "regionality of the black self." As Davis notes in "Reclaiming the South," "the recognition of place as a major aspect of identity and the reunion of blacks positioned communally to face a new day" constituted a major theme in the literary and musical productions of many self-identified black southerners, including John P. Kee.[2] Especially on his earlier recordings, Kee's sonic landscape included numerous signifiers of the black South—praying grandmothers, pickup trucks, hymn-raising elders, and bluesy guitar licks drenched in the black quartet sound.

Though Kee frequently looked back on his childhood and his southern rearing, he also spoke to contemporary issues facing young African Americans. A devout Christian who had a bout with drug addiction before breaking into the industry, the talented musician routinely confronted the harsh realities of postindustrial America and freely discussed his own personal struggles. "When I speak of deliverance," Kee testified on his album *Wash Me*, "I know what I'm talking about."[3] Drug addition, crime, violence, economic hardship—all of these issues surfaced in Kee's music, which he hoped would serve as a source of inspiration for young people. "To me, a successful role model is not always the guy who's been on top all his life," Kee said. "To me, people understand more when it's somebody who was once down, bound for destruction, and something saved them."[4]

Coming to gospel superstardom in his late twenties, Kee had a clear vision of his place in the gospel industry. He envisioned himself as a unifier, a musician who would bring diverse audiences together. Young people definitely had a special place in his heart, but he also had a deep commitment to older fans: "There are a lot of older people who love this music and still buy albums, and I want to reach them with it."[5] Kee desired a fan base reflective of the intergenerational community that loved, fostered, and protected him as a child.

North Carolina Beginnings

John Prince Kee was born on June 4, 1962, in Durham County, North Carolina. The fifteenth child of John Henry and Lizzie Mae Kee, the young John lived on the outskirts of Durham until the age of five, when his father started work as a foreman at a local brickyard. In many ways, the world in which young John entered was radically different from that of his older brothers and sisters, due in no small part to the growing political determination of African Americans in Durham.

Notwithstanding its image as a progressive southern city, Durham was racist to its core. Even when the white power structure appeared to bend in favor of African Americans, its actions were often more symbolic than substantive. As historian Christina Greene rightly points out, Durham's white power brokers were more concerned with racial harmony than with racial justice. The conflict between the city's racial moderates and more direct action–oriented civil rights organizers reached a fever pitch in the summer of 1962. Late in July, members of the Congress of Racial Equality and the NAACP picketed Eckerd's Drug Store and Howard Johnson's ice cream parlor. At Eckerd's, the issue at hand was the store's refusal to hire African Americans as salespersons, despite the fact that blacks constituted half of its customers. Likewise, Howard Johnson's was opposed to hiring African Americans in clerical positions. The restaurant had also refused to desegregate its lunch counter, even after the sit-ins of 1960 led other stores to reverse their segregation policies. Taking the lead in the fight against Howard Johnson's were black students from North Carolina Central, who in their efforts to implement change endured verbal assaults, threats of violence, consternation from conservative blacks, arrests, and sometimes imprisonment. For their refusal to pay a trespass fine for protesting Howard Johnson's, students Guytana Horton and Joycelyn McKissick were sentenced to thirty days in jail. Their arrest and subsequent jailing galvanized the civil rights community, which in August held a large rally at one of the city's movement centers, St. Joseph AME Church. Shortly after the rally, 1,500 African Americans headed to Howard Johnson's to continue their protests. These protests persisted throughout the summer as part of the "Freedom Highways" project, a CORE-directed campaign that extended from Maryland to Florida. This project eventually led more than half of the Howard Johnson's establishments in North Carolina to desegregate their lunch counters. One of the holdout restaurants was the Howard Johnson's in Durham, which in 1963 was the site of one of the largest civil rights demonstrations in North Carolina.[6] Over the next few years, Durham remained a center of political protest and grassroots activism as African Americans directed their attention to the problems of urban renewal, deindustrialization, employment discrimination, and the housing crisis.

One important center of local organizing was Union Baptist, the church home of the Kee family and hundreds of other blacks. Under the pastorate of Dr. Grady Davis, Union was a center of black spiritual life in Durham and an anchoring institution for the local civil rights movement. A dedicated member until his death in 1981, John Henry Kee lent his musical talents to the Grady Davis Choir and the Senior Male Choir.[7] Like his father, young John developed a deep love for music, routinely spending hours at the family's Walter upright piano. "I was about seven years old when I started playing that piano, and I got a lot of encouragement because music in our household was just the thing to do. And it was by playing piano that I kept my dad's attention."[8]

Showing great promise as a musician, Kee enrolled at the North Carolina School of the Arts in Winston-Salem and then graduated from there at the age of fourteen. To further develop his musical skills, he joined his brothers at Yuba College Conservatory in Marysville, California. To support himself, Kee worked as a sideman for Cameo and Donald Byrd on their visits to Northern California. On the surface, the talented youngster seemed destined for greatness, but on his route to superstardom he took several dangerous detours.

During his time in California, Kee descended into a world of drug use. He then returned to North Carolina, where he found work with the Charlotte-based Miss Black Universe pageants. His move back south was part of a national trend. Since the 1970s, the number of African Americans migrating to the South exceeded the number of those leaving the region. Especially for returning and primary migrants frustrated by the declining economic opportunities available in the rustbelt cities of the Midwest and Northeast, the metropolitan centers of Atlanta, Houston, Dallas, and Charlotte seemed much more appealing than their northern and midwestern counterparts.[9] "If ever there was a city that epitomizes the New South," boasted the June 1983 edition of *Black Enterprise*, "it is Charlotte, N.C., the largest city between Washington and Atlanta. . . . This Sunbelt city is now home to 314,000 residents—31 percent of them black—and to a burgeoning business community, which includes 500 black-owned companies."[10] For ambitious African Americans wishing to improve their lives and perhaps avoid the problems of the urban North, Charlotte was the place for them.

To many outsiders, this was a city on the move, a great place for young people with talent, ambition, and a hard work ethic. Unfortunately, Kee was not quite ready to take advantage of the city's benefits. Even after his move back south,

Kee remained a part of the drug scene—not only as a user but as a seller as well. Upon his arrival in Charlotte, he settled into the Double Oaks neighborhood, an area facing many of the problems plaguing other inner-city communities. Crime, unemployment, substandard housing, and drugs wreaked havoc on many of its residents. Drifting further away from the values of his early childhood, Kee was an active participant in Double Oaks's underworld.

A dramatic shift occurred in Kee's life in 1981, when one of his closest friends fell victim to drug-related violence. His friend's murder shook Kee to his core, forcing him to reevaluate his life: "I was seeing young men dying on the street, and I think I just made up my mind that I did not want to leave here like that. I just felt like there was a gift or something inside of me, and I didn't want to waste it."[11] The reformed drug dealer started working with a group of young singers involved in the Combination Choir, which was based in Charlotte. This marked the beginning of Kee's lifelong commitment to the local community, particularly the Double Oaks neighborhood. The choir later morphed into the New Life Community Choir, which gained national attention in the 1990s for their work with Kee.

Kee's Breakthrough

On his rehabilitation journey, Kee received major support from two of gospel's most iconic figures, James Cleveland and Edwin Hawkins. Like many aspiring musicians in the gospel field, Kee turned to the Gospel Music Workshop of America to gain a larger audience and connect with industry insiders. In 1985, Cleveland placed two of Kee's compositions, "He's My All in All" and "Jesus Can Do It," on his GMWA recording. Two years later, Kee was a featured vocalist and songwriter on Edwin Hawkins's music and arts seminar recording. That same year, Kee released *Yes Lord*, his debut with the black-owned label Tyscot. A relatively small company based in Indianapolis, Tyscot began in 1977 as a vehicle for one of its founders, Leonard Scott, to promote his church choir. The label would add to its roster a few minor gospel acts, but it was hardly on the radar of most in the gospel industry. This would change with the release of Kee's *Yes Lord*. Though the record had modest sales, it generated considerable anticipation for Kee and the New Life Community Choir's 1989 release, *Wait on Him*.

Wait on Him dipped deep into the gospel tradition yet forged its own unique path. On it are echoes of the vocal stylings of Rance Allen and Marvin Winans, the rhythmic arrangements of Willie Neal Johnson and the Gospel Keynotes and the Jackson Southernaires, and the call-and-response exchanges prevalent in the music of traditional gospel choirs. And yet, Kee was an original who delivered a sound the gospel world had never heard before. Consider, as a case in point, the foot-stomping "It Will Be Alright." The song opens with a personal testimony from Kee, who proudly claims his southern roots. Putting on his preacher hat, Kee flashes back to his childhood in Durham with a particular focus on his late father. His portrait is vivid and passionate: "I can see my daddy walking over there by that pickup truck, I can imagine in my mind being the father of sixteen children, everything wasn't going smooth all the time. But I can hear David say 'yea though I walk through the valley,' let me know that every circumstance and situation is not going to last always." The audience gives their shouts of approval as Kee recalls "his daddy singing a little song."[12] The singer then asks the crowd: "How many believe that the Lord God will make everything alright?" Guitarist Jimmy Hill then drops a few blue notes as the choir proceeds with the chorus. Feeling the weight of his past, Kee launches into the song's first verse with a line from the gospel classic "Walk around Heaven." "One of these old mornings," he rhythmically belts, "I said it won't be very long, / You going to look for me and I'll be gone on home." With each line, the NLCC responds with a forceful "Hallelujah."[13]

On the second verse, Kee turns inward again and situates his biography within a specific space and time. "I was born in Durham, North Carolina, outside the county line / I learned at an early age that Jesus was a friend of mine."[14] Not content with simply providing his audience with a sense of his regional self, Kee offers a challenge to dominant narratives about the black family's brokenness. "Fifteenth child out of sixteen children," the singer notes, "both mother and father were *there*." Here Kee complicates conventional narratives about the interiority of black life with a portrait of a two-parent African American family living on the urban/country divide. Family and religion, he lets the audience know, were anchoring forces in his life. In doing so, he provides a narrative with which many gospel listeners could identify.

Finding a receptive audience among lovers of traditional and contemporary gospel music, *Wait on Him* elevated Kee to superstar status in the black gospel world. The album climbed to #4 on the gospel charts, dominated gospel radio, and enabled Kee to launch a nationwide tour. "We're getting more requests than I can handle," Kee informed journalist Robert Darden. Though the record had a southern sound, its popularity extended beyond the Mason-Dixon Line. "'Wait on Him' is doing incredible business in New York," Kee marveled. The singer was also receiving attention from beyond the black gospel world. "We're getting calls from white churches in Texas, Washington state, even the hills of Tennessee— where the man told me all they've ever heard is 'hillbilly gospel' before now!"[15]

Wait on Him emerged at a very important juncture in gospel music, when the genre needed a fresh voice who could advance the art form, an artist who respected tradition but was not confined by it. Laying a musical foundation that would later be built upon by artists like Kirk Franklin, Kee integrated the urban contemporary flavor of the Winans and Commissioned into a choir setting.

Across the industry, artists, fans, and journalists raved over Kee's talent, immediately crowning him the "Prince of Gospel." At the 1989 Stellar Awards, Kee won in the categories of Song of the Year, Album of the Year, and Traditional Choir of the Year. The talented singer-songwriter was also nominated for a NAACP Image Award. Finally, Kee had achieved the success his late father had imagined for his gifted son.

Tapping deep into his well of creative resources, Kee continued to make new music as he toured the country promoting *Wait on Him*: "I've already begun working on music for New Life's second album," he informed his fans. "But instead of just sitting down and writing eight or 10 songs, I'm trying to find music that's in the same style as 'Wait on Him.'" Simultaneously, he worked on a solo project that embraced a more R&B, funk aesthetic: "The message is real strong and the music is attractive to young people." When discussing the upcoming project, he admitted the tension involved in seeking to "be commercial and still keep the power of the message."[16]

On August 30, 1990, Kee's second solo project, *Just Me This Time*, appeared in record stores. Far more contemporary than his choir projects, the record targeted the urban contemporary crowd. Its lead single, "Can't Nobody Do Me," combined elements of the New Jack Swing sounds of Guy and Keith Sweat with the lush harmonies of Commissioned and the Winans. But the song failed to draw much attention for the record, which paled in comparison to *Wait on Him* in terms of sales.

If the album's lackluster sales disappointed Kee, he showed no signs to his fans. The budding superstar maintained an incredibly busy schedule as he sought multiple outlets for his creativity. Along with touring across the country, Kee also formed Victory in Praise Music and Arts Seminar, which would soon record the hit song "Never Shall Forget." Victory in Praise functioned as a venue for Kee to test new ideas and showcase new talent, particularly those from his home base of Charlotte.

Building His Legacy

Kee's star continued to rise with the release of what many regarded as the *real* follow-up to *Wait on Him*: *Wash Me*. To this day, the fervor surrounding the release of *Wash Me* remains ingrained in my mind. On the album's drop date (May 7, 1991) and several weeks after, black mom-and-pop record stores, along with Christian bookstores, routinely ran out of copies. "Check back next Tuesday," the sales clerk at Gospel World in my hometown of Jacksonville shouted as customers inquired about the availability of Kee's new release. On the other side of town at Paxon Discount Christian Bookstore, the record also sold out within hours of its arrival. The same situation greeted latecomers rushing over to the black-owned D.J. Records, whose owner would yell "NO JOHN P. KEE" almost before you stepped into the store.

It was not hard to understand why gospel outlets struggled to keep the record on the shelves. *Wash Me* boasted several radio hits, most notably the title cut, "Jesus Will Make a Way," and "Jesus Is Real," a keyboard-driven jam featuring Kee and Lowell Pye on lead vocals. Within months of the record's release, church choirs across the country had incorporated "Jesus Is Real" into their repertoire as gospel stores tried to meet the high demand for the record. Beyond the radio hits, *Wash Me* also included such standout cuts as "I Must Tell Jesus," "More Like Jesus," and "Standing in the Need."

In terms of blending the old with the new, Kee had once again struck the perfect balance. Though *Wash Me* incorporated more of the Detroit contemporary gospel sound than *Wait on Him* did, Kee continued to pay homage to his North Carolina roots. On "Jesus Will Make a Way," Kee takes his listeners on another journey to his hometown of Durham. The song begins with a testimony from Kee, who recalls his childhood: "I remember as a boy, we'd all come down to the steps on Sunday, gather in a circle, somebody would start singing a song, somebody would start reading a scripture. Grandmother would start praying a prayer."[17] The centerpiece of Kee's flashback is his grandmother, who functions as the moral anchor not just for the family but for the entire community. "Grandmother's seventy-eight now," he informs the audience; "she says she will keep on praying and praising God for those who need to be encouraged." Here, Kee draws not only on his personal memories of family but also on a much deeper tradition within the African American community: the praying grandmother who holds the family together in good and bad times. The praying grandmother occupies an important position in the black religious imagination. Throughout gospel music, from the Georgia Mass Choir's "Come On in the Room" to Helen Baylor's "Testimony," there exists images of powerful grandmothers whose prayers deliver their children and grandchildren from drug addition, crime, bad marriages, and sickness.

Though 1991 was an incredibly competitive year in gospel with several highly anticipated releases, including Walter Hawkins's *Love Alive IV*, Rance Allen's *Phenomenon*, and BeBe and CeCe Winans' platinum-selling *Different Lifestyles*, Kee remained in the spotlight as his record held steady on the gospel charts, received constant airplay on traditional and contemporary gospel radio stations, and picked up numerous awards at the Stellar and the GMWA ceremonies. Kee's success was particularly meaningful as the gospel world mourned the passing of its iconic leader, Reverend James Cleveland. No individual had played a more critical role in the genre's growth over the past thirty years than Cleveland. Nor had any artist been more committed to creating the institutions to advance gospel music as an art form. Fittingly, in the year of Cleveland's passing, John P. Kee dominated the GMWA's annual Excellence Awards, winning in six categories.

In the view of many industry insiders, Kee was poised to lead gospel into a new and even more prosperous era. Vision, clarity of purpose, talent, and a deep connection to black gospel fans—Kee possessed all of these essential qualities for long-term commercial success.

Veteran executive Al Hobbs praised Kee as "unequivocally the hottest singular property in the industry."[18] To be sure, a few artists in the field sold more records. But in the view of Hobbs and many older artists, especially those who had observed Kee's earlier work with the GMWA, the North Carolina–born artist represented the best of the gospel tradition.

Cognizant of his importance to the field, Kee maintained an active recording schedule over the next three years, releasing a variety of projects with the NLCC and the Victory in Praise seminar. These projects included *We Walk by Faith*, *Lily in the Valley*, and *Colorblind*. *We Walk by Faith* captures the NLCC in top form and features inspiring vocals from gospel legend Vanessa Bell Armstrong. Coming out in late 1992, *We Walk by Faith* spent consecutive months on the top of the gospel charts. In addition to having the #1 album in the country, John P. Kee also had one of the most acclaimed gospel songs of the year: the soul-stirring "Lily in the Valley." Singing without instrumental accompaniment, Kee and the choir move the crowd with their spirited claps, deep moans, and soulful harmonies. On "Lily in the Valley," Kee shares his lead, briefly, with his grandfather, who appears at the 1:40 mark of the song. For the reminder of the song, a variety of sounds clash as Kee stretches his baritone to its limits, the choir repeats the refrain, a quartet of men interject a few doo-wop lines, and a female choir member wails "yeah, yeah, yeah."

The success of "Lily in the Valley" and *We Walk by Faith* was remarkable considering the many troubles confronting Kee's record label, Tyscot. Tyscot's distributor, Spectra Records, filed for bankruptcy in 1992. Spectra owed Tyscot more than $500,000, no small sum for the independent black-owned record company. Under these circumstances, the label proved unable to meet the rising demand for Kee's music. The news disappointed the singer but didn't surprise him: "I guess it was just a prayer that it wouldn't happen because of what's happening to our new record. *We Walk by Faith* is doing very well and I knew this would throw a rod in it."[19] Spectra's collapse made it difficult to purchase Kee's records in Christian chain stores like Family Christian Bookstores.

On the one hand, Spectra's bankruptcy was devastating for Kee and his label. On the other hand, the company's collapse freed Tyscot to entertain offers from other distributors. With one of gospel's hottest commodities on its roster, Tyscot attracted attention from the large Christian distributor Word Records, as well as from Warner Alliance. After considering many offers, Tyscot signed a distribution deal with Jive/Zomba Music Group. This deal ensured a larger market for Kee, who could now expect his music in major record stores and chains.

Zomba had high hopes for Kee. "We're working on taking John P. Kee to the next level," record executive Demetrius Alexander told industry insiders in 1994. Now, she insisted, Kee had the muscle behind him to ensure the distribution of his music in a variety of Christian and secular venues, from mom-and-pop gospel stores to larger chains like Tower Records, Sam Goody, and Circuit City. The test case for this new arrangement was Kee's 1994 release, *Colorblind*, which had a more urban contemporary sound than his New Life material. Kee also ventured into new territory thematically with more socially engaged lyrics dealing with the enduring problem of race in American society. Notwithstanding the shift in musical style and widespread distribution, *Colorblind* suffered from disappointing sales. Fortunately, Kee rebounded with his next NLCC release, *Show Up!* Labeling his sound "Sunday Morning Hip-Hop," Kee struck gold as the record moved more than 500,000 units.

Ten years after earning his first big break as a composer and performer at the 1985 GMWA convention, John P. Kee ranked as one of the most popular artists in gospel music history. His stellar recordings and electrifying performances helped redefine the gospel sound and inspired a younger generation of artists who would ensure the genre's growth into the twenty-first century. Not just a trendsetter, he was the bridge connecting the gospel of James Cleveland to the gospel of Kirk Franklin. With the artistic and commercial triumphs of Kee, the South had indeed done it again.

CHAPTER II

We Are the Drum

Take 6, the Sounds of Blackness, and the New Black Aesthetic

Out of this ferment will emerge something new.
—ISHMAEL REED in Trey Ellis, *Platitudes and
"The New Black Aesthetic"*

Though nobody's sent out any announcements yet, the '80s
are witnessing the maturation of a post-nationalist black
arts movement, one more Afrocentric and cosmopolitan
than anything that's come before. The people in this
movement find no contradiction in deriving equal doses of
inspiration from influences as diverse as Malcolm X and
Jimi Hendrix, George Clinton and George Romero, Kareem
Abdul Jabbar and Lisette Model, Zora Neale Hurston and
Alicia Kurosana . . . George Jackson and Samuel Delany,
Frederick Jameson and Reverend James Cleveland. . . .
The present generation of black artists is cross-breeding
aesthetic references like nobody's talking about yet.
—GREG TATE, *Flyboy in the Buttermilk:
Essays on Contemporary America*

The same year Spike Lee released his groundbreaking film *Do the Right Thing*,
Trey Ellis's provocative essay "The New Black Aesthetic" appeared in the literary journal *Callaloo*. In the essay, Ellis celebrated the arrival of a new generation
of African American artists primed to revolutionize the cultural landscapes of
their immediate communities and the larger world.

Alienated (junior) intellectuals, we are the more and more young blacks getting
back into jazz and the blues; the only ones you see at punk concerts; the ones
in the bookstore wearing little, round glasses and short, neat dreads; some of
the only blacks who admit liking both Jim and Toni Morrison. Eddie Murphy,
Prince, and the Marsalis brothers are just the initial shock troops because now,

in New York's East Village, in Brooklyn's Fort Greene, in Los Angeles, and in Harlem, all of us under thirty only ones are coming together like so many twins separated at birth—thrilled, soothed, and strengthened in being finally reunited.

The new crop of artists celebrated in Ellis's piece included Spike Lee, Fishbone, sisters Kellie and Lisa Jones, and brothers Reginald and Warrington Hudlin, founders of the New York–based Black Filmmaker Foundation. "Almost every month," Ellis noted, "a talented new black artist blows into town with a wild new cultural combination."[1]

Not mentioned in Ellis's piece but very much a part of this new generation of black artists revolutionizing their craft was Take 6, a group whose list of admirers ranged from Quincy Jones to Spike Lee (who featured the sextet on his *Do the Right Thing* soundtrack). Young, educated, rooted in tradition yet on the cutting edge of their art form, the members of Take 6 sampled liberally from America's rich cultural archive to create a refreshingly original sound. Their deft interpretations of Negro spirituals coupled with their doo-wop style harkened

FIGURE 19. Take 6 at the 1990 Grammy Awards. Photo by Ebet Roberts/ Redferns/Getty Images.

back to an older time in American cultural history. At the same time, their musical arrangements possessed a strong postmodernist sensibility. Like several of the artists highlighted in Ellis's "New Black Aesthetic" essay, Take 6 found a way to be both experimental and commercially successful. The group's debut album appeared on the gospel, contemporary jazz, and pop charts, garnered them two Grammys, became only the third album in black gospel history to earn gold certification from the RIAA, and received rave reviews from some of the industry's toughest critics.

Take 6's success, style, and pedigree fit perfectly in a cultural milieu that gave us Spike Lee, Tracy Chapman, Bobby McFerrin, Quincy Jones's intergenerational classic *Back on the Block*, and the explosion of smooth jazz stations across the country. The group's strong jazz sensibilities appealed to thousands of women and men who rarely listened to gospel but appreciated their superb musicianship and their commitment to the spirit of improvisation. In other words, Take 6 counted among their fans music lovers whose record collections had more Shirley Horn than Shirley Caesar, more James Moody than James Cleveland. This did not mean, however, that the group lacked appeal among gospel lovers. To the contrary, Take 6 had a strong presence in black gospel.

Popular in a variety of markets, Take 6 also had a solid base in the predominantly white, Nashville-centered, contemporary Christian music world. The sextet graced the cover of *CCM Magazine* in the 1980s, won Dove Awards in major categories, and had their music regularly played on white Christian radio stations. Their immersion in the Christian music scene was much deeper than radio play and awards. Having moved to Nashville in 1987, the group was very much a part of the city's musical culture. Moreover, the commercial success of their first two records played a critical role in Warner Brothers' decision to increase its investment in Christian music there.

The artistic and commercial triumphs of Take 6 in the late 1980s and early 1990s brought the singers into corners of the pop world previously closed off to most gospel artists. Their voices could be heard in everything from hit comedy shows to blockbuster movies.

Take 6 was not the only musical act that brought a new energy and aesthetic to the gospel scene during the 1990s. A year after the release of the sextet's second record, *So Much 2 Say*, the Minneapolis-based ensemble the Sounds of Blackness (SOB) put the music world on notice with their special blend of gospel, R&B, dance, Minneapolis funk, and Afrocentric politics. With the hit "Optimistic," "I Believe," "Testify," and "The Pressure Pt. 1," they provided a different model of how a gospel act could function musically and politically. Unapologetic in their celebration of black history and culture, the Sounds of Blackness blended perfectly with the cultural nationalist ethos of the 1990s. In fact, for many black teenagers and young adults, the pro-black music of SOB and the Afrocentric rhymes of hip-hop groups like A Tribe Called Quest seemed to grow from the same fertile soil. Diverse in their musical tastes, members of the group drew inspiration from the totality of the black experience. "You can't fully appreciate the glory hallelujah of the gospel," choir director Gary Hines insisted, "without the pain of the blues and the history of the spirituals and the complexity of jazz. You've got to acknowledge the totality of all the members together. And that's what Sounds of Blackness does."[2]

Such boldness endeared the group to many critics, including Geoffrey Himes. Feeling as if gospel needed more sonic and political punch, Himes welcomed the unique voices of both Sounds of Blackness and Take 6. In a 1994 article titled "Return of the Gospel Truth," Himes applauded the two groups for offering a sound and political message missing from other contemporary gospel acts. In his view, gospel suffered from the same overproduced and saccharine tendencies plaguing its R&B cousin, but there was hope for the genre: "Fortunately, some younger gospel artists have decided that religious faith is not mere sentiment but something more complicated that deserves music ambitious enough to accommodate true spirituality. Most prominent among these new-generation acts are Take 6, which has incorporated sophisticated jazz harmonies into gospel 'quartet' singing, and Sounds of Blackness, which has introduced its hometown Minneapolis funk into the choir setting."[3] These two groups, in Himes's estimation, were the future of gospel music—or if not the future, at least a roadmap for other musicians in the genre to explore new lyrical and sonic terrain, to create music that spoke to the political realities of the times.

So Much 2 Say: Take 6 Arrive

Coming into the national spotlight in the late 1980s, Take 6 originally consisted of tenors Claude McKnight, Mervyn Warren, David Thomas, and Mark Kibble, baritone Cedric Dent, and bass Alvin Chea. Mark Kibble's younger brother Joey joined the group in 1991 after Warren amicably left for personal and artistic reasons. There would be no further changes until 2011, when Dent departed the group to devote more time to his professorship at Middle Tennessee State University. With strong roots in the Seventh-day Adventist denomination, Take 6 began at Oakwood College, where the ensemble developed out of Claude McKnight's original group, the Gentlemen's East. A private, historically black school located in Huntsville, Alabama, Oakwood was founded in 1896, the year the Supreme Court declared "separate but equal" constitutional in its *Plessy v. Ferguson* decision. The Seventh-day Adventist Church founded the school as part of its effort to provide industrial training to the graduates of the denomination's Morning Star elementary schools. Over the years, Oakwood evolved from an industrial school to a junior college to a four-year liberal arts institution offering bachelor's degrees. All but one of Take 6's members graduated or spent time at Oakwood (Cedric Dent received his bachelor's from the University of Michigan and his master's degree in music from the University of Alabama). A confluence of circumstances eventually brought McKnight, Kibble, Warren, Dent, Thomas, and Chea together in the mid-1980s and put them on the path to superstardom. Having achieved a solid following in Alabama and Tennessee, the group decided to put together a showcase for a dozen Christian record companies. An uninvited Jim Norman of Warner Brothers decided to attend the showcase as he had been listening to the group's demo for several months. Impressed by their talents, he offered them a contract on the spot.

With the pressure of finding a label behind them, the group went to work immediately, cutting and mastering their first record in Nashville. Claude McKnight, Mark Kibble, and Mervyn Warren handled all of the arrangements and production duties. Comprising seven covers and three originals, Take 6's self-titled debut was an extraordinary collection of songs. With remarkable command, the group swing adventurously across a wide spectrum of rhythms and moods. Their innovative arrangements of such gospel classics as "Mary," "If We Ever," and "Get Away, Jordan" set a new standard of musicianship for not just gospel but vocal jazz. The same could be said of the stunning opener, "Gold Mine." The song's intricate harmonies and melodic variations coupled with its heartfelt lyrics provide the listener with the perfect introduction to the group's stunning vocals and remarkable chemistry. Take 6 then moved into the infectious "Spread Love," a wonderful showcase of the group's jazz chops. More inspirational than religious, the song netted the sextet a diverse audience of music lovers.

Nothing on gospel radio compared to Take 6's debut record. To be sure, talented groups abound in the gospel music industry, but no ensemble sounded so exquisite. Simply put, Take 6 were in a league of their own.[4]

To bring home this point, Warner Brothers used the back cover of the group's debut album as a marketing tool. The cover featured ringing endorsements from several noted musicians. Brian Wilson of the Beach Boys praised them for having "the most amazing blend of harmonies" and "some of the most ingenious arrangements and lyrics that I've heard in a long time." Equally impressed, gospel star Marvin Winans marveled at the group's innovative harmonies and dazzling vocals. Rather than viewing the sextet as a threat to his own group's popularity, Winans praised Take 6 as a groundbreaking act with a "revolutionary sound that takes gospel to another level without ever leaving its roots. I love it." Strong praise also came from Oakwood alum and actor Clifton Davis, CCM star Sandi Patty, and Gene Puerling of Singers Unlimited.[5]

Fortunately for the sextet, their debut record lived up to the hype. One of the biggest musical surprises of 1988, *Take 6* entered the gospel charts on June 18 at #23. Two months later, the record debuted on *Billboard*'s contemporary jazz charts.

So impressed was Stevie Wonder with the group's talent that he purchased 500 copies of their debut record and passed it along to family, close friends, and industry insiders. Then on the eve of two performances (August 31–September 1) at Radio City Hall, the music icon invited the sextet to join him onstage. By this time, the group had invitations pouring in from countless entertainers. The producers of CBS's new sitcom *Murphy Brown* wanted them to record the show's opening theme. And Spike Lee tapped them to perform "Don't Shoot Me" for the soundtrack of his new flick, *Do the Right Thing*. Somehow the group managed to balance these requests with their own tour dates and as they planned their studio sessions for the next project.

The group's schedule became even more hectic in early 1989, when the National Academy of Recording Arts and Sciences announced the nominees for the upcoming Grammy Awards. Much to their delight, the group was nominated for three awards. Their nomination in the category of Best Soul Gospel Group was expected, but their appearance in the Best New Artist and Contemporary Jazz categories threw them and their record company for a loop. In Grammy history, the list of the esteemed recipients of the Best New Artist Award included the Beatles, Crosby, Stills, and Nash, Bette Midler, Carly Simon, and Sade. Few believed Take 6 had a chance against the hands-down favorite Tracy Chapman; however, the media attention accompanying the nomination was sure to give the group new listeners.

As expected, Chapman won the Best New Artist award. Take 6 won in the other two categories for which they were nominated: gospel and contemporary jazz.

Ebony Men Par Excellence

On the heels of Take 6's Grammy victory, *Ebony* magazine ran a three-page story on the group, praising them as excellent models of respectable black manhood. In the article, the writer traced the group's upward climb, recounted their early years at Oakwood, detailed members' accomplishments in education, and lauded the singers for their "clean, collegiate personas, and positive-religion based messages." Their arrival, according to *Ebony*, was very much needed and welcomed "in an era when youthful role models are a rare commodity."[6] Not stated but explicitly suggested in this and other articles was Take 6's importance—for a select group of cultural brokers—as a counterpoint to hip-hop's revolution. Of course, the situation was far more complex. No doubt, Take 6 were deep in the jazz and gospel traditions. But the sextet also borrowed from the aesthetic and stylistic innovations of hip-hop.

A month after their *Ebony* feature, the group graced the cover of *CCM Magazine*, the leading magazine among white Christian music fans. The monthly rarely gave black artists its cover slot, but with the success of Take 6 and BeBe and CeCe Winans, the magazine was diversifying its content. The Winans duo had been the cover story in the February issue. Two months later, the magazine featured a full spread on Take 6, whose members discussed their evangelical commitments, their efforts to negotiate their newfound fame, and their vast musical influences. Though huge fans of jazz music, they used the interview to reiterate their indebtedness to black gospel quartets like the Fairfield Four and the Swan Silvertones. "The base from which we formed the music we're doing is basic quartet harmony, from basic quartet songs," Mark Kibble explained. "All the elements—the four-part harmony, the lead vocal, the rhythmic background and the walking bass lines are found in the old quartet songs. They just don't have extended harmonies and all the moves that we do but the elements are all the same."[7]

Amid the tremendous buzz surrounding the group, Warner Brothers finally shot a video for the single "Spread Love." The song had been out since 1988, but the label didn't finance a video for the group until May 1989. One of the most fascinating aspects of the video is its explicit attempt to situate Take 6 within a jazz rather than a gospel tradition. With multiple allusions to the bebop era, the video switches back and forth between group and individual shots. The director's framing of the group accents their dual role as singers and band members—as first-rate musicians connected to a rich lineage of African American artists. With the video's warm color palette, the place of their performance could have been 1940s New York or a jam session on the south side of Chicago in the 1960s. As a work of art deserving attention in its own right, the video falls into the category of what scholar Michael Gillespie calls "film blackness" in that it "intones contemplative measure of the past, present, and future."[8] Thanks to the video's high quality and the song's infectiousness, "Spread Love" was in steady rotation on BET's *Video Soul* and *Video Vibrations* as well as on VH1.

Loved by their fans, peers, and many of the nation's leading music critics, Take 6 teetered close to overexposure. Their songs could be heard on gospel, R&B, and jazz radio, their tour dates consistently sold out, and television shows rushed to book the fresh new act out of Nashville. They fielded numerous requests from fellow artists, including the legendary Quincy Jones. Celebrated by Jones as the "baddest vocal cats on the planet," Take 6 made several contributions to his 1989 classic, *Back on the Block*. On the breathtakingly beautiful "Setembro (Brazilian Wedding Song)," they sing with the incomparable Sarah Vaughan, who like Jones was a big fan of the group. They also lend their talents to the swinging "Wee B. Dooinit," which features Vaughan, Ella Fitzgerald, Al Jarreau, and Bobby McFerrin. Working outside the group, Mervyn Warren also contributed to the interlude "The Verb to Be." Take 6's contributions to Jones's musical gumbo, along with their inspired performance of "Don't Shoot Me" on

Spike Lee's *Do the Right Thing* soundtrack, demonstrated their ability to thrive in a variety of musical settings.

One of those settings was the jazz world. Even though Take 6 self-identified as a gospel group, many fans treated them as a jazz ensemble. In fact, the sextet received the most votes in *Downbeat's* 1989 Readers' Poll for best vocal jazz group. They were also a visible presence on the jazz festival circuit, where they shared the stage with some of their favorite musical mentors and peers.

And they did not disappoint. Top-notch performers, Take 6 amazed festival attendees as they moved from gospel to jazz. The biggest applause often came when the group went into full instrumental mode as Chea laid down the bass, Dent provided percussion, Thomas wailed with the power of an electric guitar, and the collective voices of Warren, McKnight, and Kibble functioned as the horn section. For many who religiously attended their concerts, Take 6 represented the best of both the gospel and the jazz traditions.

Crossing over into different markets had its benefits, but navigating such a diverse fan base was not always easy. "What's important to know," Claude McKnight pointed out to a reporter, "is that each situation is different, and that we don't have to beat anyone over the head to get our message across."[9] The sextet endeavored to respect the diversity of experiences, opinions, and desires within their fan base yet remain true to their evangelical commitments. As Mark Kibble explained, "We do what we do because we love the Lord. We believe we have a specific purpose in the music industry and that is to minister and share what we have through our lifestyles. Not necessarily by preaching or beating anyone over the head, but to live it and to show it and to share it."[10]

Act 2: Take 6 Return to the Studio

Still riding high off the success of their debut, Take 6 set aside time in early 1990 to complete their second CD, *So Much 2 Say*. Like their occasional tour buddies BeBe and CeCe Winans, the men felt the pressure of not just repeating but surpassing the success of their previous recording. Anything less than gold would have been a disappointment, since Warner Brothers invested a tremendous amount of money into marketing the lead single and its accompanying video.

The investment paid off. Upon its release, *So Much 2 Say* received rave reviews and sold extremely well. Take 6 avoided the sophomore slump as the record matched the debut's high standard of musical excellence. The group achieves harmonic perfection on "Come unto Me," "I'm on My Way," and "Time after Time (The Savior Is Waiting)," digs deep into the gospel quartet tradition with the soul-stirring "Something within Me," and branches out into more rhythmically complex music with "I L-O-V-E U," "So Much 2 Say," and "I Believe." On the title cut, the interludes, and the closer, "Where Do the Children Play?," the group bring a sense of mischief, humor, and openness to their work not found on the debut record. As *New York Times* reporter Will Friedwald succinctly noted, the sextet offer up "songs with passion, intelligence, musicianship and a touch of levity."[11]

Their second release won a Grammy in the Best Soul Gospel category, as well as two Dove Awards. The group also continued to pop up in unexpected places, as was the case when they appeared on the *Dick Tracy* soundtrack with country singer k. d. lang.

The implications of Take 6's phenomenal success extended far beyond the group. In the aftermath of the sextet's meteoric rise, Warner Alliance (a contemporary Christian imprint of Warner Brothers created in 1989) signed several Christian acts, including Donna McElroy, Michael English, and Vanessa Bell Armstrong's sister Margaret Bell. These artists were very different stylistically, but what label executives believed they all had in common was their crossover appeal. And by crossover, they meant the ability not only to sell in the secular market but also to garner white and black Christian music fans, as had been the case for Take 6.

Together with the hit duo BeBe and CeCe Winans, Take 6 altered many Christian record labels' sense of what was commercially possible. Their two gold records led some executives to take chances on artists they might have passed over in previous years or to increase the marketing budget for a newly signed gospel act.

But as Warner prepared to gamble on new acts, it had to respond to an unexpected change in Take 6's lineup. In 1991, Mervyn Warren departed the group in order to pursue other production and musical opportunities. His vocals, arrangements, and production had been critical to the group's commercial success. He had produced all but three of the songs on Take 6's second album, which also featured some of his finest moments as a vocalist. And who could forget his splendid arrangements on the group's debut recording? To be sure, Take 6 was an incredibly gifted group whose members possessed a variety of musical skills, but Warren would be greatly missed by the group's expanding fan base.[12]

Contemporary Gospel Meets Minneapolis Funk: The Sounds of Blackness

As Take 6 adjusted to their membership change in 1991, the gospel world embraced the arrival of another musical sensation, the Minneapolis-based ensemble Sounds of Blackness. Fueled by their top-charting hits "Optimistic," "The Pressure," and "Testify," Sounds of Blackness captured the attention of gospel, R&B, and dance fans alike with their inspirational messages, energetic performances, and Afrocentric vibe. Their first two albums struck gold, making the ensemble a household name in many African American communities. Not your ordinary gospel choir, SOB featured an eclectic group of musicians steeped in the various forms of African American music—spirituals, blues, jazz, and hip-hop. SOB's director, Gary Hines, recoiled at the label "gospel choir": "People see 30 or 40 black people singing together and singing some spiritual-oriented music, they right away think gospel. That's limited thinking. We don't think that way. Gospel is just a fraction of what this group does. If there's a label to be put on us, it's that we are a black music ensemble in the same way that there are Bach societies and so forth."[13]

Formed by Russell Knighton in 1969, the Sounds of Blackness first launched on the campus of Macalester College in St. Paul, Minnesota. Originally called the Macalester College Black Voices, the ensemble's formation was far from an isolated event. Across the nation, African American students integrating predominantly white colleges and universities formed gospel choirs as a way to maintain certain cultural traditions, strengthen themselves spiritually, and better

FIGURE 20. Sounds of Blackness video shoot in Minneapolis on August 4, 1991. Photo by Jim Steinfeldt/Michael Ochs Archives/Getty Images.

respond to the challenges of a frequently hostile environment. The names of these choirs ranged from Black Voices to Black Awakening, a reflection of the political moment and the efforts of black students to integrate their Christianity with their politics. These ensembles performed spirituals and traditional hymns, as well as the latest hits from the most popular gospel choirs and artists of the day. A testament to these choirs' growing popularity, the National Black Gospel College Choir Workshop was established in 1973 as a way to bring about better unity among black collegians seeking to preserve and advance the black sacred music tradition. The workshop held its annual meetings in Atlanta and attracted black gospel choirs from across the nation. The long list of musical ensembles participating in the convention included the Florida State University Gospel Choir, the Virginia State College Gospel Ensemble, the University of South Florida Gospel Choir, the North Carolina A&T University Fellowship Gospel Choir, the Miles College Gospel Choir, and Alabama State's Young Hearts. Intrigued by the workshop and by the possibility of cashing in on gospel's growing popularity, TSOP Records, a division of Philadelphia International, released an album featuring key performances from the 1973 convention. The first track featured several gospel ensembles, including Macalester College's Black Voices.

Made up of college students, alums, and local residents, Macalester's Black Voices expanded under the leadership of Gary Hines (who assumed the directorship in 1971), changed their name to Sounds of Blackness, and eventually became one of the most popular acts in the city. In the 1980s, the group began performing more theatrical pieces that centered on African Americans' diverse experiences. Their two most popular musicals were *Music for Martin* and *Soul of the 1960s*. The group soon caught the attention of two of the city's most famous producers, James "Jimmy Jam" Harris and Terry Lewis. In the early 1980s, Harris and Lewis received national fame for their work with Prince, their membership in the band The Time, and their production work for such acts as the S.O.S. Band, Human League, Cherrelle, and Alexander O'Neal. Harris and Lewis garnered even greater recognition in 1986 when they produced Janet Jackson's hit record *Control*. To increase their autonomy as well as advance the careers of new acts, the super-producers started their own label, Perspective. First among the label's new signees were the Sounds of Blackness.

The Sounds of Blackness had been offered recording contracts before signing with Perspective, Harris explained, "but labels wanted them to change their name to the Sounds of Music or the Sounds of Harmony—anything but Sounds of Blackness." With his years of experience in the music business, Harris understood the marketing conundrum the group's name and music posed for unimaginative secular and gospel labels. "When you specify black, that often means that it won't get much attention in the pop mainstream. Also, gospel labels wanted them for just gospel, but of course, they wouldn't do anything that limiting."[14] Fortunately, SOB found the ideal partnership with Harris and Lewis.

The Evolution of Gospel

On May 7, 1991, SOB released their Perspective debut, *The Evolution of Gospel*. The record yielded three top ten songs: "The Pressure Pt. 1," "Testify," and "Optimistic," all produced by Harris and Lewis. The rhythmically dense "The Pressure" became the first gospel song since the Mighty Clouds of Joy's "Mighty High" to reach #1 on the dance chart. Less intense but equally enjoyable was "Testify." Peaking at #7 on the dance charts, "Testify" combined Minneapolis funk with old-school gospel lyrics.

Rounding out *The Evolution of Gospel*'s trio of hits was "Optimistic," which for many R&B listeners was not just a popular single but a personal anthem. A bouncy dance tune with an inspirational message, "Optimistic" encourages the listener to remain positive amid the darkness. It beautifully communicates what scholar Craig Werner calls the gospel impulse, which doesn't deny the reality of hardship but rather emphasizes the power of faith in times of despair. The gospel impulse, according to Werner,

> consists of a three step process: (1) acknowledging the burden; (2) bearing witness; (3) finding redemption. The burden grounds the song in the history of suffering that links individual and community experiences. Black folks, like all human beings who let themselves know and feel it, have their crosses to bear. Less likely than whites to subscribe to the facile optimism of America's civic ideology, most blacks maintain an awareness of limitation, of the harsh reality that the man goin' round takin' names doesn't much care whether you've done your best to live in the light of the Lord. We don't choose our burdens; we do choose our responses.[15]

"Optimistic" acknowledges how faith and hope are not always easy concepts to believe in, let alone hold on to, but presents them as a much more viable option than despair:

> You hear the voice of reason
> Telling you this can't ever be done
> No matter how hard reality seems
> Just hold on to the dream

The lyrics, along with Ann Nesby's impassioned vocals, resonated among African American listeners, making "Optimistic" one of the hit songs of 1991. The song found a place on radio stations, in homes, and at graduation ceremonies across black America.

Looking back at their storied career, Harris and Lewis remember "Optimistic" as both their favorite and most important song. As Harris notes, "That record showed us the power of music—not about hit records, but really about how music can really move people.... As many hits as we had at that point, nobody has ever talked about a record like this: People would tell us stories about how when they feel bad that's the record they put on. It had this effect which was so much above having a hit record."[16]

With the success of "Optimistic" and the other hits on *The Evolution of Gospel*, the Sounds of Blackness helped Perspective get off to a great start in its first year. The group's debut sold extremely well, received heavy radio play, and garnered a Grammy Award. And with appearances on the hugely popular *Arsenio Hall Show*, BET's *Video Soul*, and the classic variety show *Soul Train*, SOB had a visible presence in the black pop world.

The choir's aesthetics and pro-black message meshed well with the cultural politics of the period. This was the era of Spike Lee's *Malcolm X*, A Tribe Called Quest's *Low End Theory*, and NBC's *A Different World*. Perhaps nothing better illustrated SOB's connection with this era than their video for "Optimistic." The video opens with the group singing "Chains," a song that references the brutality of slavery. The first thirty seconds of the video shows the choir draped in chains in a darkened area that could be interpreted as representing the bottom of a slave ship. Then we witness three performers engaging in an interpretative dance. A bare-chested, muscular man enters the frame at the fifty-five second mark, looks sternly into the camera, and states, "Never say die." A brief pause is then followed by the beginning notes of SOB's hit single. The video's mood then shifts from somber to joyous as SOB members sing and dance in unison. In their second video, for "The Pressure," the group doesn't deviate from the form of "Optimistic." The video opens with an interlude ("Ah Been Workin'") that references slavery, features (once again) a chiseled black man, and includes energetic dancing. One major difference, however, is the video's frenetic pace, which matches the rhythmic intensity of the song.

With strong support from black video and radio outlets, SOB was on a roll. In the fall of 1991, legendary singer Luther Vandross invited the choir to join him on a four-month tour. Touring was not easy for quite a few in the group since they held other jobs, but many took leaves of absence, intent on riding the wave of their crossover success as long as possible. Not long after ending their tour with Vandross, the group released a Christmas album, *The Night before Christmas*, in 1992. That record had as its lead single "Soul Holidays," still a favorite among African Americans during the holiday season.

As one might imagine, there was great anticipation for SOB's 1994 release, *Africa to America: The Journey of the Drum*. Theatrical in form, grounded in history, and interdisciplinary in scope, *Africa to America* is divided into three main acts. The musical drama centers on the African American odyssey in the United States, providing a beautiful artistic rendering of black folks' interracial and intraracial encounters from slavery to the present. The powerful interludes—which range from spirituals ("Ah Been 'Buked" and "Sun Up to Sundown") to spoken word ("You've Taken My Blues & Gone")—transition the listener into each major act. Digging deep into the cultural archive of black America, Sounds of Blackness sample a wide range of artists, from Billie Holiday ("Strange Fruit") to Duke Ellington ("Black Butterfly") to Langston Hughes ("You've Taken My Blues & Gone"). On "Black Butterfly," the group celebrates the beauty, genius, and perseverance of African Americans, while on "Livin' the Blues," they document the persistence of racism in the United States. Ann Nesby works her vocal magic on the up-tempo "I Believe" and the powerful ballad "A Place in My Heart." Equally impressive is the vocal work of SOB newcomer Jimmy Wright, also known as "Big Jim." Wright turned in a memorable performance on "The Harder They Are the Bigger They Fall" and "The Lord Will Make a Way."

The Evolution of Gospel may have had more radio hits, but top to bottom, *Africa to America* was the better album. Its sonic journey through the history and music of African Americans, from their roots in Africa through enslavement, Jim Crow, the Great Migration, and the civil rights and Black Power movements to the post-soul era of racial accomplishments and political setbacks, was ambitious but never boring or unnecessarily weighty. As music critic Geoffrey Himes rightly pointed out, the Sounds of Blackness and Harris and Lewis were a match made in musical heaven. "The two producers have come up with the same sort of industrial-strength rhythm tracks and soulful melodies they bring to their collaborations with Janet Jackson. The ensemble's size and mission have transformed these funk beats and pop hooks, however, from erotic scenarios into a broad tapestry of spiritual and cultural concerns." Himes was especially appreciative of the group's inspirational lyrics. "Not since the glory days of Stevie Wonder, Curtis Mayfield and the Staple Singers have major R&B stars written pop hymns of such convincing optimism. In Sounds of Blackness's Ann Nesby and Jimmy Wright, Jam and Lewis have found two superb singers to carry their message. The result is an album that blends the 'mass choir' phenomenon of the gospel world, the radio-ready funk of the pop world and a hopefulness rarely heard in these bleak days."[17] Nancy Stetson of the *Chicago Tribune* shared Himes's enthusiasm: "In less-skilled hands, the sentiments expressed in 'I'm Going All the Way' and 'Everything's Gonna Be Alright' could sound trite. But when Sounds of Blackness sings, its optimism and determination are not only believable but infectious."[18]

Infectious indeed, SOB's second release garnered them another gold certification. It was a remarkable accomplishment for a group that pursued their own path of creative expression and spirituality. Forward-thinking yet firmly rooted in the rich cultural legacy of black America, Sounds of Blackness set a new standard of musicianship *and* political engagement for gospel artists. Together with acts like Take 6 and BeBe and CeCe Winans, they showcased to the world the vast sonic and lyrical possibilities within the gospel art form. Those possibilities would become even more apparent to many within the industry with the emergence of an artist whose commercial success would surpass SOB, Take 6, and every gospel musician before him: Kirk Franklin.

Epilogue

Do You Want a Revolution?
Kirk Franklin, Yolanda Adams, and the
Beginning of a New Era in Gospel Music

On May 20, 1994, 3,000 people crammed into Calvary Temple Church in Ir-
ving, Texas, for the live recording of Kirk Franklin's highly anticipated release
Whatcha Lookin' 4. Franklin rocked the crowd for three hours, performing
thirteen songs before the enthused audience. At least nine of the songs, journalist
Lisa Collins predicted in her review of the concert, "are sure to become gospel
standards."[1] The hottest act in gospel, Franklin had taken the industry by storm
with his 1993 release, *Kirk Franklin and the Family Live*. The debut catapulted
him to a level of superstardom not experienced by any gospel artist before or
since. Over the next seven years, Franklin revolutionized the genre with his
innovative compositions and arrangements, his dynamic performances, and
his liberal sampling of black urban music and street vernacular. No individual
embodied the swagger of the hip-hop era and the commercial triumphs of the
prosperity gospel more than Franklin. With domestic record sales exceeding ten
million, Franklin stands as the most successful gospel artist of any generation.
Moreover, his multiplatinum sales and high-grossing concert tours ushered in
a new age in black sacred music.

A proud native of Fort Worth, Texas, Kirk Dewayne Franklin was born on
January 26, 1970. From the cradle, Franklin had a great deal to overcome. "My
old life, like my mother's life before me, began in confusion," Franklin somberly
reflected in 2006. "When my mother was a little girl, her mom was killed. When
my mother became pregnant with me, she was fifteen." With a teenage mother
who lacked both the desire and maturity to raise her child and an absentee father
who shirked his parental responsibilities, Franklin wrestled with abandonment
issues and low self-esteem throughout his childhood and adolescent years. Much
of the love he experienced came from his grandaunt Gertrude Franklin, who did
her best to instill within him a commitment to God and family. "At age two, she

adopted me. At age four she changed my name. She became my mama. When I was ten, she was seventy."[2]

Living with Gertrude and her husband, Jack, gave the young boy some stability and nurtured his love for music:

Jack Franklin was a piano player. He played jazz and hymns and all kinds of popular music, and he even made a living at it sometimes. He was a deacon in the church, and I'm told he had an awesome voice. . . . Gertrude told me that when

FIGURE 21. Kirk Franklin at the 2006 American Music Awards. Photo courtesy of Photofest.

Jack played the old upright piano at our house, I was hypnotized. I'd sit at Jack's feet—or sit on his knee whenever he'd let me—and I'd just listen as long as he would keep playing. . . . One day I crawled up on the bench and started picking around until I found how to make sounds like the ones I'd heard Jack playing.[3]

Soaking up these informal lessons, Franklin was playing the piano by the age of four. By the age of twelve, he was directing the adult choir at Stranger's Rest Baptist Church. Even though Franklin and his grandaunt had their personal struggles, she worked hard to help him realize his dreams, selling aluminum cans to pay for his music lessons. Traditional coursework, however, was a major challenge for Franklin, who struggled socially and academically: "All the way through school, I felt weird, strange, and like a misfit."[4] The only bright spot for him was the performing arts department, where he excelled in music, drama, and fashion. Under the guidance of Jewell Kelly, his music teacher at Oscar Dean Wyatt High School, Franklin gained invaluable training.

In local church circles, Franklin developed a reputation as a talented musician with an imaginative mind, an adventurous spirit, and something of a wild streak. His work at Stranger's Rest and later Grace Temple provided important creative outlets. A major breakthrough for the budding musician came when he hooked up with the Dallas Fort Worth Mass Choir, which was under the leadership of his former teacher Jewell Kelly. Word of Franklin's talent began to spread beyond the area in 1990, when Milton Bingham selected Franklin to direct the combined mass choir at the Gospel Music Workshop of America. Not long after his collaboration with Bingham, one of Franklin's songs, "Everyday with Jesus," appeared on the Dallas Fort Worth Mass Choir's release *I Will Let Nothing Separate Me*.

An increasingly confident Franklin decided to organize a seventeen-member ensemble called "the Family." Within months of its formation, the Family had a live recording at Grace Temple. A demo of the live recording, which occurred on July 25, 1992, caught the attention of numerous record executives in the gospel industry. One of the labels interested in Franklin was an upstart called GospoCentric, headed by the talented visionary Vicki Lataillade. A veteran in the industry, Lataillade had amassed a wealth of experience at various companies, including Light Records. With a $6,000 loan from her father's pension, she started the company with the hopes of building God's kingdom and transforming the landscape of gospel music. Her vision had an immediate effect on Franklin: "Unlike those big labels and their impressive sales pitches, Vicki didn't spend all her time boasting about how great her company was or how much money it could make for us the first six months. Instead, she talked about her passion to serve God, to spread the Word, and to change people's lives through the medium of gospel music."[5] Moved by the honesty of her pitch, Franklin signed with the company. "GospoCentric bought that original tape from me for five thousand dollars, cleaned it up, did some new voice- and sound-over dubs, then put together an incredible master and released *Why We Sing* in June of 1993."[6] Within two and half years of its release, the record was certified platinum.

When listening to Franklin's debut, one is immediately struck by his thorough attention to detail as a performer, arranger, and choir director. The choir had barely been together a year, but its members sound as if they had been performing collectively for a lifetime. The ultra-funky "He Can Handle It" and the Franklin and David Mann–led "He's Able" swing hard, while "Silver and Gold" and "Till We Meet Again" are beautiful gospel ballads. There were many great moments on the album, but the song that resonated most with gospel fans was "Why We Sing." Inaugurating a new era in gospel performance, "Why We Sing" featured Franklin reciting rather than singing his verses as the choir engaged in call-and-response. The song introduced what I regard as three hallmarks of a classic Franklin performance: tight vocals, dynamic musicianship, and an innovative arrangement. Franklin had put together an impressive debut recording, but the ambitious musician could have never imagined the overwhelming response to his music.

The record got off to an extremely good start and then picked up steam as new markets were introduced to gospel's latest sensation. By the beginning of 1994, nearly everyone in gospel seemed focused on the rising superstar. In April, Franklin cracked *Billboard*'s Top 200 Albums chart. That same month, he dethroned the Mississippi Mass Choir from the #1 position on the gospel charts. By the end of the year, Franklin's sales had hit the 300,000 mark, no easy feat for a gospel album put out by an independent label. Then in 1995, the record was certified gold, still a rare achievement in the gospel genre. The twenty-five-year-old's success brought him tremendous attention and acclaim from veterans in the field.

"There's no need for anybody to fear Kirk Franklin's success and where it will take him or the music," Shirley Caesar noted in an interview praising the newcomer. "Gospel is becoming big business. I hope they play 'Why We Sing' in a nightclub, everywhere they can play it."[7] Caesar's commentary illuminates one of the more interesting aspects of Franklin's meteoric rise: not all but many within the industry interpreted his crossover success as good for business in general. This is not to say that there was no criticism of Franklin—there most definitely was—but it was different in tone and intensity than that of other crossover acts before him.

Franklin appreciated the love and acceptance. And in return for his peers' and elders' generosity, he sought to leverage his personal success into better conditions for all gospel artists. In another article by Lisa Collins, he said, "For years, gospel artists have never gotten the same respect. We've always received second-class treatment. With sales like these, we can demand better treatment."[8]

Even though Franklin was not signed to his company, Jerry Mannery of Malaco felt the youngster's success boded well for the industry as a whole: "Franklin's success, combined with the advent of Soundscan, has proven that gospel sells at venues that were once question marks for gospel marketers—namely, Christian bookstores and mainstream retail. It has further demonstrated that urban listeners enjoy—and will buy—gospel if they are exposed to it."[9]

Mannery's colleague Milton Bingham of Savoy urged caution. "No question, there [have] been advances, but the real world in gospel is still average sales of 50,000 units. The select few should be complimented, but it hasn't changed the reality. I'm not so sure the secular world is ready."[10] But Bingham's cautionary note failed to temper the enthusiasm of some industry insiders. In her end-of-the-year report on the state of the gospel industry, Lisa Collins centered much of her conversation around Franklin, the unprecedented response to his debut, and its larger implications for the genre: "If I can't seem to stop talking about Franklin, it's because he can't seem to stop setting records and then breaking them. Hopefully he will do for gospel what Garth Brooks has done for country."[11]

Conversations around the "Franklin effect" intensified in 1996 as the industry prepared for the arrival of *Whatcha Lookin' 4*. Franklin had completed the record in the spring of 1995, but because of the phenomenal success of *Kirk Franklin and the Family Live*, GospoCentric had pushed back the release date three times. Storming to the top of the gospel charts and landing as high as #23 on the pop charts, the record won the 1997 Grammy for Best Contemporary Soul Album. Fan favorites included "Melodies from Heaven" and "Conquerors." Surpassing its predecessor in sales, *Whatcha Lookin' 4* was certified double platinum. The hits kept coming for the gospel star in 1997, when he released *God's Property from Kirk Franklin's Nu Nation*.

This record included the smash hit "Stomp," seven minutes of gospel funk. A year later, Franklin released *The Nu Nation Project*, another top seller anchored by the hits "Lean on Me," "Something about the Name Jesus," and "Revolution." On the latter song, Franklin railed at racism, absentee fathers who neglected their parental duties, and hypocritical church folk. To realize his artistic vision, he relied on an array of artists, including Bono, Mary J. Blige, Crystal Lewis, John P. Kee, Men of Standard, and even his old high school choir. Not just a trendsetter but a game changer, Franklin moved 3 million units with *God's Property* and an additional 2 million with *Nu Nation*. Crossing a variety of markets, Franklin attracted considerable attention in the secular and gospel worlds, had his videos played on BET and MTV, and grabbed the covers of monthlies ranging from *Ebony* to *Vibe*.

Franklin was not the only gospel artist enjoying great commercial success. Christian music sales exploded at a rate of 41 percent between 1996 and 1997, increasing from $381 million to $538 million.[12] This upward trend continued well into the start of the twenty-first century as the genre witnessed blockbuster releases from Fred Hammond, Yolanda Adams, Donnie McClurkin, Trin-i-tee 5:7, and CeCe Winans. Of all the crossover successes of the 1990s, Yolanda Adams might have been the most inspiring.

FIGURE 22. Yolanda Adams performing in 2005. Photo courtesy of Columbia TriStar/Photofest.

Anything but an overnight sensation, Adams had paid her dues on the gospel circuit since the 1980s. A native of Houston, Texas, Adams was the oldest child of Major Leon Adams and Carolyn Jean Adams. Though church was very much a part of their lives, Major and Carolyn Adams surrounded their children with a wide range of cultural entertainment. "My parents never said, 'You can't sing R&B,' or 'You can't sing jazz.' I just chose gospel music because it was at the heart of me, but we listened to everything in my house, from Sarah Vaughan and Ella Fitzgerald to Beethoven and Bach."[13] Adams's upbringing informed her aesthetic sensibilities, while the devastating loss of her father when she was only thirteen matured her socially and spiritually.[14]

Smart and immensely talented, Adams attended Sterling High School and then Texas Southern University, where she majored in journalism. Upon her graduation from college, she pursued a career in education as an elementary school teacher in Houston's public school system. On the weekends, she performed gospel in the greater Houston area. Soon, the world beyond the sprawling Texas metropolis learned of Adams's immense talent. A year before graduating from Texas Southern, Adams gained national attention as the lead vocalist on the Southeast Inspirational Choir's hit single "My Liberty," which was released in 1982. If you regularly listened to gospel radio or even occasionally attended church in the 1980s, you couldn't miss this song. It was everywhere. On "My Liberty," Adams displays incredible range, effortlessly moving from soprano to alto, punctuating her notes with soaring shouts and husky growls. Her jazzy runs and ad-libs would be repeated at black church services across the country. Scholar E. Patrick Johnson vividly remembered how "I got the church to shoutin' every Sunday by singing 'My Liberty.'"[15]

So impressed was Thomas Whitfield with Adams's performance that he offered to produce a solo record for her on the Sound of Gospel label. Accepting his offer, Adams released her first solo record, *Just as I Am*, in 1987. "When I first started with Thomas Whitfield, my plan was to do the album during the summer on my time off from teaching. I never dreamed of leaving the school system, and when I did, it was a huge step, but I'm so glad I took that step on faith."[16]

So, too, was the gospel world. In 1990, Adams signed with Ben Tankard's Tribute Records and elevated her career to another level with the release of *Through the Storm* in 1991. Her admiration of Shirley Horn and Nancy Wilson surfaces throughout the record, from the dramatic ballads to the up-tempo grooves. On songs like the Mervyn Warren–produced "The Only Way" and "You Know That I Know," Adams fused the spiritual fervor of gospel with the adventurous spirit of jazz. The record's finest moments, however, are the power ballads, particularly the title cut, "Even Me," and "Just a Prayer Away." Dramatic but not overwrought, "Through the Storm" was splendid. The Roberta Martin cover "Even Me" was sublime. And "Just a Prayer Away" was certain to draw attention from gospel's adult contemporary crowd. Adams's luminous voice was black gospel pop at its finest, most elegant self. "Think Whitney Houston, not Mahalia Jackson," Amy Linden once wrote in summarizing the musical talent of Adams. Linden was dead-on in her assessment.[17] Much like Houston, Adams diligently studied her vocal idols and synthesized their strengths into her own distinctive style.

Staying with the Houston comparison, we must also note how Adams's popularity soared as a result of her dynamic live performances. Consider as a case in point her legendary performance on the 1991 Stellar Awards, at which she delivered an amazing rendition of "Even Me." With her producer, Ben Tankard, at the piano, Adams stretched the Roberta Martin classic into eight minutes. The faces of various audience members were priceless as Adams interjected much-needed energy and spirit to the rather stuffy awards show. The talented singer began the song in a crystal-clear tone, upped the intensity around the minute and a half mark, and then thirty seconds later went full gospel throttle. "I need a 'right now' blessing," she shouted three times as the crowd responded enthusiastically to her ad-libs. Caught up in the moment, Shirley Caesar admiringly looked at the statuesque singer. Twenty years before, Caesar had sung the Martin standard, and now Adams was updating the tune for another generation.

The music wound down after four and a half minutes, as it was clearly time for a commercial break. But Adams was not done. "Even me, Lord Jesus," she moaned. "Bless even me Lord Jesus." Letting the Spirit take over, Adams shifted into full confessional mode: "I need a little more forgiveness, I need a little more patience, I need a little more temperance, I need a whole lot of the Holy Ghost, I need a whole lot of the HOLY GHOST."[18] Thunderous applause greeted Adams as she exited the stage with her fellow gospel peers standing in awe.

To build on the buzz of her stellar performance and the accolades and awards following the release of *Through the Storm*, Adams headed to the studio to record *Save the World*. A trio of ballads, "I'll Always Remember," "Let Us Worship Him," and "The Battle Is the Lord's," anchored the record. Written by V. Michael McKay, "The Battle Is the Lord's" assumed anthem status in the gospel community and propelled *Save the World* near the top of the charts.

Adams had all the ingredients for superstardom. And when she signed with the secular label Elektra in 1998, many predicted immediate crossover success. The media-savvy star promised to remain true to her gospel roots. "We had about 11 record companies chasing us," Adams told *Billboard*, "and this is the only secular label that told me that I didn't have to change a thing."[19]

A year after signing with Elektra, Adams released the crossover hit *Mountain High . . . Valley Low*. Critical to the record's success was the confessional "Open My Heart," a power ballad produced by the formidable team of Jimmy Jam Harris and Terry Lewis. Not just popular on gospel radio, the song became Adams's first top ten R&B hit. The song's popularity in the R&B world was a reflection of the compatibility of Adams's vocals with the lush pop sounds of black soul music. It also revealed her ability to connect with listeners in deep and meaningful ways. "Adams's genius lies in the subtlety of her faith," critic Tom Terrell observed in a *Vibe* feature. "She doesn't beat listeners over the head with Jesus like some of her contemporaries do, yet it's easy to appreciate her belief in God even if you don't share her faith."[20] With the crossover success of "Open My Heart" and outstanding cuts like "Fragile Heart," "In the Midst of It All," and the Warryn Campbell–produced/Mary Mary–penned "Time to Change" and "Yeah," *Mountain High* was eventually certified platinum. The record secured Adams's several awards, including a Grammy, appearances on well-known television shows, and much praise from her peers. When her colleague and friend Kirk Franklin commended her as "the illest singer in gospel," hundreds of thousands of music fans nodded in agreement.

To cap off the success of *Mountain High,* Adams released the live recording *The Experience* and another studio record, *Believe.* Her second studio outing for Elektra was certified gold. Shortly thereafter, the singer joined Kirk Franklin and Donnie McClurkin, a gifted singer whose hit song "Stand" played on both gospel and R&B airwaves, for the Hopewell tour. A testament to gospel's growing popularity, the tour boasted sold out audiences in cities across the nation.

Tremendous buzz surrounded the Hopewell tour, as well as the groundbreaking music coming from new acts. The first decade of the 2000s witnessed highly acclaimed releases from new acts like Mary Mary and Tonéx. With their daring infusion of hip-hop, R&B, and jazz into their music, their sartorial choices, their hobnobbing with secular musicians, and their immersion in the larger world of pop culture, these musicians transformed popular perceptions of what a gospel artist could and ought to be. And like the gospel trailblazers who came before them, they also confronted the growing pains that always comes with the genre's evolution. As their popularity increased, they grappled with new and old questions surrounding gospel's relationship to the larger world: To what extent should gospel music engage the sounds and visuals of mainstream pop culture, and how far is too far? If Hollywood came calling via reality shows, singing competitions, or even sitcoms, should they answer? How would black gospel artists relate to the white Christian industry and white televangelists, including those whose political interests and affiliations diverged from those of black gospel music's fan base? Did gospel music artists have a larger political responsibility? And would their embrace of those responsibilities reflect the conservative or progressive strands within the black church? In recent years, we have seen such issues play out in highly publicized debates surrounding gospel star Tonéx's coming out as bisexual, Kim Burrell's condemnation of gay marriage, the participation of gospel stars in the reality show phenomenon, and the gospel community's response to the many transformations within the larger political world.

Notwithstanding the art form's many challenges and changes, it has remained a source of cultural affirmation and spiritual sustenance for millions, not just in the United States but around the world. In fact, one of the most interesting developments in recent years has been the upsurge in gospel music's popularity internationally. With the geographical expansion of Pentecostalism and the rising number of charismatic churches in the Global South, Latin America and especially Africa have been important sites for the production and consumption of black gospel music forms. Of course, what also makes gospel music so vibrant as an art form is its rootedness in local communities. Beyond the airwaves and our iPods, black sacred music finds its most passionate expression among regular churchgoers in small and large congregations who still sing the music of James Cleveland, Andraé Crouch, Shirley Caesar, and other gospel pioneers. It also derives its strength from black women and men who still support organizations like James Cleveland's Gospel Music Workshop of America, which in the summer of 2017 celebrated its fiftieth anniversary.

As noted in the introduction, I was able to attend the GMWA's historic convention at the Sheraton Convention Center in downtown Atlanta. Over the course of the week, participants heard performances from established and emerging stars; rehearsed old songs and introduced new material; attended academic classes focused on the art, business, and history of gospel music; and generally enjoyed each other's fellowship. One of my most memorable moments involved a session in which James Ford, the only living member of the original GMWA board, Norma Jean Pender, former publicity director for the GMWA and Detroit radio personality, and longtime GMWA member and historian Sandra Rose discussed the organization's history and cultural significance, traded stories and memories of James Cleveland, and shared their vision of gospel's future. Eighty years old but sharp as ever, Pender, who had suffered a stroke the previous year, became quite emotional during her reflections on the organization's fifty-year journey. "We could have never imagined this," Pender informed the class as her hands gestured toward the massive convention center filled with moving bodies and spirited chatter.[21] Frequently, the Detroit resident interspersed her recollections of GMWA's beginnings with commentary on the Motor City's rebellion of 1967, which clearly weighed heavily on her mind. She seemed to be celebrating not just the progress of the organization but the making and remaking of a people. Her commentary, as well as that of other elders in attendance at the fiftieth anniversary convention, consumed my thoughts in the days following the gathering. Writing the history of gospel music entails not just documenting the stars and the hit records and the sold-out tours but also capturing what the music meant to people like Norma Pender, Sandra Rose, James Ford, and the thousands of black folks who set aside their hard-earned money to buttress the work of the GMWA. Much has changed since James Cleveland started the

GMWA in 1967, but one constant has been the centrality of gospel music in the lives of millions of African Americans.

On my drive back home, as Thomas Whitfield's "Wrapped Up, Tied Up, and Tangled Up" blared from the speakers, my thoughts turned to a Ralph Ellison quote from "Juneteenth" that still has deep resonance: "We know where we are by the way we walk. We know where we are by the way we talk. We know where we are by the way we sing. We know where we are by the way we dance. We know where we are by the way we praise the Lord on high."[22]

Notes

Introduction

1. "Two Cities Pay Tribute to Mahalia Jackson," *Ebony*, April 1972, 64.

2. "9,000 Pay Tribute to Mahalia Jackson," *Los Angeles Times*, February 2, 1972, 10.

3. "Mahalia Jackson: A Millionairess' Legacy to Blacks," *Jet*, February 17, 1972, 20.

4. "A Week of Gospel Happiness: 4,000 Church Musicians Meet in L.A.," *Ebony*, November 1972, 86.

5. Capouya, *Florida Soul*.

6. A. Ace Burgess, "Can Gospel Rock?," *Jet*, April 29, 1976, 24–26; Karima A. Haynes, "The Gospel Controversy: Are the New Songs Too Jazzy and Too Worldly?," *Ebony*, March 1992, 76–82; Roxanne Brown, "The Glory of Gospel: Will the Message Be Lost in the Contemporary Sound?," *Ebony*, May 1988, 60–66; "Has Gospel Music Become Too Contemporary?," *Jet*, August 21, 1995, 14–16, 60.

7. Geoffrey Himes, "Return of the Gospel Truth," *Washington Post*, June 26, 1994, G13.

8. Larry Robinson, interview with author, June 13, 2018.

9. "Carl B's Exclusive Interview with God's World Owner, Larry Robinson," DetroitGospel.com, October 21, 2009, http://detroitgospel.com/gods-world-needs-you-tosurvive/.

10. David Reid, interview with author, June 18, 2018.

11. David Reid interview.

12. As my book demonstrates, though, not all crossover attempts proved successful, as some gospel artists lost their fan base after switching to a secular label.

13. Haynes, "Gospel Controversy," 82.

14. Teresa Hairston interview, Mellonee V. Burnim Collection, 1881–1996, Archives of African American Music and Culture, Indiana University.

15. See Boyer, *Golden Age of Gospel*; Spencer, *Protest and Praise*; M. Harris, *Rise of Gospel Blues*; Darden, *People Get Ready!*; Heilbut, *Gospel Sound*; Williams-Jones,

"Afro-American Gospel Music"; Marovich, *City Called Heaven*; and Zolten, *Great God A'Mighty!*

16. Fortunately, digging deeper into gospel's more recent history has been made easier with the important work of scholars like Mellonee V. Burnim, Brooksie Eugene Harrington, Deborah Smith Pollard, Jon Spencer, Guthrie Ramsey, and Birgitta Johnson. In addition, historians like Shawn David Young and David Stowe provide useful insights into the contemporary Christian music genre. Harrington, "Shirley Caesar"; B. Johnson, "Back to the Heart of Worship"; D. Smith, *When the Church Becomes Your Party*; J. Spencer, *Protest and Praise*; Stowe, *No Sympathy for the Devil*; Young, *Gray Sabbath*; Ramsey, *Race Music*.

17. Geoffrey Himes, "Shout It! Gospel According to Shirley Caesar," *Washington Post*, April 3, 1987, B7.

Chapter 1. Lord Let Me Be an Instrument

1. Jon Landau, "Review: Amazing Grace," *Rolling Stone*, August 3, 1972, https://www.rollingstone.com/music/music-album-reviews/review-amazing-grace-aretha-franklin-251798/.

2. Dobkin, *I Never Loved a Man the Way I Love You*; Werner, *Higher Ground*, 126–39, 174–87.

3. Franklin and Ritz, *From These Roots*, 150.

4. Franklin and Ritz, 151.

5. See Boyer, "Overview"; and Cone, *Spirituals and the Blues*.

6. Williams-Jones, "Afro-American Gospel Music," 373.

7. Williams-Jones, 374.

8. Fowler, *Conversations with Nikki Giovanni*, 4.

9. "James Cleveland: King of Gospel," *Ebony*, November 1968, 74.

10. Dorothy Gilliam, "The 'Black Book': How It Was," *Washington Post*, March 6, 1974.

11. M. Harris, *Rise of Gospel Blues*, 180–208.

12. For a more detailed discussion of black religious life in Chicago during this period, see Marovich, *City Called Heaven*; Best, *Passionately Human*; Baldwin, *Chicago's New Negroes*, 155–92; and Pinder, *Painting the Gospel*, 25–50.

13. Best, *Passionately Human*, 2.

14. "James Cleveland: King of Gospel," 82.

15. Marovich, *City Called Heaven*, 158–60.

16. Heilbut, *Gospel Sound*, 206.

17. Salvatore, *Singing in a Strange Land*, 126.

18. "James Cleveland: King of Gospel," 82.

19. Quoted in Marovich, *City Called Heaven*, 261–62.

20. "Looters Raid Savoy Office," *Billboard*, May 23, 1960, 4.

21. For an alternative view of Savoy and Lubinsky, see Cherry and Griffith, "Down to Business."

22. For more on Savoy's importance to bebop, see DeVeaux, *Birth of Bebop*, 303–6.

23. Quoted in the liner notes, James Cleveland, *James Cleveland with the Gospel Chimes* (Savoy Records, 1962).

24. "Savoy Cites Wherefores of Spiritual Disc Boom," *Billboard*, February 27, 1965, 44.

25. Branch, *Pillar of Fire*.

26. King, *Why We Can't Wait*, 144–45.

27. James Cleveland, *Peace Be Still* (Savoy Records, 1963).

28. Cleveland, *Peace Be Still*.

29. Cleveland, *Peace Be Still*.

30. Heilbut, *Gospel Sound*, 214.

31. Cleveland, *Peace Be Still*.

32. "James Cleveland Heads Gospel Extravaganza," *New York Amsterdam News*, May 21, 1966, 22; "Gospel USA Sunday at Carnegie," *New York Amsterdam News*, September 24, 1966, 8; "James Cleveland Singers Due Oct. 27," *Pittsburgh Courier*, October 9, 1965, 15; "Pythagoras Knights Set Gospel Event," *Norfolk Journal and Guide*, October 23, 1965, A20; "James Cleveland Due Here Sunday," *New Pittsburgh Courier*, November 18, 1967, 6.

33. "James Cleveland: King of Gospel," 80.

34. "James Cleveland: King of Gospel," 82.

35. "Letters," *Ebony*, December 1968, 26.

36. "Letters," 29.

37. Ed Smith interview, August 13, 1992, Mellonee V. Burnim Collection, 1861–1996, Archives of African American Music and Culture, Indiana University.

38. Gospel Music Workshop of America's Constitution, folder 3841, Floyd McKissick Papers, Southern Historical Collection, Wilson Library, University of North Carolina, Chapel Hill.

39. L. Neal, "Resolutions," 234.

40. Touré, "We Must Create a National Black Intelligentsia," 458–59.

41. For a more in-depth analysis of the black artistic initiatives and collectives that emerged during the 1960s and 1970s, see Bracey, Sanchez, and Smethurst, *SOS—Calling All Black People*; Smethurst, *Black Arts Movement*; Napoleon Jones Henderson, "Remembering AfriCOBRA and the Black Arts Movement in 1960s Chicago," *Nka: Journal of Contemporary African Art* 30 (Spring 2012): 88; Collins and Crawford, *New Thoughts on the Black Arts Movement*; Phelps, *Visionary Women Writers of Chicago's Black Arts Movement*; Widener, *Black Arts West*; Field, Horah, and Stewart, *LA Rebellion*; and Avilez, *Radical Aesthetics and Modern Black Nationalism*.

42. "A Week of Gospel Happiness: 4,000 Church Musicians Meet in L.A.," *Ebony*, November 1972, 86.

43. See A. Cohen's *Amazing Grace*, 132–44.

44. John Abbey, "Rev James Cleveland," *Blues and Soul*, December 1972, Rock's Back Pages Library, http://www.rocksbackpages.com/Library/Article/rev-james-cleveland.

45. See Grady-Willis, *Challenging US Apartheid*; and Brown-Nagin, *Courage to Dissent*.

46. "Negroes Barred Again by Maddox's Café," *New York Times*, September 29, 1964, 26.

47. Al Haas, "12,000 Gather to Spread Gospel Music Message," *Chicago Tribune*, August 31, 1980.

48. "GMWA Director Edward M. Smith Dies at Age 59," *Billboard*, April 9, 1994, 16.

49. Woodrow T. Lewis to Floyd McKissick, September 12, 1975, folder 3851, Floyd McKissick Papers.

50. For more on the politics of Floyd McKissick, see McKissick, *Three-Fifths of a Man*; and Farrington, *Black Republicans and the Transformation of the GOP*.

51. "McKissick's New Town for Blacks Called 'Soul City,'" *Jet*, January 30, 1969, 9.

52. "Soul City Gets $14 Million from U.S. Government," *Jet*, January 24, 1974, 26.

53. Lewis to McKissick, September 12, 1975, folder 3851, Floyd McKissick Papers.

54. Edward M. Smith to McKissick, November 21, 1975, folder 3849, Floyd McKissick Papers.

55. Edward M. Smith to Jack Stewart, April 6, 1976, folder 3849, Floyd McKissick Papers.

56. Edward M. Smith to Jack Stewart, June 15, 1976, folder 3849, Floyd McKissick Papers.

57. Quoted in Link, *Righteous Warrior*, 169.

58. Fergus, *Liberalism, Black Power, and the Making of American Politics*, 217.

59. James Harper, "Power in the Choir Lofts: Gospel, the Music Motown Can't Take Away from Detroit," *Detroit Free Press*, April 20, 1975.

60. "20,000 Applaud Cleveland Black Gospel," *Billboard*, August 16, 1975, 3.

61. "ABC Move Epitomizes Expansions," *Billboard*, August 10, 1974, 70.

62. A. Ace Burgess, "Can Gospel Rock? No! James Cleveland, Yes! Mighty Clouds," *Jet*, April 29, 1976, 24–26.

63. Quoted in Burgess, 25.

64. Broughton, *Black Gospel*, 110.

65. Walter Rico Burrell, "The Gospel According to Andraé Crouch," *Ebony*, September 1982, 60.

66. See Tony Cummings, "Bishop John Francis: From the Inspirational Choir to Ruach Ministries Choir," *Cross Rhythms*, July 29, 2007, http://www.crossrhythms .co.uk/articles/music/Bishop_John_Francis_From_the_Inspirational_Choir_to _Ruach_Ministries_Choir/28292/p1/.

67. Charles L. Sanders, "The Holy Land: Top American Stars Have Israelis Shouting and Dancing in Jerusalem," *Ebony*, December 1983, 36–37, 40–42.

68. Eschen, *Satchmo Blows Up the World*; Kelley, *Africa Speaks, America Answers*.

69. Eschen, *Satchmo Blows Up the World*, 150.

70. Eschen, 151.

71. Eschen, 160.

72. Mick Brown, "Pastor Cleveland, Superstar," *The Guardian*, December 24, 1980.

73. John Ryle, *Sunday Times* (London), July 14, 1985.

74. Ryle, *Sunday Times*.

75. Jean Williams, "Word Looking to Expand, Seminars Set, Reps Hired," *Billboard,* November 7, 1981, 5.

76. Bobby Musengwa, interview with author, November 7, 2016.

77. Boyer, *Golden Age of Gospel*, 248. In the music of Hlongwane (particularly his *Crosspower Experience* 2) and Joyous Celebration, one will definitely hear the influence of Cleveland.

78. Here I draw on the observations of music critic Tom Smucker. Smucker, "Precious Lord," 168.

79. "Mightiest of Them All: The Rev. James Cleveland," *New Journal and Guide,* April 20, 1979.

80. "Mightiest of Them All."

81. Reese, *Historical Foundation, Formation and Development*, 26.

82. Ed Smith interview, August 13, 1992.

83. James Cleveland, *Recorded Live at Symphony Hall in Newark, NJ* (Savoy Records, 1984).

84. Murray, *Omni-Americans*, 58.

85. James Cleveland, *This Too, Will Pass* (Savoy Records, 1983).

86. "Illness Hospitalizes Top Gospel Recording Star," *Jet*, December 13, 1982, 45.

87. Chris Willman, "Singing the Praises of the King of Gospel: A Procession of Musical Giants Pay Their Respects to the Rev. James Cleveland in a Spiritual Tribute," *Los Angeles Times*, October 31, 1990, F9.

88. Richard Harrington, "Inspiring the Multitudes: The Rev. James Cleveland and His Gospel Legacy," *Washington Post*, February 17, 1991, G1.

89. Harrington, G1.

90. Harrington, G1.

91. Harrington, G1.

Chapter 2. A Special Kind of Witness

1. Thurman, *Jesus and the Disinherited*, 98.

2. For a broader history of the CCM industry, see Stowe, *No Sympathy for the Devil*; and Howard and Streck, *Apostles of Rock*.

3. Robert Darden, "Remembering Andrae Crouch, Dead at 72," *Christianity Today*, January 8, 2015, https://www.christianitytoday.com/ct/2015/january-web-only/remembering-andrae-crouch-dead-at-72.html.

4. See Broughton, *Too Close to Heaven*, 145. For more on Crouch's contributions to the gospel music industry, see Kidula, "Gospel of Andraé Crouch"; and Darden, *People Get Ready!*, 276–82.

5. Rodgers, *Age of Fracture*, 171, 207.

6. Deborah Evans Price, "R.I.P. Andraé Crouch: Remembering the Gospel Great's Immense Influence," *Billboard*, January 9, 2015, https://www.billboard.com/articles/news/6436383/andrae-crouch-remembering-gospel-great-influence.

7. "Our Tribute to Andraé Crouch: The Father of Modern Gospel," *Keep the Faith*, January 25, 2015, http://www.keepthefaith.co.uk/2015/01/25/our-tribute-to-andrae-crouch-the-father-of-modern-gospel/.

8. Sergii, "Andraé Crouch: He Was Certainly No Grouch," *Nairaland Forum*, January 15, 2015, http://www.nairaland.com/sergii/posts.

9. Weeks, "This House, This Music," 51.

10. *New York Amsterdam News*, August 21, 1982.

11. *Billboard*, July 28, 1979, R12.

12. P. Robinson, "Race, Space, and the Evolution of Black Los Angeles," 41.

13. See Dodge, *School of Arizona Dranes*.

14. Crouch with Ball, *Through It All*, 38.

15. Crouch with Ball, 46.

16. Quoted in the liner notes, Andraé Crouch and the Disciples, *Take the Message Everywhere* (Light Records, 1968).

17. Crouch and the Disciples, *Take the Message Everywhere*.

18. *Billboard*, February 6, 1971, 12.

19. Crouch with Ball, *Through It All*, 103.

20. Crouch with Ball, 104.

21. Crouch with Ball, 104.

22. Andraé Crouch and the Disciples, *Keep on Singin'* (Light Records, 1971).

23. "Crouch, Disciples Perform Gospel at 15 College Sites," *Billboard*, October 5, 1974.

24. Marvin Winans, speech at Rock and Roll Hall of Fame, April 12, 2015, https://www.youtube.com/watch?v=0swvIDBUwj8.

25. See Cine, *From Reconciliation to Revolution*.

26. Carson and Holloran, *Knock at Midnight*, 201.

27. Eskridge, *God's Forever Family*, 160.

28. *Time*, June 21, 1971.

29. Young, *Gray Sabbath*, 181.

30. For a history of Campus Crusade for Christ, see J. Turner, *Bill Bright and Campus Crusade for Christ*.

31. See Stowe, *No Sympathy for the Devil*, 87–96.

32. Rossinow, *Politics of Authenticity*, 12.

33. Stowe, *No Sympathy for the Devil*, 84.

34. Stowe, 86.

35. Crouch with Ball, *Through It All*, 106.

36. Quoted in liner notes, Andraé Crouch and the Disciples, *Keep on Singin'*.

37. Andraé Crouch, *"Live" at Carnegie Hall* (Light Records, 1973).

38. "Andraé Crouch Honored Again," *Billboard*, September 6, 1975, 56.

39. Crouch with Ball, *Through It All*, 72.

40. Andraé Crouch and the Disciples, *Take Me Back* (Light Records, 1974).

41. Hollie L. West, "The Gospel Music, According to Crouch," *Washington Post*, May 23, 1977.

42. Crouch with Ball, *Through It All*, 132.

43. Crouch with Ball, 132.

44. B. Johnson, "Back to the Heart of Worship," 109.

45. B. Johnson, 108.

46. White and Dallas quoted in the liner notes, Andraé Crouch, *Live in London*.

47. Darden, "Remembering Andrae Crouch, Dead at 72."

48. Jean Williams, "Crouch Dean Spurs WB's Gospel Debut," *Billboard*, June 9, 1979, 3.

49. Ed Ochs, "A Traditional Music Challenged by Change," *Billboard*, September 27, 1980, G10.

50. Ochs, G22.

51. Ochs, G22.

52. Ochs, G22.

53. Carla Darling, "Warner Bros. Issues Controversial Crouch LP," *Billboard*, November 7, 1981, 62.

54. Dennis Hunt, "Pop-Gospel: Rebel with a Cause," *Los Angeles Times*, September 24, 1982.

55. Walter Rico Burrell, "The Gospel According to Andraé Crouch," *Ebony*, September 1982, 60.

56. Darling, "Warner Bros. Issues New Controversial Crouch LP," 62.

57. Richard Harrington, "A Soft Crouch, an Uncertain Mills," *Washington Post*, August 20, 1982.

58. Marie Moore, "Andraé Crouch Thinks S. African Boycott 'Stupid,'" *New York Amsterdam News*, August 21, 1982.

59. William Seraile, "What Message Did Rev. Andraé Crouch Deliver in S. Africa?," *New York Amsterdam News*, September 4, 1982.

60. "Andraé Crouch Arrested on Cocaine Rap in L.A.," *Jet*, November 29, 1982.

61. "Andraé Crouch Arrested," *Baltimore Afro-American*, November 20, 1982; "Grammy Winner Faces Drug Charge," *Chicago Tribune*, November 13, 1982; "Police Arrest Gospel Singer on Drug Possession Charge," *New York Times*, November 15, 1982.

62. "Cocaine Charges Dismissed against Crouch and Turner," *Jet*, December 6, 1982.

63. Bob Darden, "Gospel Lectern," *Billboard*, March 22, 1986, 60.

64. Quincy Jones, *The Color Purple* (Qwest, 1986).

65. Cullen, *Restless in the Promised Land*, 101.

66. For an analysis of this performance, see Dyson, *Reflecting Black*, 35–60.

67. Dyson, 58.

68. Chris Williams, "Producer Bill Maxwell Discusses the Winans Sophomore, Tomorrow, on Its 30th Anniversary," *Waxpoetics*, May 29, 2004, https://www.waxpoetics.com/blog/features/producer-bill-maxwell-discusses-the-winans-tomorrow-on-its-thirtieth-anniversary/.

69. Marvin Winans, speech at Rock and Roll Hall of Fame.

Chapter 3. Hold My Mule

1. Shirley Caesar, *Live . . . in Chicago* (Rejoice Records, 1988).

2. Caesar, *Live . . . in Chicago*.

3. Harrington, "Shirley Caesar," 82.

4. J. Johnson, *God's Trombones*, 5.

5. Caesar, *Lady, the Melody, and the Word*, 93.

6. Sanders, "Pentecostal Ethics and the Prosperity Gospel," 150.

7. Caesar, *Lady, the Melody, and the Word*, 157.

8. Gilkes, "Shirley Caesar and the Souls of Black Folk," 12.

9. "First Lady of Gospel," *Ebony*, September 1977, 98. See also "Gospel Star Shirley Caesar Says Female Pastors Ok!," *New Pittsburgh Courier*, August 10, 1985.

10. For a broader reading on black women and their relationship to feminism, see Collins, *Black Feminist Thought*; Cannon, *Black Womanist Ethics*; hooks, *Ain't I a Woman?*; Hull, Scott, and Smith, *All the Women Are White*; Guy-Sheftall, *Words of Fire*; and V. Watkins, "New Directions in Black Women's Studies."

11. Caesar, *Lady, the Melody, and the Word*, 10.

12. Washington, "Durham, North Carolina, a City of Negro Enterprises"; Brown, *Upbuilding Black Durham*; Frazier, "Durham, Capital of the Black Middle Class"; Weare, *Black Business in the New South*.

13. Brundage, *Southern Past*, 234.

14. Frazier, "Durham, Capital of the Black Middle Class," 333.

15. Interview with Hallie Caesar by Glenn Hinson, May 21, 1979 (H-0194), in the Southern Oral History Program Collection, Series H: Piedmont Industrialization (04007H), Southern Historical Collection, Wilson Library, University of North Carolina at Chapel Hill.

16. Caesar, *Lady, the Melody, and the Word*, 34.

17. See W. Turner, *United Holy Church of America*; and W. Turner, "East Coast Celebration of Azusa."

18. Caesar, *Lady, the Melody, and the Word*, 33.

19. Caesar, 33.

20. Caesar, 18.

21. Charlie T. Roach, box 231, Southern Oral History Program Collection, Southern Historical Collection, Wilson Library, University of North Carolina, Chapel Hill.

22. Caesar, *Lady, the Melody, and the Word*, 35.

23. Caesar, 62.

24. Marovich, *City Called Heaven*, 234.

25. Bob Darden, "Shirley Caesar: Singing Evangelist," *Rejoice!*, Summer 1990, 9.

26. Caesar, *Lady, the Melody, and the Word*, 73.

27. Caesar, 81.

28. Caesar, 80.

29. "HOB Doubled '66, Billing Promotion, New Acts," *Billboard*, January 20, 1968.

30. Caesar, *Lady, the Melody, and the Word*, 93.

31. Shirley Caesar, *My Testimony* (HOB Records, 1968).

32. Shirley Caesar, *Stranger on the Road* (HOB Records, 1968).

33. "Gospel Singer Performs before SRO Audiences," *New Journal and Guide*, July 20, 1968.

34. Eleanor Blair, "Shirley Caesar Teaches Gospel in a Running Sermon of Songs," *New York Times*, July 31, 1972.

35. Hollie West, "Church-Like Concert by Shirley Caesar," *Washington Post*, September 8, 1969, B6.

36. See S. Watkins, "Black Is Beautiful and It's Bound to Sell"; and Deburg, *New Day in Babylon*.

37. Shirley Caesar, *No Charge* (HOB Records, 1975).

38. Darden, "Shirley Caesar," 8.

39. Darden, 8.

40. David Nathan, "First Lady of Gospel: Shirley Caesar," *Blues and Soul*, January 17, 1978, https://www.rocksbackpages.com/Library/Article/shirley-caesar-the-first-lady-of-gospel.

41. M. J. Musik, "Record Ratings," *New York Amsterdam News*, September 17, 1977.

42. Caesar, *Lady, the Melody, and the Word*, 120.

43. Eskridge, *God's Forever Family*, 231–35.

44. "Executive Spotlight: James Bullard, Word Records," *Totally Gospel*, November 1986, 11.

45. Richard Harrington, "Hail to Shirley Caesar," *Washington Post*, February 18, 1983.

46. Caesar, *Lady, the Melody, and the Word*, 142–43.

47. Quoted in B. Harrington, "Shirley Caesar," 43–44.

48. Caesar, *Lady, the Melody, and the Word*, 155.

49. "Shirley Caesar: Putting the Gospel Truth into Politics," *Ebony*, December 1988, 70.

50. Shirley Caesar interview, WTVD Videotape Collection, 1976–1992, VT-4929/166, Special Collections, Wilson Library, University of North Carolina, Chapel Hill.

51. Anderson, *Durham County*, 422.

52. Shirley Caesar interview, WTVD Videotape Collection.

53. Caesar, *Lady, the Melody, and the Word*, 144–45.

54. Caesar, 147.

55. Caesar, 148.

56. Caesar, *Live . . . in Chicago*.

57. C. Cohen, *Boundaries of Blackness*; A. Harris, *AIDS, Sexuality, and the Black Church*.

58. Caesar, *Live . . . in Chicago*.

59. Caesar, *Live . . . in Chicago*.

60. Caesar, *Live . . . in Chicago*.

61. Caesar, *Live . . . in Chicago*.

62. This performance is an excellent case of how Caesar used the sermonette to connect with audiences. Once again, the work of Brooksie Harrington is insightful: "By presenting a subject in story form, her listener becomes emotionally involved just as they become physically and emotionally involved with her music. Somehow Caesar has perfected her verbal artistry to the point that whichever mode of performance she calls upon, she entreats her audience to become a part of that performance. She

appeals to their emotional interests by 'putting it right down front where they can get it.' She also chooses themes, motifs, and plots that most people can identify with and appreciate." Harrington, "Shirley Caesar," 118.

63. Sinclair Ward, "FMHA Policies Harm Minorities, Group Says," *Washington Post*, November 27, 1987.

64. Geoffrey Himes, "Shout It! Gospel According to Shirley Caesar," *Washington Post*, April 3, 1987.

Chapter 4. A Wonderful Change

1. Ida Peters, "Rev. James Cleveland, Hawkins Family, 7,000 at WYCB's Second Anniversary," *Baltimore Afro-American*, August 30, 1980, 11.

2. Peters, 11.

3. Jean Williams, "Panel Discusses Breaking Acts Internationally," *Billboard*, October 25, 1980, 63.

4. Self, *American Babylon*, 82. For more on the culture and politics of black Oakland, see Murch, *Living for the City*; and R. Spencer, *Revolution Has Come*.

5. Lawrence E. Davies, "Black Panthers Denounce Policemen," *New York Times*, April 3, 1968, 12.

6. Reginald Hildebrand, "The First Family of Gospel Music," *Oakland Magazine*, November 30, 2009, http://www.oaklandmagazine.com/Oakland-Magazine/December-2009/The-First-Family-of-Gospel-Music.

7. Jones, *Touched by God*, 91.

8. Hildebrand, "First Family of Gospel Music."

9. Jesse Hamlin, "Good News for Gospel," *San Francisco Chronicle*, October 8, 1988, C3.

10. *Jet*, September 25, 1969, 66; *Jet*, November 6, 1969, 80; *Jet*, June 17, 1971, 66.

11. Ed Ochs, "Soul Sauce," *Billboard*, May 3, 1969, 29.

12. Daniel Goldberg, "1969—Gospel Makes Great Industry Strides," *Billboard*, August 16, 1969, S16.

13. Rick Moss interview with Henry Delton Williams, African American Museum and Library at Oakland, May 22 and June 14, 2007, Internet Archive, https://archive.org/details/caolaam_000119/caolaam_000119_t01_access.HD.mov.

14. Jones, *Touched By God*, 95.

15. Twila, "Gospel Musicians: Tramaine and Walter Hawkins," *Christian Herald*, October 1980, 37.

16. Gamson, *Fabulous Sylvester*, 226–27, 270–71.

17. "Words of the Week," *Jet*, August 27, 1981, 40.

18. "Gospel Album Topped Record Charts," *New York Amsterdam News*, July 20, 1985, 25.

19. Quoted in liner notes, Walter Hawkins, *Love Alive* (Light Records, 1975).

20. Hawkins, *Love Alive*.

21. Hawkins, *Love Alive*.

22. Hawkins, *Love Alive*.

23. Walter Hawkins, *Love Alive II* (Light Records, 1978).

24. Stephen Styles, "Joel Smith," *Modern Drummer*, September 2012, https://www.moderndrummer.com/article/september-2012-joel-smith.

25. *Billboard*, December 22, 1979, 40.

26. Hollie I. West, "The Hawkins Family," *Washington Post*, July 19, 1978, E3.

27. "Walter Hawkins Says Fans Can't Fathom His 'Downs,'" *Jet*, August 30, 1979, 64.

28. Williams, "Panel Discusses Breaking Acts Internationally," 63.

29. "Words of the Week," *Jet*, February 19, 1981, 32.

30. Robert K. Oermann, "Barriers Fall as Black Gospel Eyes Pop Venues," *Billboard*, October 3, 1981, G33.

31. Karen Mary Platt, "The Hawkins Family: Singing to the Glory of God," *Contemporary Christian Music*, July 1980, 27.

32. "Words of the Week," *Jet*, February 19, 1981, 32.

33. "Light Pacts Hawkins," *Billboard*, July 3, 1982, 54.

34. Jean Williams, "Soul Sauce," *Billboard*, March 31, 1979, 133.

35. *Billboard*, April 28, 1979, 50.

36. Perry Lang, "Black Church's AIDS Shelter: Oakland Congregation's 'Ark' is Outside the Mainstream," *San Francisco Chronicle*, August 27, 1990, A8.

37. Cliff, "Gospel Legend Walter Hawkins Passes," *The Gospel Blog*, http://thegospelblog.com/gospel-legend-walter-hawkins-passes/ (accessed March 24, 2020).

Chapter 5. Higher Plane

1. Robert Christgau, "Christgau's Consumer Guide," *Village Voice*, January 30, 1978, https://www.robertchristau.com/get_artist.php?name=Al+Green.

2. Mick Brown, *The Guardian*, July 16, 1984.

3. Christgau, *Christgau's Record Guide*, 173.

4. Green and Seay, *Take Me to the River*, 11–12.

5. Z. Robinson, *This Ain't Chicago*, 41.

6. Hughes, *Country Soul*, 6.

7. Hughes, 128.

8. Don Snowden, "Al Green Firmly in the Gospel Groove," *Los Angeles Times*, January 26, 1985, FI.

9. For a closer read on the cultural significance of Green's music, see Awkward, *Soul Covers*, 81–133; and Friskics-Warren, *I'll Take You There*, 57–63.

10. Green and Seay, *Take Me to the River*, 19.

11. Bob Palmer, "Let's Stay Together," *Rolling Stone*, March 30, 1972, https://www.rollingstone.com/music/music-album-reviews/lets-stay-together-187330/.

12. Peter Bailey, "Al Green: The Apostle of Love and Happiness," *Ebony*, November 1973, 105.

13. Bailey, 105.

14. Al Green, *Call Me* (Hi Records, 1973).

15. Acham, *Revolution Televised*, 56.

16. David Nathan, "Al Green: Soul Minister Al Aims to Get Next to You," *Blues and Soul*, July 1976, https://www.rocksbackpages.com/Library/Article/al-green-soul-minister-al-aims-to-get-next-to-you.

17. Greil Marcus, "The Belle Album," *Rolling Stone*, February 23, 1978, https://www.rollingstone.com/music/music-album-reviews/the-belle-album-200886/.

18. Green and Seay, *Take Me to the River*, 332.

19. Green and Seay, 333.

20. Jean Williams, "Word Records Stretching Out, Wooing Al Green," *Billboard*, September 13, 1980, 36.

21. Julie Chenault, "Al Green Succeeds in Switch from Soul to Gospel," *Jet*, April 23, 1981, 41.

22. Don Snowden, "Pop Beat: Al Green Firmly in the Gospel Groove," *Los Angeles Times*, January 26, 1985, F1.

23. Tom Carson, "Belle," *Rolling Stone*, March 18, 1982, https://www.rollingstone.com/music/music-album-reviews/higher-plane-250755/.

24. Christgau, *Christgau's Record Guide*, 173.

25. Andy Gill, "Higher Plane," *New Musical Express*, April 3, 1982.

26. Gill, "Higher Plane."

27. Bob Darden, "Al Green's Transcendent Reality," *CCM Magazine*, May 1992.

28. Geoffrey Himes, "Al Green: Sanctity and Sexuality on a Higher Plane," *Musician*, April 1983.

29. Christgau, *Christgau's Record Guide*, 173.

30. Robert Palmer, "The Pop Life: Al Green at His Peak With Gospels," *New York Times*, July 27, 1983, C18.

31. Z. Robinson, *This Ain't Chicago*, 16.

32. "Al Green Is a Soul Survivor," *Billboard*, April 18, 1987, 27.

Chapter 6. *The Only Thing Right Left in a Wrong World*

1. Karlyn Barker, "Stevie Wonder Arrested in Apartheid Protest," *Washington Post*, February 15, 1985.

2. For more on the anti-apartheid struggle in the United States, see R. Robinson, *Defending the Spirit*, 125–63; Nesbitt, *Race for Sanctions*, 138–56; and Meriwether, *Proudly We Can Be Africans*.

3. Though each member's name is Winans, the group is collectively known as the Winans (not the Winanses). Likewise, in much of the writing that has been done about the various family members, including BeBe and CeCe (discussed in chapter 9), the plural used is often "the Winans," a convention I follow in this book.

4. For more on the use of the jeremiad in the African American and American political theory and literary tradition, see Moses, *Black Messiahs and Uncle Toms*; Howard-Pitney, *African American Jeremiad*; Bercovitch, *American Jeremiad*; Glaude, *Exodus!*; Hubbard, "David Walker's 'Appeal' and the American Puritan Jeremiadic Tradition"; Harrell, "Call to Consciousness and Action"; and Harrell, *Origins of the African American Jeremiad*.

5. The Winans, *Let My People Go* (Qwest, 1985).

6. The Winans, *Let My People Go.*

7. See Cheryl Jenkins Richardson, "Motown Sound Inspires Winans' Gospel Music," *Chicago Sun-Times*, April 17, 1987; Roxanne Brown, "The Glory of Gospel: Will the Message Be Lost in the Contemporary Sound?," *Ebony*, May 1988; Lee Hildebrand, "Gospel Singing Brothers Hit the Pop Charts," *San Francisco Chronicle*, May 4, 1986; Alona Wartofsky, "More Like This," *Washington Post*, June 4, 1990.

8. Christopher Heron, "Fred Hammond Talks about His Particular Tastes, Ideas, and Perspectives on Music, Food, and Faith," Blackgospel.com, September 30, 2014, http://blackgospel.com/2014/gospelartists/interviews/interview-fred-hammond/.

9. James Harper, "Power in the Choir Lofts: Gospel, the Music Motown Can't Take Away from Detroit," *Detroit Free Press*, April 20, 1975.

10. Stephanie Cofield, "Mattie Moss Clark," *Spirit Filled* 1 (1985): 12.

11. Cofield, 12.

12. Cofield, 13.

13. "The Clark Sisters: Career Takes a Turn on the Serious Hit Scene," *New Journal and Guide*, October 22, 1986.

14. Barney Hoskyns, "The Clark Sisters: Is the Lord Bored with Disco?," *New Musical Express*, August 27, 1983, https://www.rocksbackpages.com/Library/Article/the-clark-sisters-is-the-lord-bored-with-disco.

15. Hoskyns, "Clark Sisters."

16. Kristine McKenna, "'Gospel': The 'Marriage' Is Successful," *Los Angeles Times*, June 17, 1983.

17. Janet Maslin, "Screen: Gospel Concert," *New York Times*, December 23, 1983.

18. David Leivick and Frederick A. Ritzenberg, dirs., *Gospel* (Aquarius, 1983).

19. Cooper, *Pop Culture Considered as an Uphill Bicycle Race*, 163.

20. Hoskyns, "Clark Sisters."

21. Cooper, *Pop Culture Considered as an Uphill Bicycle Race*, 170.

22. Quoted in Harold, "Almighty Fire," 31.

23. Tim Smith, "Introducing the Winans," *Contemporary Christian Music*, October 1981, 7.

24. Chris Williams, "Producer Bill Maxwell Discusses the Winans Sophomore Album, Tomorrow, on Its 30th Anniversary," *Waxpoetics*, May 29, 2014, http://www.waxpoetics.com/blog/features/producer-bill-maxwell-discusses-the-winans-tomorrow-on-its-thirtieth-anniversary/.

25. Ritz, *Messengers*, 109–10.

26. "Religion: The Spirit Guides a Laid-Back Fred Hammond," *USA Today*, December 8, 1997.

27. James Attlee, "Commissioned: Detroit's Hitmaking R&B Gospel Team," *Cross Rhythms*, August 1, 1991, http://www.crossrhythms.co.uk/articles/music/Commissioned_Detroits_hitmaking_RB_gospel_team/36490/p1/.

28. "Commissioned: They've Topped the Charts Again and They're Headed for Another National Tour," *Totally Gospel*, March/April 1989, 35.

29. Melanie Clark, "Interview with Fred Hammond," Gospelflava.com, http://gospelflava.com/articles/fredhammond.html (accessed March 24, 2020).

30. For more on black religion in Detroit, see Dillard, *Faith in the City*; Salvatore, *Singing in a Strange Land*; Pehl, *Making of Working-Class Religion*, 183–207; Brown and Harfield, "Black Churches and the Formation of Political Action Communities in Detroit," 151–70.

31. Thomas B. Edsall, "Discomfort over Drugs and Decay Loosens Young's Grip on Detroit," *Washington Post*, March 31, 1989.

32. Quoted in Billingsley, *It's a New Day*, 134. For more information on the postindustrial black church, see Carruthers and Haynes, *Blow the Trumpet In Zion*; R. Smith, *New Day Begun*; Lee, *T. D. Jakes*; Walton, *Watch This*; and Owens, *God and the Government in the Ghetto*.

33. See Sugrue, *Origins of the Urban Crisis*; Thompson, *Whose Detroit?*; and Kinney, *Beautiful Wasteland*.

34. Winans and Winans, *Mom and Pop Winans*, 53.

35. Warren Brown, "Detroit Writes Off a Disaster," *Washington Post*, October 5, 1982.

36. Bill Peterson, "Detroit's Soup Kitchens Crowded for Holidays," *Washington Post*, December 29, 1982.

37. Clark Sisters, *Sincerely* (New Birth Records, 1982).

38. The Winans, *Decisions* (Qwest, 1987).

39. Karima A. Haynes, "The Gospel Controversy: Are the New Songs Too Jazzy and Too Worldly?," *Ebony*, March 1992, 78.

40. Bob Darden, "Gospel Lectern," *Billboard*, December 3, 1988, 25.

41. Haynes, "Gospel Controversy," 78.

42. Heilbut, *Gospel Sound*, 335.

43. Lynn Voedisch, "Gospel Singer Winans Finds Salvation Is Sweet," *Chicago Sun-Times*, April 17, 1988, 6.

44. George, *Death of Rhythm and Blues*, x.

45. See Gennari, *Blowin' Hot and Cool*; Linda Williams, "A Young Musician Trumpets a Revival of Traditional Jazz," *Wall Street Journal*, September 24, 1986.

46. Gray, *Cultural Moves*.

47. Haynes, "Gospel Controversy," 78.

48. Jon Pareles, "Old and New Blend in Gospel Music," *New York Times*, August 8, 1986.

49. Tim A. Smith, "Taking the Gospel Higher," *CCM Magazine*, December 1985, 16.

50. Kris Needs, "The Winans," *ZigZag*, February 1986, https://www.rocksbackpages.com/Library/Article/the-winans.

51. Needs, "The Winans."

52. "Black Gospel," *Billboard*, October 11, 1986, 60.

53. Tim A. Smith, "Marvin Winans: Helping to Take Gospel Music in a New Direction," *Totally Gospel*, March 1988, 28.

54. Stephen Holden, "Music: The Winans, Gospel," *New York Times*, October 14, 1987, C26.

55. M. Neal, *Soul Babies*, 85.

56. Mark Marymount, "The Winans Break Out," *USA Today*, May 4, 1990.

57. Tim A. Smith, "It's Time for the Winans," *CCM Magazine*, September 1990, 19.

58. Geoffrey Himes, "Clark Sisters and Al Green," *Washington Post*, April 5, 1984, D14.

59. Jon Pareles, "Old and New Blend in Gospel Music," *New York Times*, August 8, 1986.

60. Bob Darden, "Gospel Lectern," *Billboard*, March 26, 1989, 29.

61. *Ordinary Just Won't Do* was the group's last record with Light. In 1989 they signed with Benson and in 1990 released *State of Mind*, which was the last record to feature all of the original members of Commissioned as Keith Staten and Michael Brooks departed the band after its release. Staten would be replaced by Marvin Sapp, who would go on to have a productive solo career after his brief stint with Commissioned. Then in 1994, Fred Hammond and Michael Williams departed the group to pursue other ventures.

62. "Fred Hammond," *Ebony*, June 2000, 60.

Chapter 7. If I Be Lifted

1. Marovich, *City Called Heaven*, 262.

2. "Reverend Milton Brunson's Thompson Community Choir: A Legacy of Success," *Totally Gospel*, May 1988, 30.

3. Achy Obejas, "Reaching Out with Gospel: Music Helps Minister Bring Message to Young People," *Chicago Tribune*, June 12, 1992, E1.

4. Howard Reich, "Voice of Chicago Gospel Falls Silent," *Chicago Tribune*, April 3, 1997, http://www.chicagotribune.com/news/ct-xpm-1997-04-03-9704030106-story.html.

5. Obejas, "Reaching Out with Gospel," E1.

6. Bob Hunter, "Tommies Choir Wins Stature in Gospel Field with Many Firsts," *Chicago Defender*, January 15, 1963.

7. "Stardom: Praising the Lord in Song," *Chicago Defender*, August 25, 1975, 18.

8. Terri Schultz, "Peace Possible? He Says 'No' but His Choir Is Singing 'Yes,'" *Chicago Tribune*, June 25, 1970, S3.

9. Floyd, *Power of Black Music*, 198.

10. Tim Smith, "Rev. Milton Brunson and the Thompson Community Singers: Giving God the Praise!," *Totally Gospel*, May 1988, 33.

11. Obejas, "Reaching Out with Gospel," E1.

12. *Chicago Sun-Times*, April 7, 1997.

13. Karima A. Haynes, "The Gospel Controversy: Are the New Songs Too Jazzy and Too Worldly?," *Ebony*, March 1992, 78.

14. John Fountain, "Gospel Music Stays in Tune with Times," *Chicago Tribune*, March 2, 1990.

Chapter 8. Through It All

1. John Rockwell, "Record Industry's Sales Slowing after 25 Years of Steady Growth," *New York Times*, August 28, 1979.

2. Lisa Collins, "In the Spirit," *Billboard*, April 29, 1995, 42.

3. Jones, *Touched by God*, 196.

4. Jones, 197.

5. "Born to Sing: Vanessa Bell Armstrong," *CCM Magazine*, March 1986, 12.

6. Cassandra Spratling, "Grammys Call Modest Gospel Singer," *Detroit Free Press*, February 11, 1984, 5B. Vanessa Armstrong also gained attention as the lead soloist on the Voices of Heaven 1972 song "Put a Little Love in Your Heart."

7. "Born to Sing," *CCM Magazine*, March 1986, 13.

8. Vanessa Bell Armstrong, *Peace Be Still* (Onyx Records, 1983).

9. Spratling, "Grammys Call Modest Gospel Singer," 5B.

10. Larry McKeithan, "The Gospel Connection: Working Soulfully for God," *New York Amsterdam News*, October 15, 1983.

11. "Expert Choices," *U.S. News and World Report* 100 (May 5, 1986), 67.

12. Quoted in Carpenter, *Uncloudy Days*, 312.

13. Dyson, *Michael Eric Dyson Reader*, 374.

14. Peter Jones, "Zomba Group Is a 'Creative Family,'" *Billboard*, June 21, 1986, 60.

15. Vanessa Bell Armstrong interview with Marvin Winans, *Vanessa Bell Armstrong* (Jive, 1987).

16. Vanessa Bell Armstrong interview with Marvin Winans.

17. Collins, "In the Spirit," 42.

18. Collins, 42.

19. Lisa Collins, "Gospel Proves a Commercial Blessing in Its Own Right in '95," *Billboard*, December 23, 1995, 54.

Chapter 9. Hold Up the Light

1. Granger, *CCM Presents the 100 Greatest Albums in Christian Music.*

2. Sparrow gave BeBe and CeCe Winans a $44,000 budget for *Heaven*.

3. Quoted in Harold, "Almighty Fire," 31.

4. Emily Johnson, "A Theme Park, a Scandal, and the Faded Ruins of a Televangelism Empire," *Religion and Politics*, October 28, 2004, http://religionandpolitics.org/2014/10/28/a-theme-park-a-scandal-and-the-faded-ruins-of-a-televangelism-empire/. For more on PTL and televangelism, see Bowler, *Blessed.*

5. Winans and Reems, *On a Positive Note*, 109.

6. Winans and Reems, 109.

7. For more on the racial politics of Charlotte, see Lassiter, *Silent Majority*; and Graves and Smith, *Charlotte, NC.*

8. Winans and Reems, *On a Positive Note*, 175.

9. Winans and Reems, 105.

10. Wigger, *PTL.*

11. Paul Baker, "Sparrow Records: 10th Anniversary Brings New Luster to Roster of Largest Gospel Independent," *Billboard*, October 11, 1986, G6.

12. Deborah Evans Price, "Pop Writer/Producer Keith Thomas Overcoming Nashville's Country Stigma," *Billboard*, October 14, 1995, 45.

13. Bob Darden, "Gospel Lectern," *Billboard*, July 16, 1988, 44.

14. Winans and Reems, *On a Positive Note*, 160.

15. Bob Darden, "Gospel Lectern," *Billboard*, July 9, 1988, 55.

16. Darden, 55.

17. Darden, 55.

18. "Whitney Houston and CeCe Winans Talk about Their Musical Friendship," *Jet*, October 9, 1995, 59–60.

19. Hugh Boulware, "Gospel Truths: New Lyrics Restate an Old-Fashioned Faith for BeBe and CeCe Winans," *Chicago Tribune*, July 23, 1989, K4.

20. Terri Rossi, "Rhythm Section," *Billboard*, February 11, 1989, 26.

21. Karima A. Haynes, "The Gospel Controversy: Are the New Songs Too Jazzy and Too Worldly?," *Ebony*, March 1992, 78.

22. Charles A. Turner, "Letters," *Ebony*, June 1992, 18B.

23. Geoffrey Himes, "Gospel Born-Again Beat," *Washington Post*, August 21, 1991, B7.

24. Edwin Smith, *Rejoice*, October/November, 1991, 28.

Chapter 10. Outside the County Line

1. John P. Kee, *Wait on Him* (Tyscot Records, 1991).

2. Davis, "Reclaiming the South," 63.

3. John P. Kee, *Wash Me* (Tyscot Records, 1991).

4. Tommy Tomlinson, "The Gospel According to Kee," *Charlotte Observer*, February 27, 1994.

5. Robert Darden, "New Life's 'Wait on Him' Is an Overnight Hit for John P. Kee," *Billboard*, February 24, 1990, 45.

6. Greene, *Our Separate Ways*.

7. "Obituary," *Carolina Times*, January 31, 1981.

8. Jones, *Touched by God*, 239.

9. Stack, *Call to Home*; Pendergrass, "Perceptions of Race and Region"; Gmelch, "Return Migration"; Long and Hansen, "Trends in Return Migration to the South."

10. David D. Porter and Rosalyn Gist Porter, "The Changing Profile of Charlotte," *Black Enterprise* 13 (June 1983): 180.

11. Jones, *Touched by God*, 242.

12. Jones, 242.

13. Jones, 242.

14. Jones, 242.

15. Darden, "New Life's 'Wait on Him' Is an Overnight Hit for John P. Kee," 45.

16. Darden, 45.

17. Kee, *Wash Me*.

18. Bil Carpenter, "The Lifeline of the New Life Community Choir," *Rejoice*, February/March 1992, 8.

19. Lisa Collins, "In the Spirit," *Billboard*, March 6, 1993, 41.

Chapter 11. We Are the Drum

1. Ellis, "New Black Aesthetic," 243.

2. Michel Martin, "Sounds of Blackness: Songs of Hope in Hard Times," NPR,

December 29, 2011, https://www.npr.org/templates/transcript/transcript.php?storyId=144426378.

3. Geoffrey Himes, "Return of the Gospel Truth," *Washington Post*, June 26, 1994, https://www.washingtonpost.com/archive/lifestyle/style/1994/06/26/return-of-the-gospel-truth/487b6658–028d-47ad-860c-55bf0e554d6a/.

4. The group's singularity would be a point of emphasis in the strong endorsements featured on the back cover of their debut.

5. Liner notes, Take 6, *Take 6* (Warner Alliance, 1989).

6. "Take 6," *Ebony*, March 1989, 74.

7. "Take 6 Takes Off!," *CCM Magazine*, April 1989, 20.

8. Gillespie, *Film Blackness*, 13.

9. Mike Joyce, "The Crossover A Capella of Gospel's Take 6," *Washington Post*, July 20, 1988, C7.

10. *Jet*, August 28, 1989, 40.

11. *New York Times*, October 14, 1990.

12. It bears noting that Take 6 continued to thrive in his absence. The group's fourth album, *Join the Band*, yielded the hit "Biggest Part of Me" and achieved gold status. Over the next decade Take 6 maintained their busy schedule of touring and recording and remained at the cutting edge of the gospel genre. The group's musicianship remained unrivaled, as did their widespread crossover appeal.

13. Dennis Hunt, "Sounds of Blackness Aided by Uncompromising Allies," *Los Angeles Times*, December 21, 1991.

14. Hunt, "Sounds of Blackness Aided by Uncompromising Allies."

15. Werner, *Change Is Gonna Come*, 69.

16. Steve Appleford, "Jimmy Jam and Terry Lewis: Our Life in 15 Songs," *Rolling Stone*, October 9, 2015, https://www.rollingstone.com/music/lists/jimmy-jam-and-terry-lewis-our-life-in-15-songs-20151009/sounds-of-blackness-optimistic-1991–20151008.

17. Himes, "Return of the Gospel Truth."

18. Nancy Stetson, "Sounds of Blackness Africa to America: The Journey . . .," *Chicago Tribune*, August 11, 1994.

Epilogue

1. Lisa Collins, "In the Spirit," *Billboard*, June 11, 1994, 36.

2. Ritz, *Messengers*, 181.

3. Franklin, *Church Boy*, 148.

4. Franklin, 102.

5. Franklin, 148.

6. Franklin, 149.

7. Lisa Collins, "In the Spirit," *Billboard*, July 22, 1995, 30.

8. Lisa Collins, "Gospel Proves a Commercial Blessing in Its Own Right in '95," *Billboard*, December 23, 1995, 54.

9. Lisa Collins, "Gospel's Glory Days Are Here: Genre May Be Forging into Mainstream," *Billboard*, August 19, 1995, 34.

10. Collins, 34.

11. Collins, "Gospel Proves a Commercial Blessing in Its Own Right in '95," 54.

12. "Hottest Gospel Stars: African American Artists Take Music to a Higher Level," *Ebony*, August 1998, 74.

13. Andrew Gilbert, "Yolanda Adams Brings an R&B Pulse to the Sounds of Worship," *San Diego Union-Tribune*, August 10, 2006.

14. Carpenter, *Uncloudy Days*, 10.

15. E. Johnson, *Sweet Tea*, 185.

16. Lisa Collins, "In the Spirit," *Billboard*, July 8, 1995, 32.

17. Amy Linden, "Back Talk," *Vibe*, October 2006, 151.

18. See Yolanda Adams's performance at the 1991 Stellar Awards on YouTube, https://www.youtube.com/watch?v=jzvCtGbA8Gw.

19. *Billboard*, September 12, 1998, 47.

20. Tom Terrell, "Soul Power: Yolanda Adams Is on a Mission from God to Bring Gospel Music to the Masses," *Vibe*, December 2000, 165.

21. Norma Pender lecture, GMWA's 50th Anniversary Celebration, Atlanta, June 2017.

22. Ellison, *Juneteenth*, 130.

Selected Bibliography

Manuscript Collections

Behind the Veil Collection: Documenting African American Life in the Jim Crow South, William R. Perkins Special Collections Library, Duke University, Durham, North Carolina

Black Print Culture Collection, Stuart A. Rose Manuscript, Archives, and Rare Book Library, Emory University, Atlanta, Georgia

Mellonee V. Burnim Collection, 1861–1996, Archives of African American Music and Culture, Indiana University, Bloomington

William Clair Turner Papers, William R. Perkins Special Collections Library, Duke University, Durham, North Carolina

Wilson Library, University of North Carolina, Chapel Hill
    Southern Historical Collection
        Floyd McKissick Papers
        Southern Oral History Program Collection
    Special Collections
        WTVD Videotape Collection, 1976–1992

Newspapers and Serials

Baltimore Afro-American
Billboard
Black Enterprise
Black World
Blues and Soul
Carolina Times
CCM Magazine (previously *Contemporary Christian Music*)
Charlotte Observer
Chicago Defender
Chicago Sun-Times

Chicago Tribune
Christianity Today
Crisis
Cross Rhythms
Detroit Free Press
Ebony
The Guardian
Independent
Jet
Los Angeles Times
Melody Maker
Musician
Musicline
New Journal and Guide
New Musical Express
New Pittsburgh Courier
New York Amsterdam News
New York Times
Norfolk Journal and Guide
Oakland Magazine
Opportunity
Pittsburgh Courier
Rejoice
San Diego Union-Tribune
San Francisco Chronicle
Spire Comics
Spirit Filled
Sunday Times (London)
Totally Gospel
USA Today
U.S. News and World Report
Vibe
Village Voice
Wall Street Journal
Washington Post
Waxpoetics

Secondary Sources

Acham, Christine. *Revolution Televised: Prime Time and the Struggle for Black Power.* Minneapolis: University of Minnesota Press, 2004.

Alexander, Estrelda Y. *Black Fire: One Hundred Years of African American Pentecostalism.* Downers Grove: IVP Academic, 2011.

Anderson, Jean Bradley. *Durham County: A History of Durham County, North Carolina.* Durham: Duke University Press, 2011.

Avilez, GerShun. *Radical Aesthetics and Modern Black Nationalism.* Urbana: University of Illinois Press, 2016.

Awkward, Michael. *Soul Covers: Rhythm and Blues Remakes and the Struggle for Artistic Identity.* Durham: Duke University Press, 2007.

Baker, Houston A., Jr. *Turning South Again: Rethinking Modernism/Re-Reading Booker T.* Durham: Duke University Press, 2001.

———. *Why I Don't Hate the South.* New York: Oxford University Press, 2007.

Baldwin, Davarian L. *Chicago's New Negroes: Modernity, the Great Migration, and Black Urban Life.* Chapel Hill: University of North Carolina Press, 2007.

Bercovitch, Sacvan. *The American Jeremiad.* Madison: University of Wisconsin Press, 1980.

Best, Wallace D. *Passionately Human, No Less Divine: Religion and Culture in Black Chicago, 1915–1952.* Princeton: Princeton University Press, 2005.

Billingsley, Scott. *It's a New Day: Race and Gender in the Modern Charismatic Movement.* Tuscaloosa: University of Alabama Press, 2008.

Bone, Robert, and Richard A. Courage. *The Muse in Bronzeville: African American Creative Expression in Chicago, 1932–1950.* New Brunswick: Rutgers University Press, 2011.

Bowler, Kate. *Blessed: A History of the American Prosperity Gospel.* New York: Oxford University Press, 2013.

Boyd, Michelle R. *Jim Crow Nostalgia: Reconstructing Race in Bronzeville.* Minneapolis: University of Minnesota Press, 2008.

Boyer, Horace. *The Golden Age of Gospel.* Urbana: University of Illinois Press, 2000.

———. "An Overview: Gospel Music Comes of Age." *Black World* 23 (November 1973): 42–48, 79–86.

Bracey, John H., Jr., Sonia Sanchez, and James Smethurst, eds. *SOS—Calling All Black People: A Black Arts Movement Reader.* Amherst: University of Massachusetts Press, 2014.

Branch, Taylor. *Pillar of Fire: America in the King Years, 1963–1965.* New York: Simon and Schuster, 2007.

Broughton, Viv. *Black Gospel: An Illustrated History of the Gospel Sound.* Poole, UK: Blandford Press, 1985.

———. *Too Close to Heaven: The Illustrated History of the Gospel Sound.* London: Midnight Books, 1996.

Brown, Leslie. *Upbuilding Black Durham: Gender, Class, and Black Community Development in the Jim Crow South.* Chapel Hill: University of North Carolina Press, 2009.

Brown, Ronald E., and Carolyn Hartfield. "Black Churches and the Formation of Political Action Committees in Detroit." In *Black Churches and Local Politics: Clergy Influence, Organizational Partnerships, and Civic Empowerment,* edited by R. Drew Smith and Fredrick C. Harris, 151–70. Lanham, MD: Rowman and Littlefield, 2005.

Brown-Nagin, Tomiko. *Courage to Dissent: Atlanta and the Long History of the Civil Rights Movement.* New York: Oxford University Press, 2012.

Brundage, W. Fitzhugh. *The Southern Past: A Clash of Race and Memory.* Cambridge, MA: Harvard University Press, 2005.

Burford, Mark. *Mahalia Jackson and the Black Gospel Field.* New York: Oxford University Press, 2019.

Butler, Anthea D. *Women in the Church of God in Christ: Making a Sanctified World.* Chapel Hill: University of North Carolina Press, 2007.

Caesar, Shirley. *The Lady, the Melody, and the Word: The Inspirational Story of the First Lady of Gospel.* Nashville: Thomas Nelson, 1998.

Cannon, Katie. *Black Womanist Ethics.* Atlanta: Scholars Press, 1988.

Capouya, John. *Florida Soul: From Ray Charles to KC and the Sunshine Band.* Gainesville: University of Florida, 2017.

Carpenter, Bil. *Uncloudy Days: The Gospel Music Encyclopedia.* San Francisco: Hal Backbeat Books, 2005.

Carson, Clayborne, and Peter Holloran, eds. *A Knock at Midnight: Inspiration from the Great Sermons of Reverend Martin Luther King, Jr.* New York: Hachette Books, 2001.

Carruthers, Iva E., Frederick D. Haynes III, and Jeremiah A. Wright Jr. *Blow the Trumpet in Zion: Global Vision and Action for the Twentieth Century.* Minneapolis: Fortress, 2005.

Cherry, Robert, and Jennifer Griffith. "Down to Business: Herman Lubinsky and the Postwar Music Industry." *Journal of Jazz Studies* 10, no. 1 (Summer 2014): 1–24.

Christgau, Robert. *Christgau's Record Guide: Rock Albums of the '80s.* New York: Pantheon, 1990.

Cine, David. *From Reconciliation to Revolution: The Student Interracial Ministry, Liberal Christianity, and the Civil Rights Movement.* Chapel Hill: University of North Carolina Press, 2016.

Cleage, Albert B., Jr. *The Black Messiah.* New York: Sheed and Ward, 1968.

Cohen, Aaron. *Amazing Grace.* New York: Continuum, 2011.

Cohen, Cathy J. *The Boundaries of Blackness: AIDS and the Breakdown of Black Politics.* Chicago: University of Chicago Press, 1999.

Collins, Lisa Gail, and Margo Natalie Crawford, eds. *New Thoughts on the Black Arts Movement.* Newark: Rutgers University Press, 2006.

Collins, Patricia Hill. *Black Feminist Thought: Knowledge, Consciousness, and the Politics of Empowerment.* 2nd ed. New York: Routledge, 1991.

Cone, James H. *The Spirituals and the Blues.* Maryknoll, NY: Orbis, 1972.

Cooper, Carol. *Pop Culture Considered as an Uphill Bicycle Race: Selected Critical Essays (1979–2001).* New York: Nega Fulo Books, 2006.

Crouch, Andraé, with Nina Ball. *Through It All.* Waco: Word Books, 1974.

Cullen, Jim. *Restless in the Promised Land: Catholics and the American Dream.* Lanham, MD: Rowman and Littlefield, 2001.

Darden, Robert. *People Get Ready! A New History of Black Gospel Music.* New York: Continuum, 2004.

Davis, Thadious M. "Reclaiming the South." In *Bridging Southern Cultures: An Interdisciplinary Approach,* edited by John Lowe, 57–76. Baton Rouge: Louisiana State University Press, 2005.

———. *Southscapes: Geographies of Race, Region, and Literature.* Chapel Hill: University of North Carolina Press, 2011.

Deburg, William L. Van. *New Day in Babylon: The Black Power Movement and American Culture, 1965–1975.* Chicago: University of Chicago Press, 1992.

DeVeaux, Scott Knowles. *The Birth of Bebop: A Social and Musical History.* Los Angeles: University of California Press, 1999.

Dillard, Angela D. *Faith in the City: Preaching Radical Social Change in Detroit.* Ann Arbor: University of Michigan Press, 2006.

Dobkin, Matt. *I Never Loved a Man the Way I Love You: Aretha Franklin, Respect, and the Making of a Soul Music Masterpiece.* New York: St. Martin's Press, 2004.

Dochuk, Darren. *From Bible Belt to Sunbelt: Plain-Folk Religion, Grassroots Politics, and the Rise of Evangelical Conservatism.* New York: Norton, 2011.

Dodge, Timothy. *The School of Arizona Dranes: Gospel Music Pioneer.* Plymouth: Lexington Books, 2013.

Dyson, Michael Eric. *The Michael Eric Dyson Reader.* New York: Basic Books, 2004.

——. *Reflecting Black: African American Cultural Criticism.* Minneapolis: University of Minnesota Press, 1993.

Ellis, Trey. "The New Black Aesthetic." *Callaloo* 38 (Winter 1989): 233–43.

Ellison, Ralph. *Juneteenth: A Novel.* New York: Random House, 2000.

Eschen, Penny M. Von. *Satchmo Blows Up the World: Jazz Ambassadors Play the Cold War.* Cambridge: Harvard University Press, 2006.

Eskridge, Larry. *God's Forever Family: The Jesus People Movement in America.* New York: Oxford University Press, 2013.

Farrington, Joshua D. *Black Republicans and the Transformation of the GOP.* Philadelphia: University of Pennsylvania Press, 2016.

Fenderson, Jonathan. *Building the Black Arts Movement: Hoyt Fuller and the Cultural Politics of the 1960s.* Urbana: University of Illinois Press, 2019.

Fergus, Devin. *Liberalism, Black Power, and the Making of American Politics, 1965–1980.* Chapel Hill: University of North Carolina Press, 2010.

Field, Allyson Nadia, Jan-Christopher Horak, and Jacqueline Najuma Stewart, eds. *L.A. Rebellion: Creating a New Black Cinema.* Oakland: University of California Press, 2015.

Floyd, Samuel A., Jr. *The Power of Black Music: Interpreting Its History from Africa to the United States.* New York: Oxford University Press, 1995.

Fluker, Walter Earl, and Catherine Tumber, eds. *A Strange Freedom: The Best of Howard Thurman on Religious Experience and Public Life.* Boston: Beacon Press, 1998.

Forman, Murray, and Mark Anthony Neal. *That's the Joint!: The Hip-Hop Studies Reader.* New York: Routledge, 2004.

Fowler, Virginia C., ed. *Conversations with Nikki Giovanni.* Jackson: University of Mississippi Press, 1992.

Franklin, Aretha, and David Ritz. *Aretha: From These Roots.* New York: Crown, 1999.

Franklin, Kirk. *Church Boy: An Autobiography.* Nashville: Word Publishing, 1998.

Frazier, E. Franklin. "Durham, Capital of the Black Middle Class." In *The New Negro: An Interpretation,* edited by Alain Locke, 333–40. New York: Arno Press, 1968.

Friskics-Warren, Bill. *I'll Take You There: Pop Music and the Urge of Transcendence.* New York: Continuum, 2005.

Gamson, Joshua. *The Fabulous Sylvester: The Legend, the Music, the Seventies in San Francisco*. New York: Henry Holt, 2005.

Gennari, John. *Blowin' Hot and Cool: Jazz and Its Critics*. Chicago: University of Chicago Press, 2006.

George, Nelson. *The Death of Rhythm and Blues*. New York: Plume, 1998.

Gilkes, Cheryl Townsend. "Shirley Caesar and the Souls of Black Folk: Gospel Music as Cultural Narrative and Critique." *African American Pulpit* 6, no. 2 (Spring 2003): 12–16.

Gillespie, Michael Boyce. *Film Blackness: American Cinema and the Idea of Black Film*. Durham: Duke University Press, 2016.

Glaude, Eddie S., Jr. *Exodus! Religion, Race, and Nation in Early Nineteenth-Century Black America*. Chicago: University of Chicago Press, 2000.

Gmelch, George. "Return Migration." *Annual Review of Anthropology* 9 (1980): 135–59.

Grady-Willis, Winston A. *Challenging US Apartheid: Atlanta and Black Struggles for Human Rights, 1960–1977*. Durham: Duke University Press, 2006.

Granger, Thomas. *CCM Presents the 100 Greatest Albums in Christian Music*. Eugene: Harvest House, 2001.

Graves, William, and Heather A. Smith. *Charlotte, NC: The Global Evolution of a New South City*. Athens: University of Georgia Press, 2010.

Gray, Herman. *Cultural Moves: African Americans and the Politics of Cultural Representation*. Los Angeles: University of California Press, 2005.

Green, Al, and Davin Seay. *Take Me to the River*. New York: Harper Entertainment, 2000.

Greene, Christina. *Our Separate Ways: Women and the Black Freedom Movement in Durham, North Carolina*. Chapel Hill: University of North Carolina Press, 2005.

Guralnick, Peter. *Sweet Soul Music: Rhythm and Blues and the Southern Dream of Freedom*. 1986. Reprint, New York: Harper Perennial, 1994.

Guy-Sheftall, Beverly, ed. *Words of Fire: An Anthology of African-American Feminist Thought*. New York: New Press, 1995.

Harold, Claudrena. "Almighty Fire: The Rise of Urban Contemporary Gospel Music and the Search for Cultural Authority in the 1980s." *Fire!!!* 1, no. 1 (2012): 25–48.

Harrell, Willie J., Jr. "A Call to Consciousness and Action: Mapping the African-American Jeremiad." *Canadian Review of American Studies* 36, no. 2 (2006): 149–80.

———. *Origins of the African American Jeremiad: The Rhetorical Strategies of Social Protest and Activism, 1760–1861*. Jefferson, NC: McFarland, 2011.

Harrington, Brooksie Eugene. "Shirley Caesar: A Woman of Words." PhD diss., Ohio State University, 1992.

Harris, Angelique. *AIDS, Sexuality, and the Black Church: Making the Wounded Whole*. New York: Peter Lang, 2010.

Harris, Michael W. *The Rise of Gospel Blues: The Music of Thomas Andrew Dorsey in the Urban Church*. New York: Oxford University Press, 1992.

Heilbut, Anthony. *The Gospel Sound: Good News and Bad Times*. 1975. Reprint, New York: Limelight Editions, 1997.

hooks, bell. *Ain't I a Woman? Black Women and Feminism*. Boston: South End Press, 1981.

Howard, Jay R., and John M. Streck. *Apostles of Rock: The Splintered World of Contemporary Christian Music*. Lexington: University of Kentucky Press, 1999.

Howard-Pitney, David. *The African American Jeremiad: Appeals for Justice in America*. Philadelphia: Temple University Press, 2005.

Hubbard, Dolan. "David Walker's 'Appeal' and the American Puritan Jeremiadic Tradition." *Centennial Review* 30 (1986): 331–46.

Hughes, Charles. *Country Soul: Making Music and Making Race in the American South*. Chapel Hill: University of North Carolina Press.

Hull, Gloria T., Patricia Bell Scott, and Barbara Smith, eds. *All the Women Are White, All the Blacks Are Men, but Some of Us Are Brave: Black Women's Studies*. New York: Feminist Press, 1982.

Jackson, Jerma A. *Singing in My Soul: Black Gospel Music in a Secular Age*. Chapel Hill: University of North Carolina Press, 2004.

Johnson, Birgitta J. "Back to the Heart of Worship: Praise and Worship Music in a Los Angeles African-American Megachurch." *Black Music Research Journal* 31, no. 1 (Spring 2011): 105–29.

Johnson, E. Patrick. *Sweet Tea: Black Gay Men of the South*. Chapel Hill: University of North Carolina Press, 2011

Johnson, James Weldon. *God's Trombones: Seven Negro Sermons in Verse*. New York: Viking Press, 1927.

Jones, Bobby. *Touched by God: Black Gospel Greats Share Their Stories of Finding God*. New York: Pocket Books, 1998.

Kelley, Robin D. G. *Africa Speaks, America Answers: Modern Jazz in Revolutionary Times*. Cambridge, MA: Harvard University Press, 2012.

Kidula, Jean. "The Gospel of Andraé Crouch: A Black Angeleno." In *California Soul: Music of African Americans in the West*, edited by Jacqueline Cogdell Djedje and Eddie S. Meadows, 294–320. Los Angeles: University of California Press, 1998.

Kimble, Lionel., Jr. *A New Deal for Bronzeville: Housing, Employment, and Civil Rights in Black Chicago, 1935–1955*. Carbondale: Southern Illinois University Press, 2015.

King, Martin Luther, Jr. *Why We Can't Wait*. New York: Penguin Books, 1964.

Kinney, Rebecca J. *Beautiful Wasteland: The Rise of Detroit as America's Postindustrial Frontier*. Minneapolis: University of Minnesota Press, 2016.

Lassiter, Matthew D. *The Silent Majority: Suburban Politics in the Sunbelt South*. Princeton: Princeton University Press, 2006.

Lee, Shayne. *T. D. Jakes: America's New Preacher*. New York: New York University Press, 2005.

Link, William A. *Righteous Warrior: Jesse Helms and the Rise of Modern Conservatism*. New York: Macmillan, 2008.

Long, Larry H., and Kristin A. Hansen. "Trends in Return Migration to the South." *Demography* 12, no. 4 (1975): 601–14.

Marcus, Greil. *Mystery Train: Images of America in Rock 'n' Roll Music*. New York: Plume, 2008.

Marovich, Robert M. *A City Called Heaven: Chicago and the Birth of Gospel Music.* Urbana: University of Illinois Press, 2015.

McBride, James. *Kill 'Em and Leave: Searching for James Brown and the American Soul.* New York: Spiegel and Grau, 2016.

McDonough, Jimmy. *Soul Survivor: A Biography of Al Green.* New York: De Capo Press, 2017.

McKissick, Floyd. *Three-Fifths of a Man.* New York: Macmillan, 1969.

Meriwether, James H. *Proudly We Can Be Africans: Black Americans and Africa, 1935–1961.* Chapel Hill: University of North Carolina Press, 2002.

Miller, Karl Hagstrom. *Segregating Sound: Inventing Folk and Pop Music in the Age of Jim Crow.* Durham: Duke University Press, 2010.

Miller, Monica R., Anthony B. Pinn, and Bernard "Bun B" Freeman. *Religion in Hip Hop: Mapping the New Terrain in the US.* New York: Bloomsbury, 2013.

Moses, Wilson J. *Black Messiahs and Uncle Toms: Social and Literary Interpretations of a Religious Myth.* University Park: Pennsylvania State University Press, 1982.

Murch, Donna Jean. *Living for the City: Migration, Education, and the Rise of the Black Panther Party in Oakland, California.* Chapel Hill: University of North Carolina Press, 2010.

Murray, Albert. *The Omni-Americans: Black Experience and American Culture.* New York: Outerbridge and Dienstfrey, 1970.

Neal, Larry. "Resolutions." In *SOS—Calling All Black People: A Black Arts Movement Reader*, edited by John H. Bracey Jr., Sonia Sanchez, and James Smethurst, 234–39. Amherst: University of Massachusetts Press, 2014.

Neal, Mark Anthony. *Soul Babies: Black Popular Culture and the Post-Soul Aesthetic.* New York: Routledge, 2002.

Nelson, Angela M. S. "Why We Sing: The Role and Meaning of Gospel in African American Popular Culture." In *The Triumph of the Soul: Cultural and Psychological Aspects of African American Music*, edited by Ferdinand Jones and Arthur C. Jones, 97–126. Westport, CT: Praeger, 2000.

Nesbitt, Francis Njubi. *Race for Sanctions: African Americans against Apartheid, 1946–1994.* Bloomington: Indiana University Press, 2004.

Owens, Michael. *God and Government in the Ghetto: The Politics of Church-State Collaboration in Black America.* Chicago: University of Chicago Press, 2007.

Pehl, Matthew. *The Making of Working-Class Religion.* Urbana: University of Illinois Press, 2016.

Pendergrass, Sabrina. "Perceptions of Race and Region in the Black Reverse Migration to the South." *Du Bois Review: Social Science Research on Race* 10 (2013): 155–78.

Perry, Imani. *Prophets of the Hood: Politics and Poetics in Hip Hop.* Durham: Duke University Press, 2004.

Phelps, Carmen L. *Visionary Women Writers of Chicago's Black Arts Movement.* Jackson: University Press of Mississippi, 2013.

Pinder, Kymberly N. *Painting the Gospel: Black Public Art and Religion in Chicago.* Urbana: University of Illinois Press, 2016.

Pollard, Deborah Smith. *When the Church Becomes Your Party: Contemporary Gospel Music*. Detroit: Wayne State University Press, 2008.

Ramsey, Guthrie P., Jr. *Race Music: Black Cultures from Bebop to Hip-Hop*. Los Angeles: University of California Press, 2003.

Reese, Charles F. *The Historical Foundation, Formation and Development: From a Dream and a Vision*. Palm Beach: Gospel Music Workshop of America Publications, 2004.

Ritz, David. *Messengers: Portraits of African American Ministers, Evangelists, Gospel Singers, and Other Messengers of "the Word."* New York: Doubleday, 2005.

Robinson, Paul. "Race, Space, and the Evolution of Black Los Angeles." In *Black Los Angeles: American Dreams and Racial Realities*, edited by Darnell Hunt and Ana-Christina Ramón, 21–59. New York: New York University Press, 2010.

Robinson, Randall. *Defending the Spirit: A Black Life in America*. New York: Plume, 1999.

Robinson, Zandria F. *This Ain't Chicago: Race, Class, and Regional Identity in the Post-Soul South*. Chapel Hill: University of North Carolina Press, 2014.

Rodgers, Daniel T. *Age of Fracture*. Cambridge, MA: Harvard University Press, 2011.

Rose, Tricia. *Black Noise: Rap Music and Black Culture in Contemporary America*. Middletown, CT: Wesleyan University Press, 1994.

Rossinow, Doug. *The Politics of Authenticity: Liberalism, Christianity, and the New Left in America*. New York: Columbia University Press, 1998.

Salvatore, Nick. *Singing in a Strange Land: C. L. Franklin, the Black Church, and the Transformation of America*. Urbana: University of Illinois Press, 2006.

Sanders, Cheryl J. "Pentecostal Ethics and the Prosperity Gospel: Is There a Prophet in the House?" In *Afro-Pentecostalism: Black Pentecostal and Charismatic Christianity in History and Culture*, edited by Amos Yong and Estrelda Y. Alexander, 141–52. New York: New York University Press, 2011.

Self, Robert O. *American Babylon: Race and the Struggle for Postwar Oakland*. Princeton: Princeton University Press, 2003.

Sides, Josh. *L.A. City Limits: African American Los Angeles from the Great Depression to the Present*. Los Angeles: University of California Press, 2003.

Smethurst, James Edward. *The Black Arts Movement: Literary Nationalism in the 1960s and 1970s*. Chapel Hill: University of North Carolina Press, 2005.

Smith, R. Drew. *A New Day Begun: African American Churches and Civic Culture in Post–Civil Rights America*. Durham: Duke University Press, 2003.

Smucker, Tom. "Precious Lord: New Recordings of the Great Gospel Songs of Thomas A. Dorsey," In *Stranded: Rock and Roll for a Desert Land*, edited by Greil Marcus, 161–70. New York: Da Capo Press, 2007.

Spencer, Jon Michael. *Protest and Praise: Sacred Music of Black Religion*. Minneapolis: Augsburg Fortress Publishing, 1990.

Spencer, Robyn C. *The Revolution Has Come: Black Power, Gender, and the Black Panther Party in Oakland*. Durham: Duke University Press, 2016.

Stack, Carol B. *Call to Home: African Americans Reclaim the Rural South*. New York: Basic Books, 1996.

Stowe, David W. *No Sympathy for the Devil: Christian Pop Music and the Transformation of American Evangelicalism*. Chapel Hill: University of North Carolina Press, 2011.

Sugrue, Thomas J. *The Origins of the Urban Crisis: Race and Inequality in Postwar Detroit*. Princeton: Princeton University Press, 1996.

Thompson, Heather Ann. *Whose Detroit? Politics, Labor, and Race in a Modern American City*. Ithaca: Cornell University Press, 2002.

Thurman, Howard. *Jesus and the Disinherited*. 1949. Reprint, Boston: Beacon Press, 1996.

Touré, Askia Muhammad. "We Must Create a National Black Intelligentsia in Order to Survive." In *Black Nationalism in America*, edited by John H. Bracey, Jr., August Meier, and Elliott Rudwick, 452–62. New York: Bobbs-Merrill, 1970.

Turner, John G. *Bill Bright and Campus Crusade for Christ: The Renewal of Evangelicalism in Postwar America*. Chapel Hill: University of North Carolina Press, 2008.

Turner, William C. "An East Coast Celebration of Azusa: Theological Implications." *Journal of Pentecostal Theology* 16, no. 1 (2007): 32–45.

———. *The United Holy Church of America: A Study in Black Holiness-Pentecostalism*. Piscataway, NJ: Gorgias Press, 2006.

Vincent, Rickey. *Funk: The Music, the People, and the Rhythm of the One*. New York: St. Martin's Griffin, 1996.

Walker, Wyatt Tee. *"Somebody's Calling My Name": Black Sacred Music and Social Change*. Valley Forge, PA: Judson Press, 1979.

Walton, Jonathan L. *Watch This! The Ethics and Aesthetics of Black Televangelism*. New York: New York University Press, 2009.

Washington, Booker T. "Durham, North Carolina, a City of Negro Enterprises." *Independent* 70 (March 30, 1911): 642–50.

Watkins, S. Craig. "Black Is Beautiful and It's Bound to Sell: Nationalist Desire and the Production of Black Popular Culture." In *Is It Nation Time? Contemporary Essays on Black Power and Black Nationalism*, edited by Eddie S. Glaude Jr., 189–214. Chicago: University of Chicago Press, 2002.

———. *Hip Hop Matters: Politics, Pop Culture, and the Struggle for the Soul of a Movement*. Boston: Beacon Press, 2005.

Watkins, Valethia. "New Directions in Black Women's Studies." In *The African American Studies Reader*, edited by Nathaniel Norment Jr., 229–40. Durham: Carolina Academic Press, 2006.

Weare, Walter B. *Black Business in the New South: A Social History of the NC Mutual Life Insurance Company*. Durham: Duke University Press, 1993.

Weeks, Melinda E. "This House, This Music: Exploring the Interdependent Interpretive Relationship between the Contemporary Black Church and Contemporary Gospel Music." *Black Music Research Journal* 25, no. 1–2 (Spring–Fall 2005): 43–72.

Werner, Craig. *A Change Is Gonna Come: Music, Race, and the Soul of America*. Ann Arbor: University of Michigan Press, 2006.

———. *Higher Ground: Stevie Wonder, Aretha Franklin, Curtis Mayfield and the Rise and Fall of American Soul*. New York: Crown, 2005.

West, Cornel. *Brother West: Living and Loving Out Loud, a Memoir*. New York: Smiley Books, 2010.

Whiteis, David. *Southern Soul-Blues*. Urbana: University of Illinois Press, 2013.

Widener, Daniel. *Black Arts West: Culture and Struggle in Postwar Los Angeles*. Durham: Duke University Press, 2010.

Wigger, John. *PTL: The Rise and Fall of Jim and Tammy Faye Bakker's Evangelical Empire*. New York: Oxford University Press, 2017.

Williams-Jones, Pearl. "Afro-American Gospel Music: A Crystallization of the Black Aesthetic." *Ethnomusicology* 19, no. 3 (September 1975): 373–85.

Winans, BeBe, and Timothy Willard. *The Whitney I Knew*. Nashville: Worthy Publishers, 2012.

Winans, CeCe, and Renita J. Weems. *On a Positive Note: Her Joyous Faith, Her Life in Music, and Her Everyday Blessings*. New York: Pocket Books, 1999.

Winans, David, Delores Winans, and Lisa T. Grosswiler. *Mom and Pop Winans: Stories from Home*. Santa Ana, CA: FMG Press, 1992.

Young, Shawn David. *Gray Sabbath: Jesus People USA, the Evangelical Left, and the Evolution of Christian Rock*. New York: Columbia University Press, 2015.

Zolten, Jerry. *Great God A'Mighty! The Dixie Hummingbirds: Celebrating the Rise of Soul Gospel Music*. New York: Oxford University Press, 2003.

Index

CLAUDRENA N. HAROLD is a professor of African American and African Studies and History at the University of Virginia. She is the author of *New Negro Politics in the Jim Crow South* and *The Rise and Fall of the Garvey Movement in the Urban South, 1918–1942.*

Music in American Life

Long Steel Rail: The Railroad in American Folksong (2d ed.)   *Norm Cohen*
The Golden Age of Gospel   *Text by Horace Clarence Boyer; photography by*
    Lloyd Yearwood
Aaron Copland: The Life and Work of an Uncommon Man   *Howard Pollack*
Louis Moreau Gottschalk   *S. Frederick Starr*
Race, Rock, and Elvis   *Michael T. Bertrand*
Theremin: Ether Music and Espionage   *Albert Glinsky*
Poetry and Violence: The Ballad Tradition of Mexico's Costa Chica
    John H. McDowell
The Bill Monroe Reader   *Edited by Tom Ewing*
Music in Lubavitcher Life   *Ellen Koskoff*
Zarzuela: Spanish Operetta, American Stage   *Janet L. Sturman*
Bluegrass Odyssey: A Documentary in Pictures and Words, 1966–86
    Carl Fleischhauer and Neil V. Rosenberg
That Old-Time Rock & Roll: A Chronicle of an Era, 1954–63   *Richard Aquila*
Labor's Troubadour   *Joe Glazer*
American Opera   *Elise K. Kirk*
Don't Get above Your Raisin': Country Music and the Southern Working Class
    Bill C. Malone
John Alden Carpenter: A Chicago Composer   *Howard Pollack*
Heartbeat of the People: Music and Dance of the Northern Pow-wow
    Tara Browner
My Lord, What a Morning: An Autobiography   *Marian Anderson*
Marian Anderson: A Singer's Journey   *Allan Keiler*
Charles Ives Remembered: An Oral History   *Vivian Perlis*
Henry Cowell, Bohemian   *Michael Hicks*
Rap Music and Street Consciousness   *Cheryl L. Keyes*
Louis Prima   *Garry Boulard*
Marian McPartland's Jazz World: All in Good Time   *Marian McPartland*
Robert Johnson: Lost and Found   *Barry Lee Pearson and Bill McCulloch*
Bound for America: Three British Composers   *Nicholas Temperley*
Lost Sounds: Blacks and the Birth of the Recording Industry, 1890–1919
    Tim Brooks
Burn, Baby! BURN! The Autobiography of Magnificent Montague
    Magnificent Montague with Bob Baker
Way Up North in Dixie: A Black Family's Claim to the Confederate
    Anthem   *Howard L. Sacks and Judith Rose Sacks*
The Bluegrass Reader   *Edited by Thomas Goldsmith*
Colin McPhee: Composer in Two Worlds   *Carol J. Oja*
Robert Johnson, Mythmaking, and Contemporary American Culture
    Patricia R. Schroeder
Composing a World: Lou Harrison, Musical Wayfarer   *Leta E. Miller and*
    Fredric Lieberman

Fritz Reiner, Maestro and Martinet   *Kenneth Morgan*
That Toddlin' Town: Chicago's White Dance Bands and Orchestras, 1900–1950
    Charles A. Sengstock Jr.
Dewey and Elvis: The Life and Times of a Rock 'n' Roll Deejay   *Louis Cantor*
Come Hither to Go Yonder: Playing Bluegrass with Bill Monroe   *Bob Black*
Chicago Blues: Portraits and Stories   *David Whiteis*
The Incredible Band of John Philip Sousa   *Paul E. Bierley*
"Maximum Clarity" and Other Writings on Music   *Ben Johnston, edited by*
    Bob Gilmore
Staging Tradition: John Lair and Sarah Gertrude Knott   *Michael Ann Williams*
Homegrown Music: Discovering Bluegrass   *Stephanie P. Ledgin*
Tales of a Theatrical Guru   *Danny Newman*
The Music of Bill Monroe   *Neil V. Rosenberg and Charles K. Wolfe*
Pressing On: The Roni Stoneman Story   *Roni Stoneman, as told to Ellen Wright*
Together Let Us Sweetly Live   *Jonathan C. David, with photographs by*
    Richard Holloway
Live Fast, Love Hard: The Faron Young Story   *Diane Diekman*
Air Castle of the South: WSM Radio and the Making of Music City
    Craig P. Havighurst
Traveling Home: Sacred Harp Singing and American Pluralism   *Kiri Miller*
Where Did Our Love Go? The Rise and Fall of the Motown Sound
    Nelson George
Lonesome Cowgirls and Honky-Tonk Angels: The Women of Barn Dance Radio
    Kristine M. McCusker
California Polyphony: Ethnic Voices, Musical Crossroads   *Mina Yang*
The Never-Ending Revival: Rounder Records and the Folk Alliance
    Michael F. Scully
Sing It Pretty: A Memoir   *Bess Lomax Hawes*
Working Girl Blues: The Life and Music of Hazel Dickens   *Hazel Dickens and*
    Bill C. Malone
Charles Ives Reconsidered   *Gayle Sherwood Magee*
The Hayloft Gang: The Story of the National Barn Dance   *Edited by Chad Berry*
Country Music Humorists and Comedians   *Loyal Jones*
Record Makers and Breakers: Voices of the Independent Rock 'n' Roll Pioneers
    John Broven
Music of the First Nations: Tradition and Innovation in Native North America
    Edited by Tara Browner
Cafe Society: The Wrong Place for the Right People   *Barney Josephson,*
    with Terry Trilling-Josephson
George Gershwin: An Intimate Portrait   *Walter Rimler*
Life Flows On in Endless Song: Folk Songs and American History
    Robert V. Wells
I Feel a Song Coming On: The Life of Jimmy McHugh   *Alyn Shipton*
King of the Queen City: The Story of King Records   *Jon Hartley Fox*

The University of Illinois Press
is a founding member of the
Association of University Presses.

University of Illinois Press
1325 South Oak Street
Champaign, IL 61820-6903
www.press.uillinois.edu